Not Just Child's Play

Not Just Child's Play

Emerging Tradition and the
Lost Boys of Sudan

Felicia R. McMahon

University Press of Mississippi • Jackson

www.upress.state.ms.us

The University Press of Mississippi is a member of the Association of American University Presses.

Copyright © 2007 by University Press of Mississippi
All rights reserved
Manufactured in the United States of America

Print-on-Demand Edition
∞
Library of Congress Cataloging-in-Publication Data

McMahon, Felicia R., 1950–
Not just child's play : emerging tradition and the lost boys of Sudan / Felicia R. McMahon.
—1st ed.
p. cm.
Includes bibliographical references and index.
ISBN-13: 978-1-57806-987-3 (cloth : alk. paper)
ISBN-10: 1-57806-987-4 (cloth : alk. paper) 1. Didinga (African people)—New York (State)—Syracuse—Folklore, 2. Didinga (African people)—New York (State)—Syracuse—Social conditions. 3. Refugees—Sudan. 4. Refugees—New York (State)—Syracause. 5. Sudan—Folklore. 6. Sudan—Social conditions. 7. Syracuse (N.Y.)—Social conditions.
1. Title.
DT155.2.D53M36 2007
305.896'5—dc22

2007007044

British Library Cataloging-in-Publication Data available

To Carl Oropallo, "found father" of the Lost Boys in Syracuse

Contents

Acknowledgments

I would like to express my gratitude to my husband and colleague, John M. McMahon, for nurturing my work through the process of researching and writing this book and to Craig Gill, Editor-in-Chief, who noticed my article in the *Journal of American of Folklore* and subsequently encouraged me to submit my monograph to the University Press of Mississippi. Special thanks are due to Atty. Carl Oropallo at St. Vincent de Paul Church, to Ann Mayes of Constantia, New York, to foster parents Rob Rogers and Barb Rogers of Otisco, New York, and to Harvey Pinyon, caseworker at Catholic Charities Refugee Resettlement Services, for unending hours of volunteering with the Sudanese people in Syracuse. Robert Baron, Brian Sutton-Smith, John Alley, Lee Haring, Thomas van Buren, and anonymous reviewers made valuable suggestions; native DiDinga speakers Paul Atanya, Charles Lino, Marino Mauro, Joe Nachungura, Dominic Raimondo, Benjamin Virgilio, and Ursula Virgilio provided the song translations in DiDinga and English. At Syracuse University, I am indebted to Chris DeCorse, Eric Holzworth, and Robert Rubinstein for institutional support, and to Geoffrey Gould at Binghamton University for generously allowing use of his photograph for the cover. Colleen Hamilton provided meticulous copyediting. Funding for the public programs described in this book was provided by the New York State Council on the Arts and the New York Council for the Humanities, an affiliate of the National Endowment for the Humanities. I am grateful to Rev. Darius Oliha Makuja and all the DiDinga people whom I met for teaching me about their culture. Portions of the proceeds from the sale of this book will be donated to the Lost Boys Chapter in Syracuse and the DiDinga of St. Vincent de Paul Church.

Not Just Child's Play

Introduction

During their forced migration from south Sudan in the 1990s, many male children of Dinka, DiDinga, and other ethnic groups lost connection with their parents and elders. According to folklore, refugee workers named the group of children who walked hundreds of miles en masse to refugee camps Lost Boys after the unaccompanied group of male children in the story of Peter Pan. The recontextualized traditions, performed in diaspora by the "Lost Boys," represent the continuation of their journey. The communally danced songs of the DiDinga, one of the several ethnic groups of Lost Boys, are documented for the first time in this work. Rather than mere vehicles for transmission of oral tradition, these songs constitute a strategy by which the young men proudly position themselves not as victims of war but as preservers of DiDinga culture and as harbingers of social change.

A brief explanation is in order here concerning the context from which the ideas in this book emanate. This investigation of one group of refugee youth was prompted by a single chance encounter. My meeting with the DiDinga men was one of those proverbial life coincidences rich with profound consequences. Like many people in other American cities to which the Lost Boys of southern Sudan immigrated, I was at first only vaguely aware of this small community of young parentless male refugees living in upstate New York. I did not seek them out, nor they me. The fact that these now young men lived through their long journey from their homeland to safety and eventually to the United States is nothing less than a miracle. Yet it was nothing more than chance that I met them at all. Almost a year after their arrival in our city, I contacted the local Catholic Charities Refugee Resettlement Services to invite recent relocated people from Bosnia, Burma, Ukraine, and Sudan to my university class. That is when their amazing story of survival began to unfold for me.

Long after I invited them to my classroom and eventually to my home, I struggled to understand the complexities of their traditions. Polite and quiet in demeanor, they were simply going about their daily lives in their new home. Their rich culture and their tragic stories were unknown to most Americans. Even now, some six years later, after national media coverage (for example, on

CBS's Sixty Minutes II), the remarkable narrative of these young men, who have lost fathers and mothers, brothers and sisters and who for all intents and purposes are now orphans, is just being told (Bixler 2005; G. B. Deng 2006; B. Deng et al. 2005; Dau 2007; Williams 2005). The compelling stories of all the Sudanese refugees are tragic, of course, but none more so than those of the Lost Boys. After decades of civil war in their native land, in the late 1980s thousands of Sudanese children, some as young as six and seven years of age, fled forced conscription by rebel armies and trekked to Ethiopia. Most of the female children did not survive the ordeal. Many of the survivors remained in refugee camps in Ethiopia until, in 1991, a newly elected government there expelled them. Finding themselves returned to Sudan with civil war again threatening, in 1992, some of the boys continued walking more than 600 kilometers into northwest Kenya, where Kakuma and other camps were established to protect them. Some, such as Charles and Lino, whose stories are recounted later in this book, were imprisoned by officials at the Kenyan border; many others died in a war they did not understand and for which they were not responsible: "These children have seen their countrymen fighting one another for reasons they scarcely understand. They have seen dead and mutilated bodies. They have seen people killed or dying of starvation. They have been forced to abandon helpless friends and relatives on the roadside as they fled the fighting" (Zutt 1994, 2). Members of the Dinka people in addition to a smaller group of DiDinga men now comprise the total of 75 Sudanese Lost Boys who arrived in Syracuse in 2001 after the United States offered 3,000 young men safe haven in several cities throughout the United States.

Until they talked to me about their traditional village lives prior to the war, I did not fully comprehend how different life is for the many refugees who come to the United States from rural, remote regions of the world such as southern Sudan. The realization that I, an adult, could never have survived if the situation were reversed was a startling one, especially when I read Mary Pipher's comment, "Picture yourself dropped in the Sudanese grasslands with no tools or knowledge about how to survive and no ways to communicate with the locals or ask for advice. Imagine yourself wondering where the clean water is, where and what food is, and what you should do about the bites on your feet, and your sunburn, and the lion stalking you. Unless a kind and generous Sudanese takes you in and helps you adjust, you would be a goner" (2002, 63). I continue to marvel at the resilience of this group of young men who have maneuvered their way in the United States with no parents or elders here to advise them. And, as most Americans who come in contact with them agree, their exuberant friendliness brings authentic joy into an otherwise comfortable American life. The young men are cheerful, bright, and genuinely playful. We are privileged to be in the United States, James told me on several occasions. But his comment does not reveal the entire story: The refugee camps from which Americans believe they "rescued" the Lost Boys are by-products of a First World ideology which is "military rather than humanistically oriented" (Hrvatin and Senk 2004, 77).

I chose to write an interpretive ethnography, a first person narrative, which would have relevance for the young men as well as for fieldworkers (Ellis and Bochner 1996; Goodall 2003). For five years the DiDinga and I collaborated on public programs that ultimately revealed a playful nostalgia, inevitably reflecting their dislocation to the West. Close analysis of these recontextualized public performances for DiDinga and American audiences demonstrates how the young men communicated their own transnational identity through memories of childhood play.

A careful analysis of the processes of identity and hybridization is essential for understanding the contemporary development known as "transnationalism." In today's world, public sector professionals are coming in contact with more and more groups whose cultural identities are transnational; that is, they maintain dual identities that can be said to involve both the globalization and the localization of culture. As a consequence of this globalization, the local and the global become intertwined, and the traditions emerging from this contemporary development are said to be transnational. *Transnationalism* here is defined as "the processes by which immigrants forge and sustain multi-stranded social relations that link together their societies of origin and settlement. We call these processes transnationalism to emphasize that many immigrants today build social fields that cross geographic, cultural, and political borders" (Basch et al. 1994, 7). Refugees, a particular kind of immigrant, do not have a choice about immigration. Displaced as a result of war, genocide, and forced relocation, the DiDinga are "refugees," that is, dislocated people, forced to live in a new country.

In addition to the documentation of traditions in a new context, the cultural intervention debate among folklorists is central to this inquiry. For relocated people, "access to the welfare state wasn't their problem. They had lost their roots. The loss of their culture, and the subsequent disintegration of their communities' sense of cohesion, was the problem" (Graves 2005, 2). Although public folklorists have long defended cultural intervention, others point out that even the best intentions can entail psychic, social, or economic costs to the very groups whose traditions are being "validated" (Whisnant 1983, 261). For the Lost Boys, however, cultural intervention may be the only way to validate their cultures, ensuring the likelihood of high cultural self-esteem (N'Diaye 1997; Owens 1999).

Although there is some disagreement about the issue of authenticity, folklorists in general agree that they must tread cautiously, ensuring their own self-reflexivity before engaging in public-sector work with any group (Baron 1999).

Yet public-sector folklorists are faced today with scarce resources and limited venues for the performance of traditional arts for these dispossessed groups: "Cultural conservation is a relatively new term that refers to the efforts of organizations and individuals to encourage and support the right of diverse cultures to continue dancing, drumming, singing, and living as they wish. . . . By validating a culture publicly, its expressive forms are strengthened and, therefore, more likely to continue. In a very real sense, festivals help cultures overcome what could be called low cultural self-esteem" (Owens 1999). In my own work as a public folklorist, I witnessed a growing self-esteem among the young men, expressed in their emerging traditions performed for new audiences. Emergence is the dynamic process basic to the performance of every group's shared expressive behavior, which folklorists call "tradition." In performance, traditional behaviors are selected and reformulated by a group for presentation of a shared group identity. Tradition is the means for identifying, affirming, and valuing uniqueness and personal history: "If tradition is a people's creation out of their own past, its character is not stasis but continuity; its opposite is not change but oppression, the intrusion of a power that thwarts the course of development. Oppressed people are made to do what others will them to do. . . . Acting traditionally, by contrast, they use their own resources—their own tradition, one might say—to create their own future, to do what they themselves want to do" (Glassie 1995, 396). Therefore, tradition, like identity, is a dynamic process because it is never static (Hymes [1975] 1981; Bauman 1978, 1986; Glassie 1995). Simply stated: historical periods cannot be replicated; situations change; overtly, expressive behaviors may give the appearance of being frozen in time, but implicitly, new meanings are continually emerging in new contexts.

To avoid the misperception of folklore as reified persistent cultural items, performance scholars today emphasize "contextualization" because verbal arts are "so susceptible to treatment as self-contained, bounded objects separable from their social and cultural context of production and reception" (Bauman and Briggs 1990, 79). These theorists argue that the measure of a performer's competence depends on how well the performance resonates aesthetically with a specific audience (Briggs 1988, xv). Groups forced to migrate to new locations such as the United States may be less concerned with their relationship to hegemonic American society than with maintaining cultural authenticity. Performance frames for multiple audiences may be "relatively clear and stable or they may be ambiguous and shifting" (Bauman, Sawin, and Carpenter 1992, 28).

Understanding how tradition emerges in these new contexts is essential for public-sector folklore because when introducing traditional performers to new audiences through new frames, responsibility falls squarely on the shoulders of the presenting folklorist (Baron 1999).

For academic folklorists, the study of performances in the public sector by diasporic groups provides insight that contributes to understanding how hybrid identity emerges. At the same time, these performances are not performed in the homeland context, thus raising the issue of "authenticity" (Rynearson 1996). In this book, I demonstrate that an authentic diasporic identity can be "defined" when the variables affecting the emergence of the tradition are identified. In my own fieldwork, I was confronted with immediate obstacles because there is no written record of DiDinga folklore and therefore no prior publication of DiDinga songs and dances performed in the original context. DiDinga culture is based entirely in orality, lacking an official orthography for the language. Further, for the DiDinga young men, the performance of a group identity is complicated by the very facts of life circumstances: This group of males was separated from adults when they were quite young; they were never initiated into adulthood, so in the eyes of their DiDinga community, they have the status of children. Prior to immigrating to the United States, they lived for over 10 years in a refugee camp in Kenya without contact with adult members of their DiDinga community.

As important are the new hurtles the young men confronted in the United States. Like most refugees, on a daily basis they had to decide which parts of their culture to maintain: "They performed a delicate balancing act in deciding which aspects of their old culture will suit them in the United States and which will be a liability" (Bixler 2005, 190). Unspoken cultural signals confused them and, as a result, they often behaved shyly in public.[1] In Sudan they had been marginalized because they were not Arabs; here in the United States they were forced to accept the opposite of the classic American assimilation model because they are not white. In the United States the young men experience a racialized identity for the second time:

> For blacks in particular, the classic assimilation model is nothing more than a bad joke. Unlike Latin Americans and even some Asians, blacks don't stand a chance of becoming white and benefiting from the institutions and connections available to white people. In fact, all they can become is another type of traditional American: black American. But this form of assimilation doesn't offer the same opportunities that white assimilation offers European immigrants. So to succeed in the United States, modern African immigrants have to adopt the

very opposite of the classic assimilation model. To survive in this country, they work hard to preserve their cultural distinctions rather than blend with African-Americans. (Mudede 2001)

This strained relationship between African immigrants and African Americans only underscores the far-reaching and long term effects of racism, evident in globalization and the way it affects the lives of groups, such as the DiDinga, living in diaspora.

The ways in which the West is implicated in global processes is mentioned here because it should be part of every scholarly comparative and historical work which aims to understand performance of identity and authenticity as it applies to diasporic groups. William Safran defines "diaspora" as an expatriate minority group that meets six criteria: (1) members are dispersed from an original center to at least two peripheral places; (2) members maintain a memory, a vision, or a myth about their homeland; (3) the community believes it is not fully accepted by the host country; (4) members expect to return one day to their ancestral home; (5) the community is committed to support or restoration of the homeland; (6) members share a group identity that is defined by a continuing relationship with the homeland (1991, 83–84). By Safran's definition, the DiDinga are unequivocally a diasporic group. As a diasporic performance group, they communicate a hybrid identity to new audiences.

The organization of this ethnography traces folklorist-informant collaboration to understand how cultural conservation efforts can contribute to identity formation. In chapter 1 the reader is introduced to the forces that caused the forced migration of the young men. Chapter 2 chronicles the initial fieldwork encounter with this diasporic group. Chapter 3 focuses on difficulties I faced theorizing about traditions never documented in the original context. Chapter 4 concentrates on entextualization as a means to understand emerging tradition. In chapter 5 a recontextualized performance is analyzed as kinesthetic communication through the lens of Richard Schechner's dramaturgical model of "restored behavior." Next, chapter 6 problematizes the public folklorist as cultural mediator. Chapter 7 recounts my meeting with the "Lost Girls" to show how the young women subvert male-dominated traditions by creating their own hybrid identity. The diagram suggested in the conclusion demonstrates how it is possible to track the historical shifts, changes, and directions of tradition performed in diaspora. By tracking these shifts, I realized that early socialization in the form of childhood play traditions contributed to the young men's transnational identity, now emerging in the United States.

Men Meet
(But Mountains Do Not)

Omoto eeta holonga omotohorometa
DiDinga proverb

Ironically, documentation of the traditions of war refugees began while
I was teaching a university course entitled Beauty in Cross-Cultural
Perspective. Prior to this course, I had not considered introducing my
American students to the cultures of the many refugee groups now living in
our city. Later, I recognized the oversight and wanted to honor the living traditions of all residents in the neighborhood surrounding our university by including traditional artists from Bosnia, Burma, and Sudan in this university-wide
Symposium on Beauty at Syracuse University. After meeting the small group
of DiDinga men, I recognized the importance of providing a written record of
their oral culture. This led me to investigate how this group came to consensus
about appropriate and meaningful song traditions performed outside of their
natural cultural context (McMahon 2002, 2005). Eventually, I focused on the
negotiation process related to aesthetics and identity, as the young DiDinga
men (ages 14–21 when they first arrived) selected, discarded, or recombined
dance-songs learned throughout their lives as children in their rural villages, as
refugees in camps in Kenya, as students in missionary schools in Nairobi, and
as residents in an urban American environment. To provide a record that would
have relevance for the DiDinga community, I used a novel inductive methodology: I described the procedure I used, the comments of the young men, and
the insights I had as I observed. The difficulties of my investigative efforts were

compounded because although anthropologists have extensively researched the Nuer and Dinka in Sudan, the only published book on the DiDinga has not been translated from the German. Other published articles are scattered and obscure, mostly attempts by linguists to classify the isolated DiDinga language. Moreover, one anthropologist calls the DiDinga an "anthropological anomaly" (Fetterman 1992).

For this reason, I decided to focus exclusively on the DiDinga, the lesser-known group. Shortly after my first encounter with the DiDinga, I began an exhaustive search in order to locate the few published sources on the DiDinga. Faced with a paucity of published information, none on DiDinga dances and songs, I was forced to rely on early published memoirs from the 1920s and 1930s by missionaries and by one scholar in particular, Jack Herbert Driberg, the first and only anthropologist to publish information about DiDinga folklore. Although Archibald Tucker published *Tribal Music and Dancing in the Southern Sudan (Africa) at Social and Ceremonial Gatherings* (1933b), the first record of dance-songs of the other little-known groups in the southern Sudan, his book does not provide contextual information, and the song traditions of the DiDinga are not included. No documentation of dance-song traditions from any group in the southern Sudan has been published, with the exception of *The Dinka and Their Songs* (1973), Francis Deng's seminal study on a culturally related Nilotic pastoral group in southern Sudan. For historical and anthropological background, I relied on *Logik und Leben: Kulturelle Relevanz der DiDinga und Longarim, Sudan* by Andreas Kronenberg (1972b) and, to a lesser degree, an unpublished doctoral dissertation by Marilyn Harer Fetterman (1992), who lived among the DiDinga in Sudan during 1977–78 and again in 1980–81. As a folklorist, I was surprised that neither scholar documented the songs of the DiDinga. I would never have the opportunity to live among the DiDinga, but I knew from meeting the young men that history and culture are preserved in DiDinga song, as in many other cultures in Sudan. In fact, there is bare mention of the DiDinga in any publication. However, in spite of these limitations, without published sources it would have been difficult for me to rely solely on interviews with the young men, for whom English is their fourth language. I had never visited Sudan, so it would take me much longer to understand the ways that these young men, now wearing the label of refugees, expressed a viable group identity within an American framework.

Also, to date there are no publications to guide folklore research with the many refugee groups in the United States. Although I would have opportunities to observe the continuity or discontinuity in the young DiDinga men's traditions as they continued to evolve, the dilemma was how to adequately interpret these emerging traditions, now being performed outside of their natural context. It would be two years before I would have the good fortune of observing DiDinga traditional dance in its original context. And even then, that opportunity would be limited to a home video made by a DiDinga elder who returned to Canada from a refugee camp in Kenya. It was critical, therefore, for me to simultaneously spend hours in the library while conducting the necessary interviews with the young men. Waiting for sources to arrive through interlibrary loan often caused delays in analysis of my interviews with the young men. On a daily basis, I needed to confirm whether I accurately understood the traditions they were describing because I had not observed them in the natural context. Later, as I organized the chapters for this book, I integrated the data to accurately represent the pitfalls of this type of fieldwork, ranging from false starts, tedious interviews, and language limitations to scant available publications.

As important for future scholarship is the inclusion of original DiDinga dance-songs with singer commentaries. Folklorists will recognize the significance of recording the songs as my informants instructed me to. Unlike linguistic scholars who use a standardized orthography created by nonnative speakers, I did not alter the written texts or translations of my DiDinga informants. Moreover, these translations from DiDinga to English were written by native DiDinga speakers. My methodology, therefore, differs from a totally linguistic approach.

At the same time, there can be no accurate understanding of these song traditions without recognizing the role of globalization in the emergence of their traditions. *Global* here is understood as the hybrid nature of cultural practices resulting from shifting national, ethnic, and political boundaries. Understanding the global processes which brought the young men to the United States is central to understanding their emerging traditions: "Every public performance operates within or as part of a network of technical, economic, and social activities. . . . The 'actual performance' is nested within both technical and economic situations that extend in time, space, and kind beyond what is going to happen on stage" (Schechner 2002, 209). For the DiDinga dancers, every performance was linked to Sudan's civil war, which has disrupted the lives of not only their families but that of every man, woman, and child in southern Sudan. Britain, the United States, the former Soviet Union, and other Western powers have also contributed to this dire situation through colonialism and arms trade.

According to reports by the U.S. Committee on Refugees (USCR) and other world agencies, the Sudanese have suffered more war-related deaths during the past 15 years than any single population in the world. The current phases of the war began in 1983, pitting the rebel Sudanese Peoples Liberation Army and Movement (SPLA) and its allies against the government of Sudan and its military and allies. Since 1983, the SPLA has been fighting for equality for the largely Christian south against the Arabic-speaking Islamic north. This war has cost the lives of over 2 million people. The death toll is greater than all the fatalities in Bosnia, Kosovo, Afghanistan, Chechnya, Somalia, and Algeria combined. Today, there are still 4 million Sudanese displaced within their own country, and the young DiDinga men whom I know are only a few of the 350,000 refugees who fled to neighboring countries, unable to return to their war-ravaged homes. In July 2002 the Sudanese government and southern rebels reached an initial agreement to hold a referendum that gave the south the option to secede from the north after a six-year interim period. Because the Arab League wanted to see a unified Sudan, during the first round of talks the government exempted the southern Christian and animistic Sudanese from Islamic sharia law.

But the war in Sudan is more complicated than a simple north-south territorial conflict or a fight between Christians and Muslims. Prior to independence from British rule in 1956, the colonial powers used divisive tactics to control north and south Sudan. According to Francis Mading Deng, who is Dinka, this led to "Islamization" to unify the country when the British left in 1956 because "[t]heir successors' policy for fostering unity was to reverse the trends of separate development and promote Islamization and Arabization. The southerners, for the most part unfavorably disposed to Muslim-Arab culture by bitter history, opposed it. Violent upheavals were first generated in 1955, a year before independence, when a battalion of the Southern Corps mutinied, sparking off a revolt in the south during which several hundred Northern Sudanese and an equal number of Southerners lost their lives" (1973, 3). The south was introduced to weapons by the Soviets while in turn the United States backed the north. Later, when the Soviets withdrew, the United States reversed its support and backed the rebel armies in the south to fight against the Arabic north. Although each of the DiDinga expressed gratitude for living in the United States, the complicity of the United States in their country's civil war was not lost on them. They guardedly acknowledged Western involvement if I persisted with questions about the war in Sudan:

Felicia: The war in Sudan, it still goes on?

Simon: Yes, it will never get finished.

F: Why is that?

Charles: I don't know, like I read on the internet, they say, they stop the war, but not really stop, but they still fighting.

Simon: Actually, don't blame Africa!

F: No? Why not?

Simon: Why they are fighting? Blame the West!

F: And what did the West do?

Simon: You know, the West, they think Africa is like a testing ground for missiles.

F: Where are they doing that? Testing missiles?

Simon: Well, they say, they import big guns, ammunitions from Portugal, America, European countries. They say that in Africa we're supposed to be united like United States of America. The person who proposed that was an Arab so the West thinks, they want to Islamize the whole of Africa, that's why they do this kind of thing. It is because of the foreign policies of the big Super Powers. They think the world belongs to them. They don't care about the lives of people around. So there is no way to express their views except to do something crazy so others will understand their problems.

In this interview, the young men express ambivalence about western motives in Africa. Simon comments that peace is futile ("It will never get finished"), a belief shared by millions of Sudanese: "War has divided the lives of southern Sudanese of nearly half a century. Since independence from Great Britain in the late 1950s, armed conflict has been the principal medium to promote the divided visions which southerners and northerners have for the culture of Africa's second largest nation" (Holtzman 1999, 15). Ironically, with its 1 million square miles, there is nowhere to escape. There is no one in Sudan who has not been affected by this war. In 2004, the conflict spread to western Sudan where the mostly black Muslim populations are now engaged in armed conflict against the Islamic Khartoum government.

A substantial number of deaths, however, also resulted from intertribal fighting among southern Sudanese rebel armies (F. M. Deng 1995). Many DiDinga and Dinka young men in Syracuse witnessed the mistreatment of their own families by neighboring rebel soldiers. In the United States, the majority of the young male Sudanese refugees are Dinka who insist that the intertribal murder of civilians is a misunderstanding among brothers and not an issue for international concern. However, from the DiDinga perspective alone, it is more than mere misunderstanding. Because of the domination of the DiDinga by not only northern Islamic groups but also Christian and animistic groups such as the Dinka and Nuer in the south, what might appear to be a traditional song about warriors and cattle raiding of long ago between DiDinga and their neighbors, such as the Toposa, can also have hidden meanings as protest against the atrocities committed by Islamic government soldiers from the north as well as by southern Sudanese rebel armies against southern Sudanese civilians.

The recontextualized dance-songs that the DiDinga later performed for American audiences would re-present the effects of the global processes described above. However, songs were equally nostalgic, playfully concerned with love and hunting. In their ancestral home, songs had been connected to specific community events. For example, mocking songs are sung during impromptu events called *gyrikot*, while story songs about hunting are sung for *nyakorot*, a full-scale celebration that focuses on the accomplishments of warriors. Political songs are also sung for *nyakorot*, which can include *oli* (also *olé*; unrelated to the Spanish *olé*), the bullsongs created when adult men tend their cattle. Usually a bullsong is sung by its creator but, if his song becomes renowned, it will be sung by others during full-scale *nyakorot*. The DiDinga men told me that *nyakorot* is "really DiDinga"; by contrast, *gyrikot* is said to have been adopted from neighboring "enemy" groups in Uganda, and the DiDinga claim, "Now it is ours." Rather than hybridization, *gyrikot* demonstrates what folklorists call cultural syncretism, that is, the combining of cultural elements from two or more distinct groups, which gives rise to a new expressive behavior with a new meaning.

Reorienting Performance Theory

Folklorists today understand tradition as "process." Dell Hymes first stressed the need to understand the underlying structure of a traditional performance as "emergent in action" ([1975] 1981), moving from the emphasis on entextualized texts. Later performance theorists demonstrated that tradition is not mere reiteration; it is linked to a community's communicative repertoire; that is, performances are understood and constructed as part of an extended succession of intertextually linked recontextualizations (Bauman and Briggs 1990; Bauman 2004). Building on these theories, Ray Cashman asserted the need to reconsider the entextualization of traditional forms: "In returning to the text itself, we can see, simply put, what is old and what is new. Seeing how the text draws from or reframes tradition—how it depends on the authority of tradition and/or pointedly neglects elements of discourse that have come before—helps us better understand the possible meanings. . . . In doing so, we also come to better understand tradition and the process of its construction" (2000, 53). Cashman's research is based on written sources, but his understanding of the importance of comparative analysis lies at the heart of hybrid dance-songs performed in diaspora.

Yet current performance theories originating in linguistic models fail to address the transnational situation of refugees. For the young men, a fixed point in space and time is lacking, and there is no simple relationship between people and place, past and present. A reoriented performance theory must address "diaspora" as a transnational social organization in which members relate first and foremost to the homeland: "The setting (or the equivalent) cannot appear at a crucial point in chapter one. For refugees there is no such fixed setting; this is, indeed, *the whole point about them*, regrettably missed in many refugee studies. Moreover, it is this point which clearly distinguishes migrants from refugees. Migrants 'decide' to leave and to recreate their life in another place; refugees are torn away from their homeland and still cling to it. In the case of refugees *everything* that should normally define them in a socio-cultural context is non-existent, or rather, still back home" (A. B. Steen, quoted in Wahlbeck 1998, 4). While living in the United States, the young men continue to relate primarily to Sudan where, at one time, they had their own play culture, related to adult DiDinga culture but different (Pellegrini and Smith 2005). Like many African groups, DiDinga children "play at culture" as a form of socialization. These performances, modeled on adult behaviors, are considered play because they occur outside of adult ritualistic contexts (Gosso et al. 2005, 229). Thus, the notion that "culture is the name of the game" became increasingly apparent during the course of my documentation of the Lost Boys' traditions performed in diaspora.

"Restored behavior," a concept introduced by Richard Schechner, is particularly relevant for understanding the process of tradition performed in diaspora (1985). Schechner recognized that play is at the heart of all performance. His ideas on theatricality are apt for understanding all recontextualized performance, especially restored behavior, in which cultures understand themselves reflexively and explain themselves to others (Roach 1996b, 215). Like verbal art, recontextualized dance is creative yet governed by cultural connections reflected in the performer's self-awareness. Innovation and spontaneity are reconciled in restored behavior because every performance in a new context is the epitome of "repetition with a difference," with meaning communicated to multiple audiences through kinesthetic imagination (Roach 1996a, 46). Thus, while repetition may restore a cultural item, it changes it in ways that both provide stability and shape it for new contexts. Schechner's concept of restored behavior also contributes to understanding recontextualization and metacommunication or "keying," that is, the way a performance is framed, as well as the role of the audience in the performance (Bauman 1978). More recently, folklorists have argued for a refinement of his performance theory that extends the aesthetics of performance to reflexivity of performer and audience. From this perspective, performance includes "the performer's awareness of him or herself as a participant in an interaction, his or her signaling of this awareness, and the reciprocal phenomena experienced by the audiences" (Berger and Del Negro 2002, 63).

For this reason, I have included the voices of the young men and their audiences to show how meaning is primarily communicated through kinesthetic communication, an approach that requires a synthesis of linguistic (Hymes, Bauman, Cashman) and dramatic theories (Schechner, Roach) applied to these traditions. This approach combines performance as the enactment of poetic forms, "a special, artful mode of communication, the essence of which resides in the assumption of accountability to an audience for a display of communicative competence, subject to the evaluation for the skill and effectiveness with which their act of expression is accomplished" (Bauman 1989, 177–78), and performance as social or cultural drama, twice-behaved behaviors or "restored behaviors," which are "performed actions that people train to do, that they practice and rehearse" (Schechner 2002, 22). The complexity of these recontextualized performances can be demonstrated in the following example.

Recontextualization and the Emergence of Song

In July 2002, I first heard the DiDinga sing *Ichayo*, which translates simply to "fighting," during a performance in the parking lot of the Thompson Memorial AME (African Methodist Episcopal) Zion Church in Auburn, New York. The audience for the performance was mainly African American with no prior exposure to DiDinga language or culture. Although a program with historical and cultural information I had written was distributed, the ensuing questions after the young men's performance demonstrated the audience's strong desire to connect with an African heritage and, at the same time, exposed the audience's complete unfamiliarity with DiDinga culture. When the young men attempted to explain the cultural differences between DiDinga and Dinka, who were both performing that day, several members of the African-American audience insisted, "But don't you think at one time you were one people?" The DiDinga and Dinka, who are linguistically quite distinct and culturally only on the surface similar, merely stood still—and blinked in amazement. Both Dinka and DiDinga insisted, "We are different tribes." Although it would have been impossible for me to step in and explain the debate over the usage of the word *tribe*, I did try to clarify the cultural differences between the two groups, who, according to the archaeological evidence, originally migrated to south Sudan from very different parts of Africa. All of the Dinka and DiDinga continued to refer to their respective communities both here and in Sudan as "tribes." I was not unaware of the cultural baggage that this term carries because extensive literature has shown the term to be a product of racism and exploitation (Amselle and M'Bokolo 1985; Cohen and Middleton 1970; Fried 1975; Humesco 1997). However, the DiDinga, more so than the Dinka, may very well be one of the few ethnographically known groups to possess all the characteristics of this anthropologically theoretical type of human social organization: they are from the remote DiDinga Hills; they are a small group of no more than 30,000–50,000 people (Abeles and Peltier-Charrier 1979); unlike a chiefdom, they have no centralized authority.[1] All DiDinga are pastoralists with localized kin groups that act independently but occasionally unite for collective action. The DiDinga society contains age-sets and clans, which integrate the segments of the tribe, and within the warrior system there are mechanisms to inhibit violence between these segments. As children the DiDinga and Dinka form play groups which later develop into the age-sets in which they remain members for life. This phenomenon creates a more solid child group in which there is a rich play tradition, which may explain what was being reinvoked in this and later recontextualized performances (Gosso et al. 2005). However, for the American audience, the Dinka and DiDinga remained simply one "Sudanese tribe."

After the performance, all of the dancers seemed surprised by this degree of American unfamiliarity with Sudan and its numerous "tribes." Indeed, because the audience was made up of mainly American Christians, most giggled when the DiDinga mentioned their continued tradition of polygamy, which is still practiced by many Christian Dinka and DiDinga and other groups in south Sudan. Yet, even after the dancers realized the audience's general lack of familiarity with their cultures, the young men demonstrated their traditional artistic virtuosity through coordinated rhythmic movements and vocal agility through quickly changing musical keys. The audience was stunned. One American expressed what many of us were thinking: "They (the dancers) appeared to transport themselves back to Sudan—and at one point, I too felt they took us with them." The power of this performance could never be properly captured on video or in print because, as John Miles Foley has so aptly quipped, "The play's the thing (and not the script)" (2002, 184). When I later met with the young men to review the videotapes in my home, their comments supported

Foley's statement but in a literal way that even Foley may not have expected: When asked why they were laughing during one of the first songs I ever heard them perform for the public, the young men told me that a playful teasing exchange between Fortunato and Lino had been taking place during the dance. Fortunato substituted Lino's name in a song which made Lino a cuckolded husband whose masculinity is questioned when his wife writes a love letter to another man.

Later, this episode became the key to understanding the inherent ludic element in the traditions of these young men. But in addition to playful substitutions, in recontextualized performance, the traditional DiDinga audience's lively criticism was missing. In spite of limitations, each time the young men performed, the American audience's enjoyment of the men's rhythms and dance movements was obvious, thus indicating the performers' ability to successfully communicate to new audiences.

However, when I was working on the translations for these dance-songs with the singers, it became increasingly clear that outsiders could never fully appreciate culture-specific oral-poetic language such as this. Even when the songs are translated into English by the singers themselves or by DiDinga adults, it is extremely difficult for even English-speaking DiDinga to render their meaning. Some of the words have been adopted from their traditional enemies, the Toposa, and DiDinga elders whom I met later admitted that the DiDinga themselves do not know the meanings of these words. Yet, the Toposa words contribute to DiDinga aesthetics. I relied on the translations of the DiDinga young men and then checked them with elder Paul Antaya, a Canadian DiDinga musician who had taken a three-day bus trip to perform with the young men for the second *nyakorot* in our region. After speaking extensively with Paul, I realized the subtlety in what I thought were relatively straightforward texts:

Ichayo hotongutho lota
They fought a gun battle until they lay on the ground.
Ichayo hotongutho lota
They fought a gun battle until they lay on the ground.
Ichayo gore baoko nyao
They fought a gun battle during the war of Nyao.
Ichayo hotongutho lota
They fought a gun battle until they lay on the ground.
Ichayo loholia hotonguthu lota
The children fought a gun battle until they lay on the ground.

When I asked the performers to explain the text, they merely commented: "It's a nice song" and "It's about a tribal war so it is about DiDinga men who really fought and didn't give in." They suggested to me pride in the bravery of the DiDinga warriors usually associated with cultural acceptance of cattle raiding, which traditionally has been the root of almost all intertribal warfare. Yet, they admitted, "Cattle raiding is destructive."

The repetition of this song is characteristic of all DiDinga songs. The refrain is repeated unless the lead singer inserts another line and changes the octave. When the soloist returns to the original octave, he is indicating that the song is about to end. The reference to "they" in this song is intentionally vague. According to the singers, the song describes one particular historic battle between the DiDinga and their traditional enemies, the Toposa (whom the DiDinga claim are hostile to them to this day). Battles often relate to cattle raiding, which occurs among many of the ethnic groups. The use of "children" (*loholia*) for warriors is an example of special language; like the repetition and the parallelism of most DiDinga songs, it is fundamental to the song's meaning as well as to its inherent power. It is not a question of redundancy but rather impact: The art of oral poetry emerges *through* rather than *in spite of* its special language. From this, it follows that for oral poets repetition is the symptom, not the disease. Their recurrent language is not redundant but connotatively explosive (Foley 2002, 184). Although the DiDinga word for "children" is used, the song is sung by villagers in order to encourage young men to continue the hereditary fight, which usually involves cattle raiding. The reference to children is essentially facetious in this context because this song is praise for young adult males who have already been initiated and granted warrior status. It is also ironic because modern Sudanese armies on all sides have literally conscripted male children to fight in an adult war. "Fighting" refers to ethnic conflicts over cattle raiding as well as to the killing of DiDinga civilians during the current civil war. Many of the songs such as *Ichayo*, which the DiDinga identify as old ones, can also be new; they can imply recent wars and political events in addition to the original historical battles. When sung for American audiences, the commingling of old and new meanings may in fact produce a hybrid, that is, two distinct reference points forging a new identity for the performers not as warriors but as refugees of that war. None of the young men explained the song in this way, but because of their new life experiences and education, *warrior* for them has taken on new meaning.

Other songs, however, were designated "new" songs, because they may be transitory. For example, during one performance, the Lost Boys sang *Tinga Tinga Lobulingiro*, a strangely upbeat tune that is the bullsong composed by Peter

Lorot (whose bull name is Lobulingiro), a commander of a DiDinga rebel army. One young man explained that the song had become "popular," so they sang his bullsong to honor Lobulingiro because he killed another commander: "Go DiDingaland and fight back. That one is a new one." Importantly, unlike traditional (old) songs, this new song is not highly repetitive, and examples of parallelism as well as special language are absent. Dancers formed the traditional dance circle of *nyakorot* but remained motionless until the song was finished. At that point, they resumed their clockwise movement using a traditional jump called *ngothi* to 2/4 meter. Also, unlike the old song, in which nuance is subtle, this one is specifically tied to one particular event and person, and anyone familiar with the history and politics of Sudan can understand the message. Prior to the first public performance, the inclusion of the song was heatedly debated by the DiDinga on several occasions. By consensus, both songs were eventually included, although initially the soloist argued that *Sadik* was not a traditional (old) song but rather a new popular one and should not be performed for Americans. But once the decision was made to include these two songs, the DiDinga also sang *Ee Uket Nohoni* (Why are you torturing us like this?). By contrast, songs such as *Tinga Tinga Lobulingiro*, which the young men called new songs, incorporate specific references to people and current events. Yet both old and new songs are sung to the same duple meter, with a soloist taking the lead. The chorus, which is the traditional audience, answers in call and response. In other words, whether the texts were traditional or new, the melody and the delivery remained traditional. In essence, all DiDinga songs are both old and new because the DiDinga often express themselves in a traditional, succinct manner without naming specific people or places. I also came to realize that nice songs, however militant, meant songs that expressed bravery, resistance, and a positive outcome for the DiDinga.

I noted that sometimes it was only the soloist, the eldest in the group, who knew the songs, and he was the one who introduced these songs to the group, demonstrating how an individual's repertoire can increase that of the group. The fact that only the soloist understood the references did not seem to hamper this process. In his work decades earlier among the Zande of Sudan (unrelated linguistically or culturally to the DiDinga), E. E. Evans-Pritchard wrote that it was usually the melody that remained consistent, while the degree of understanding among other singers varied:

All these songs have meaning but the degree of meaning varies. Their meaning is not doubtful in their context in their creator's mind, for they refer to persons or events known to him. The meaning conveyed to those who sing and hear them depends upon the degree to which they are acquainted with the persons or happenings referred to. I have not found that there was any difficulty in getting the author to give me a clear commentary but I have often found that other people, though they knew and sang the songs, had only a vague sense as to their meaning. Meaning in both its qualities of sound and sense undergoes many phonetic and grammatical changes. Generally speaking we can say that it is melody and not the sense which matters, or, as we say in common parlance, it is the tune which matters and not the words. (1928, 449)

Although Zande dance in Sudan was the focus of his seminal study, Evans-Pritchard provided no documentation of the song texts or music associated with the dances he studied. Since that time, no ethnomusicologists have provided documentation of southern Sudanese music. On the surface, it may appear that it is the melody and not the meaning that matters; to a greater degree, this may be true when DiDinga songs are recontextualized for American audiences. In the original village context, pithy songs serve as a newspaper, referring back to specific incidents or specific people but remaining somewhat in flux. The songs refer to a collective authority which controls individual actions in the present. The DiDinga singers also demonstrated a facility with metrical structures and even, when they admitted their unfamiliarity with song texts, responded appropriately to the call of the soloist, who would string together several songs and improvise.

My documentation of individual songs over time revealed subtle changes that the soloist made which adapted the message but not necessarily the outward form. This is not to be unexpected because "the instability of a folklore text is the result of its emergent, processual character, stressing the dialectic of innovation and tradition within community-based expressive culture, and the relations between the performer and audience" (Titon 1995, 439). But I wondered, Who determined the repertoire of this group? The group's repertoire included many story songs with texts so succinct that they remained enigmatic to outsiders. For example, when I inquired about his early childhood in Sudan, the young soloist became animated as he recalled the African tradition of using colored clay to paint designs on the mud walls of DiDinga homes, especially at Christmas time. The others described individual compounds as "beautiful." It was only after several conversations about homes in Sudan that I understood why the group always included the song *Lobalu*, which they initially performed for my university class. A recollection from their boyhoods, *Lobalu* is a warning to all young men because it implies that in order to find brides men must prove they can provide for them. It is important that houses, built on steep slopes, both conform to DiDinga aesthetics and are strong enough to endure during the rainy seasons. "DiDingaland," as the young men call their homeland, stretches for 1,600 square miles and has an elevation of 7,000 feet. Common sense said that nostalgia was playing an important role in the traditions of these men. Yet simultaneously, the young men also deliberately parodied the song, subverting its authoritative warning. Thus, "(t)exts may make us, but we also make texts; we translate, we represent. Texts in this sense are always nostalgic, longing for experience" (Titon 1995, 446). In other words, a kind of hybridization of these texts as they related to childhood memory and identity was also occurring.

The question still remained whether the young men were adequately familiar with DiDinga tradition. They had been separated from adults since childhood, later schooled in Swahili and English, and there were traditions they had not performed since that early separation. After escaping, each young man lived for 10 years in a refugee camp together and eventually attended missionary schools in Kenya. Their interpretations of the texts sometimes differed from the elder who later checked their translations for me. Yet, the grammatical structure of DiDinga language left spaces open for the young men to interpret in their own ways. I suspected that their songs might be based on how they had understood them when they were children and how, since they were members of this most powerless group, parody continued to play out in their song traditions.

Eventually, this process would elucidate how traditions are adapted, become unique to subgroups such as children, and are hybrid. By viewing their recontextualized performances as restored behavior, that is, "strips of behavior which can be arranged or reconstructed independent of causal systems which brought them into existence" (Schechner 1985, 35), what I saw and heard was something not invented (Rynearson 1996) but rather authentic and meaningful for this small group. The young men were communicating a DiDinga child's understanding of the danced songs now performed by young men. In Sudan and other African countries, it is common for children's games to be exact representations of adult behaviors. In this way, the young men preserved a shared childhood tradition. They were in effect creating their own kind of hybrid for American audiences, before whom the young men represented themselves as warriors, not children.

Because of the continuing civil war in Sudan, I knew it was impossible for me to visit DiDingaland to learn more about these traditions. It was necessary, therefore, that I rely on descriptive memories of the young men about DiDinga dance traditions and to honor their traditions as they were emerging in a new context. Later, I would learn that other DiDinga elders in the United States fully approved of the young singers efforts to perform their traditional songs. One visiting DiDinga elder described the young men's warrior dances as "cute," confirming my belief that this was actually a form of childhood play. I learned that some of the versions sung by the young men did not change when DiDinga elders pointed out to the young men that they did not fully understand the song's traditional meaning. It was then that I fully realized that the young men had created their own hybrid on which nostalgia was acting. As "immature" as some of the songs might have appeared to the elders, these traditions were the ones the young men shared and would continue to perform as adults in a new context.

On the surface, none of the DiDinga young men's songs appeared complex enough to warrant what scholars call an in-depth text-centered approach. The issue here is that parody expressed through words or gesture might not fully reveal the song to be a hybrid. For example, applying Dennis Tedlock's microanalysis (1983) to the DiDinga songs would give the impression that all of these aspects of an oral performance can be adequately represented in print, but this approach would not be complex enough to reveal the parody in these songs and dances. A more revealing approach was to include the singers' commentaries as they were reviewing a videotape or listening to a cassette tape after the performance. Later, I would make note of the ways that the dances seemed to affirm this group's solidarity. As I learned more about DiDinga culture, I realized that their dance-songs were suggestive of DiDinga social structure, in which the youth are at the bottom. The all-male dance formations (which later would include the Lost Girls taking a position at the end of the line), call and response technique, as well as the song texts, represented traditional DiDinga hierarchies. By applying Hymes's notion of "speech act" (see chapter 8) to the components of these music events, it was possible to gain an understanding of the way DiDinga music conveys DiDinga social codes in artistic form.

However, capturing the music in print is not easy. The lively and highly repetitive antiphonal melodies of this group, based on the pentatonic scale, are composed spontaneously even when performed in Sudanese villages, so no two melodies are performed in exactly the same way. DiDinga songs possess unique musical characteristics, such as frequently changing modes, and different songs are often strung together with little or no break or change in melody or rhythm. Musical accompaniment is unique because, unlike other neighboring Surmic-speaking groups, until recent contact with other African groups, the DiDinga did not use the drum. For the most part, songs are unaccompanied by instruments, except for a *tooeri* (reed trumpet), occasional *hedemeta* (handheld rattles made from dried gourds), or *chugurena* (small bells worn on the forearms and thighs). Rather, percussion is produced by stomping the feet while clapping and

Left to right: Fortunato, Dominic R., Simon, and Charles demonstrate *gyrikot* rhythms in their Syracuse apartment, 2002. Photo: Felicia McMahon.

standing in a line, and when females are present, a male-female formation called *padan* begins. During *nyakorot*, the movements also include *ngothi* (jumping in rapid sequence).

All the young men in Syracuse knew *padan* and *ngothi*. Even without instruments such as *hedemeta*, the young men improvised the sound by using aluminum pans and tin trays with forks and knives from their kitchen. When I offered them wooden instruments, which I bought for them at a store specializing in African wares, they politely accepted the instruments only to perform on the next occasion with the aluminum pans.

I thought that perhaps they had misplaced the instruments, until they continued to prefer metal whistles, knives, and forks in order to produce accompaniment for their songs. However, when I purchased two horse- and cow-tail fly whips and when community members donated African thumb pianos, they did use them. Interestingly, the DiDinga tell me that their word for the fly whip is *nyalado*, a word borrowed from the hostile Toposa. Thus, their incorporation of cultural objects from the Toposa and from countries such as Kenya and the United States also demonstrates a dynamic cultural transaction. Although *nyakorot*, in which *padan* is central, was danced and sung in the "truly DiDinga" way and one of the DiDinga performers said, "*Padan* is our identity," the musical instruments used during the dance also contribute to its syncretism. To reinforce my assumption that cultural syncretism was occurring, the young men frequently told me that DiDinga traditions are "like taking from many groups but now it is ours." I observed this process occurring again when, soon after performing with Africans from Ghana, the young men also requested that I provide a drum for their next public performance.

Like many other east African groups, in addition to political songs, the men most frequently danced and sang mocking songs such as *Mariah*, during which the tempo increases until it culminates in an insult or reprimand. The songs frequently included references to appropriate love relationships between young men and women, community censure of adultery, premarital sex, and appropriate gender roles. *Gyrikot* is the genre that is favored by DiDinga youth in Sudan. In the United States, *gyrikot* lent itself to many performance opportunities because it is a vigorous dance tradition that could be appreciated by non-DiDinga speakers. One young DiDinga explained a young man's preference for this tradition because "*gyrikot* is all based in love stuff." The most obvious example of love stuff follows:

Soloist: *Ai Mariah hanyaki thong*
Ai Mariah hanyaki thong
Maria says, I'm pregnant.
Yes, Maria says, I'm pregnant.
Chorus: *Ai Mariah hanyaki thong*
Ai Mariah hanyaki thong
Maria says, I'm pregnant.
Yes, Maria says, I'm pregnant.
Soloist: *Ee tira thiga da*
Yes, so let us see you give birth.
Chorus: *Arita hina gi ci ereketa*
Ee Ai Mariah hanyaki thong
Instead, she is giving birth to it.
Yes, Maria says, I'm pregnant.

Initially, they told me that the translation for the last line was, "She is just fat." It was not until a year later that they told me what the song really implied. The song is framed as a repetitive conversation. Repetition, according to Foley, is critical for impact. In this song, the repetition signals community disapproval of Maria's behavior. Humor is used (she is giving birth to something we do not recognize as human) to convey a serious warning about premarital sex: outside of the institution of marriage, sex has its consequences. Among the DiDinga, sometimes an unmarried woman, like an unmarried man, might have multiple relationships. In this song, Maria tells her lover that she is pregnant. But DiDinga society has no way to scientifically determine fatherhood. This poses difficulties for many men and judges who rely on physical similarity of the child to the father, a process that takes time. In this song, Maria claims that she is pregnant by one of her lovers whom she believes is definitely the father of her child. But she is chided that she could be giving birth to "it," or "something we do not know," since the father's identity, human or not, is uncertain. Because of the subtlety in this verbal play, the insult, "it," might go unnoticed even by linguists. As the young men explained, in Maria's case, the insult implies not only that Maria is promiscuous but that perhaps her offspring is not human and therefore she mated with an animal. In this manner, few words are sung, but one word is loaded with meaning encapsulated in this shorthand form.

At that point, I realized how difficult it would be to interpret the meanings of these pithy songs for American audiences without lengthy introductions or comprehensive written texts that included grammatical or historical information as well as translations. The songs were not hybrid in form, yet they were hydrid in meaning. They were not exactly incomplete, nor were they overtly combined or recombined. Simply, the young men were playing at a childhood tradition, thus preserving performances of DiDinga childhood dance-song games in which they imitated adult music events they recalled from childhood. As I began to document the performances outside of the natural contexts, after each performance I asked the young men to repeat their interpretations of the songs. Sometimes this took the form of informal conversation as we reviewed a video while we sat on my living room floor and drank soda. Sometimes these situations were more formal taped question-and-answer interviews at the young men's apartment after I found another published source on DiDinga history. Eventually, I learned that although DiDinga abuse songs and political songs are common, the genre of song which is held in highest regard is the *oli*, a term for the male bullsong. Yet most of the young men whom I met had not progressed through an initiation to warrior status, and thus none wore the black feather indicating the completion of the initiation that gave a man the privilege to sing a fully composed *oli*. Although none had yet composed full-fledged bullsongs, some did recall the beginning stage for the bullsongs of their youth composed for the man's favorite bull. During adolescence, a son is given a calf that he must raise and for which he alone is responsible. To do this, he must compose a song to his bull. This is the song that will soothe the bull throughout its lifetime; it is the song that the man will use to call his bull to follow him home after grazing. The importance of the *oli* for a man's identity and the centrality of the bull in DiDinga culture is difficult for Americans to understand but was revealed to me and my husband, John, during a lengthy exchange with several of the young men at my home (described in detail in chapter 5).

I did not have the opportunity to meet DiDinga women because at that time there were no female DiDinga refugees in Syracuse. Indeed, there are few sources that mention women's traditional songs (Kronenberg 1972b). Since cattle raiding continues to occur in the refugee camps among a variety of ethnic groups, traditionally one role of women's songs has been to encourage cattle raiding by singing praise songs to sons who are successful in these raids. In reaction to the destructive effects of this practice, however, many Sudanese women from neighboring groups have recently tried to end this tradition by changing the content and meaning of the songs to something less confrontational (Akabwai 2001). In Sudan, women do not perform in public because male performance is privileged. In the United States, the recontextualized performances of the Lost Girls subverted a traditional male-dominated performance.

Much of what is classified as tradition or invention is affected by the rhetoric surrounding the event. Like identity, tradition is always in flux—even if externally the expression appears to remain the same. Because times change and people change, no tradition, no identity can be truly static. But how does one decide which traditions are tied to this group since issues of identity are at stake here? And who does so? To address these questions, it was necessary to consider the recontextualized dance-songs as restored behavior in order to grasp how the dance-songs related to the group's hybrid identity as uninitiated DiDinga males, as refugees from Sudan, and as young black men now living in the United States. Because of their life circumstances, nostalgia and parody remain strong forces, and many of the songs were based in childhood song games. Their racial identities vis-à-vis both the African-American and dominant white cultures and my role in cultural intervention seemed to have less impact on their traditions than I had anticipated.

The question of whether I should engage in cultural intervention remained foremost in my mind. However, the young men had limited space where they could perform *gyrikot* or *nyakorot*. They lived in cramped apartments and their neighbors were concerned about their "noise." Their songs were always accompanied by dance, and this required outdoor space. In some cases, my questions jogged their memories, an experience which they described as "like a flashback" to their childhood, and they would become animated as they talked among themselves about songs they had not heard since they were children. The question became a moot point when Dominic R. said, "I carried the song in my heart" until I had suggested that he perform it for me. My suggestion had prompted our collaboration, in which the young men began to consider new performance "frames." When Dominic R. left Syracuse in 2002 to join his estranged brother, whom he learned was living in Salt Lake City, he wrote to me, "You are very interested in our DiDinga culture which I appreciate the way you are try to gather all our information which I support too. Thank you for that and keep it up!" Two years later, I visited Dominic R. in Salt Lake City, where I learned that he had initiated and organized a men's group which sang traditional DiDinga and Dinka songs for new audiences. It was then that I fully realized cultural conservation efforts can make an important contribution to lives in an increasingly globalized world.

2

Encountering Ethnography

Lotim holia thoti ahacaani ba ngani ngati holo akani ho
The baboon, the black-footed. Who betrayed you for not farming?
Lotim holia thoti ahacaani ba ngani ngati holo akani ho
The baboon, the black-footed. Who betrayed you for not farming?
Adak lotimi mana ci Lonyume
The baboon ate Lonyume's farm produce.
Lotim holia thoti ahacaani ba ngani ngati holo akani ho
The baboon, the black footed. Who betrayed you for not farming?
Adak lotimi mana ci Kulanga
The baboon ate Kulanga's farm produce.
Lotim holia thoti ahacaani ba ngani ngati holo akani ho
The baboon, the black footed. Who betrayed you for not farming?
Traditional DiDinga children's song

I first heard the young Sudanese men's church choir at a Sunday Catholic mass at St. Vincent de Paul's Church in Syracuse, New York. Prior to the mass, the church's choral director explained that the young men frequently sang in English and Swahili, rather than their native tongue, while playing African rattles. After the mass, I asked to talk with the young men. At the time, I did not realize that the DiDinga were singing without the Dinka on that particular day.[1] When I was introduced as "Professor McMahon," they seemed as curious about me as I was about them. I explained that I would like to invite them to the university to sing, but first I would like to hear them

29

during rehearsal. They appeared not to understand my request, so I asked when they practiced. They replied, "We don't practice. We just sing." The singing that I heard sounded so polished that I wondered whether perhaps they had not understood my request. I repeated my question. They repeated their answer. We then agreed that I would visit them the following Sunday at their apartment to talk about my invitation.

Because I had just been introduced to the young men, I wanted to have some basic understanding of their culture before our appointment. At the library, I found Francis Mading Deng's book *The Dinka and Their Songs* (1973). Since I was meeting the young men at noontime at their apartment, I decided to bring assorted bagels and juice in order to create an informal social atmosphere. Although I prepared a few questions, I wanted to avoid the appearance of an interview, which might make them uncomfortable. As many researchers have noted, an interview is not a communicative norm in all cultures and can be misunderstood because "[s]ome potential respondents are drawn from communities whose sociolinguistic norms stand in opposition to those embedded in the interview. This is likely to be the case in groups that do not feature the interview as an established speech-type. Lacking experience in this means of relating, such individuals are less likely to be able and willing to adhere to its rules. The farther we move away from home, culturally and linguistically, the greater the problem" (Briggs 1986, 3). Rather, through casual conversation it might be easier to elicit information about the young men's musical traditions before they came to my classroom.

This was a naive assumption because I had no familiarity with DiDinga culture, and worse, I assumed all of the young men were Dinka. Much later, I learned that Swahili had been their lingua franca in the refugee camps, and that there were two distinct linguistic groups living in Syracuse, the Dinka and the DiDinga. In Syracuse, the two groups used English to communicate, although English is their fourth language. When they sang together, the complex rhythms were so beautifully harmonized that I was certain that they practiced together frequently.

Unknown to me, there was also the issue of status. As a professor, I would possess a high degree of status in DiDinga culture; but as a middle-aged married woman, I would not. If I were a man, I would be *eet chi obi*, from *obi*, which literally translates to "big man." *Eet chi obi* is used for a man who holds a position of power, such as a professor, judge, or a DiDinga chief or elder. The word *galac*, which originally meant "white man," is sometimes used for a man who is of senior rank or has a university education, but there are no such words for women. The DiDinga use several phrases to indicate status among outstanding men but none for women. *Eet chi obi* is "a big man," but it has several meanings: (1) an elderly or older man, being big (advanced) in age (*eet chi maka* is more commonly used to refer to age); (2) a mature man, being big in experience; and (3) a man with big (great) authority or power and class. In the latter category would be judges, professors, army generals, government officials, chiefs, and DiDinga of senior rank in their respective age-sets. More difficult for translation is the subtle difference between *eet chi egenyithi* and *egenyith eeti nicie gerret*. If the man is called *eet chi egenyithi*, he is a gifted man or a genius, but *egenyith eeti nicie gerret* means a man extraordinarily clever or knowledgeable but not necessarily gifted.

Thus, in a culture which I later learned has ten words for father and one word for mother, it was a rather novel experience for the young singers to interact with me. To the young men my position was not only anomalous but worse, ambiguous. However, when I arrived at their apartment, I was greeted politely and briefly by several of the men, many of whom then disappeared into other rooms. Charles, the oldest in the group, sat with me in his living room as I asked cursory questions about where they were born. As the young men drifted in and out of the living room, I had difficulty associating background information with the individuals. I avoided all personal questions and references to the Sudanese civil war, which might make them uncomfortable. Instead, I inquired about their opinions of the United States, about their lives in Syracuse, their courses at the community college, and their jobs. Although their English was good, their answers were constrained by limited vocabularies and my unfamiliarity with their language. When I began to ask directly about *dit*, the Dinka word for the traditional male bullsong, they said that they did not know the word. When I asked about the colorful beaded vests for which the Dinka are renowned, they said they did not know about such things. I then suspected that their lack of cultural knowledge was due to their separation from their families at early ages. Then I overheard the young men speaking among themselves, so I asked if they were speaking Dinka. It was then that I learned the word DiDinga, which they described as an "entirely different language." The difference, they explained, was so great that the two groups communicated in Arabic or, in the United States, in English. After I apologized for my ignorance, I used the opportunity to ask them if *they* would teach *me* what I needed to know before they came to my classroom. They reassured me that this was a common mistake which was not "too bad" because both DiDinga and Dinka were cattle herders and sang bullsongs.

The young men told me that they sang together in a Dominican missionary school in Nairobi under the leadership of Charles because he was the oldest, now about age 21. It was in Nairobi that they learned to harmonize in the western choral tradition. It was at the University of Nairobi that the DiDinga competed with the Dinka in a dance competition where they won first place "over the Dinka." After one intensive hour, I was overwhelmed. I realized that during the following weeks I would need to interview them for an hour or two and then return again with follow-up questions for each interview hour. In the meantime, I asked that each write a short biography that I could share with my students. A few weeks later, Charles was the only one who handed me his "story":

> I am the son of Lino Mamur Akwagira born in Chukudum in the year 1980 and raised in Nahichode.[2] I am DiDinga by tribe and Sudanese by nationality. DiDinga is found in equatorial part of southern Sudan. In 1983 the southern part of Sudan and northern part of Sudan involved in war. However, war has 18 years. In 1985 the great and long lasting war reached the land of minority tribe so called DiDinga. And in 1990 my father said, "Go and die outside but not inside." He then sell his belongs and told us to go outside the world. Seven boys and one lady [sister] has decide to moved out off the war and search a better place for living in peace. In 1991 December I strike from Sudan to Kenya in two days. Therefore I found a non [nun] who deliberately taking her time to help the needy like me and my brother. Back home in DiDingaland only Father, Mother and lady. Therefore in Kenya, Nairobi I join the school from lower-high school, when I finish in 2000. At same time in Kenya during that period I do learn a lot of things e.g. better life, a great education, a cross-country where I become champion in 1998–1999 and I have a lot of certificate with me, and the greatest of all is a singing e.g. church song tradition and learning of tones voices [harmonizing]. This is where it's get good to me. And in any singing, I have a great confident whether [it] is in another language I will [am able]. In church song, I am elected a director of choir in 1995 and lead choir for 6 years. In this case, I cannot forget my voice as soloist in 1998 when we are performing cultural dance in Kenyatta International Conference center and emerged #1.

It would be another year before Charles would tell me the details about how as a ten-year-old boy he rescued his seven-year-old brother before he fled from his village. Carrying George in his arms, Charles ran to the woods where the two boys hid until nightfall. For four days, the two children had no food or water. They walked by night and slept by day to avoid "hostile" animals and their traditional enemies, the Toposa, "who are very, very hostile. They will kill us." While fleeing, their cousin Lino, also 10 years old, discovered Charles and

George in the woods. Lino did not write his biography; however, two years later he allowed me to videotape his tragic narrative:

I was born in Sudan, in a place called Chukudum. Our first born is a boy and he is about 25 now. I am the second born, now about 21. I got three younger sisters. My parents are subsistence farmers. They keep cattles and farming so mostly they farmed to provide food for us. When I was nine years old, the conflict which start in 1981 reach our village when I was nine years and the situation was not good. Living conditions was [that] there was a lot of killing. The soldiers forced the young boys nine years and onward to fight the Khartoum regime, the ruling government, so most of the boys were forced to go in to join the army. Actually, my brother went—he was forced, he didn't go willingly but he was forced and I saw I would be the next victim to join the army. I left home without knowing where I was going in the forest. I met up with Charles and his younger brother and it was like I was really happy to meet them there once again since we grew up in the same village. We did everything together. So it was first like back at home again *but* it was in a different place—it was a forest with so many other young men and boys headed for a place. I didn't even know [where we were going]. We went like [for] four nights and four days with no food, no water. Surviving was really very difficult. Since it was a long distance and I was young, I couldn't even walk at times. Sometimes I would drop back. Some were very generous and they would take my hand and keep me going. It took us a long time to get to the border of Kenya. As soon as we reached the border, the Kenyans ambushed us. So it was like, maybe this was the end of life because they took us into custody and questioned us: Why we are doing? Why we are entering? We told them we just run because of the war and the situation which was back in Sudan. They kept us in custody for a few days. Then the chief informed the United Nations that there are some people who trespassed. So the United Nations came and, you know, found out we are the boys who ran because of the conflict, because of the war in Sudan. Then they gave us some food. At least life became easier, compared to before because we could eat sometimes. We could get a meal of corn and beans for a few days. So they took us to the camp which was in a place in Nairobi called Thika so we stayed in the camp for a few months.

Coincidentally, just prior to hearing Lino's story, I had read *Dark Star Safari: Overland from Cairo to Cape Town*, in which writer Paul Theroux describes Thika as "a congested maze of improvised houses and streets thick with lurking kids and traffic and an odor of decrepitude: sewage, garbage, open drains, the stink of citified Africa" (175, 2003). I was, therefore, always reluctant to ask the DiDinga for more details about their lives in refugee camps. From the beginning of my relationship with them, it was Charles, the oldest in the group, who became the group's interlocutor. I relied on Charles to tell me if some subjects were too sensitive. When he hesitated, saying "I don't know" or "It may not be good," I knew I was asking questions that might make the young men uncomfortable. I relied on Charles to ask the others whether they wanted to talk with me, but this was not without difficulty because he frequently forgot to mention it to the others. If I called to inquire about their availability on a specific day and hour, Charles always insisted, "Just come." Since I preferred to designate a specific time and to have him confirm it with the others, it took Charles and me some time before we were in agreement about organizing group meetings. But it remained a problem to get the men together in one place. They were very busy attending school and held full-time jobs at different locations. Their individual schedules were very different, and they lived in different parts of the city. Transportation was an issue until the men soon bought used cars. Further, I taught in Syracuse, but my home in Tully was 27 miles south of the city, and I worried when they drove to visit me because their secondhand cars were in such poor condition. In spite of the difficult logistics, we met on several occasions prior to the group's first performance at Syracuse University.

It was Dominic R. who resolved our scheduling dilemma by telling the other men, "She is saying we need to be organized." As Charles and I became accustomed to working together, he too recognized the need to confirm the meetings with me, while I accepted that he needed to wait until the last minute to do so. One day I asked how DiDinga traditionally arranged meetings in Sudan only to learn that it is common to point to the sun to indicate time. When I asked how they arranged gatherings among villages, he said, "We send a messenger." I took this to mean that events were spontaneous and that meetings began when everyone finally arrived. My assumption was right: Among the DiDinga, there is no concept of being "tardy" or "on time." My eventual realization that they had grown up in a world without watches, clocks, or calendars meant that my education about the world through the eyes of the DiDinga had begun. I had acquired the cultural understanding of a DiDinga child.

It would be many months before I grasped the degree of the cultural adjustment that the young men made in just a few months in our country. Complex issues remained on the conceptual level: There are no DiDinga words for "time" and "space," which in DiDinga are relative. If asked whether something is "far" by a young man, the DiDinga may say no, but if the same question is posed by an old man, the DiDinga would say yes. This is logical from a DiDinga perspective because it takes an older person longer to move from one place to another. Interestingly, this is similar to a Western understanding of outer space: When we talk about light-years, we are actually thinking about measurements of distance in terms of time, how long it takes before we can see an object from the earth's perspective. Because the DiDinga often express themselves in relative time and space, I frequently left our meetings feeling dazed, but I could never quite put my finger on the reason for my confusion until I read about traditional life in rural Sudan. It took me about a year before I no longer experienced this feeling of disorientation. I would remark to my husband that when I was with my informants, I was experiencing a parallel world, not separate from but existing within an American context.

From all outward appearances, the young men had no such disorientation. They quickly adapted to a new American life. They even seemed to do so with ease. After a long search, I found a copy of Michele Rosato's DiDinga-English dictionary (1980), which enabled me to point to DiDinga words during our interviews. I was not surprised to find that there is no word for "time" in DiDinga language. It was then that I understood that time among people in today's world could be relative and not necessarily determined by rigid Western ways of thinking. In other parts of the world, such as the rural Sudan, time is still determined by work, such as harvesting, or by an occasion to celebrate seasonal events or ceremonies.[3] Further library research led me to descriptive DiDinga words for time that meant "first light," "dawn," and the "loosing of cattle" (B. A. Lewis 1972, 27). To describe the day as it progresses, DiDinga say it is first "ugly," then "hot," and then "deep" (B. A. Lewis 1972, 27). According to Lewis and other researchers, groups like the DiDinga-Murle employ poetic references to indicate the passage of time such "the belly of the night" (midnight). To indicate approximately 8:00 a.m. to 9:00 a.m., the DiDinga say, *Kikiya kora lukora*, literally, "The sun is mounting up" (Driberg 1931, 182); but to indicate high noon, the DiDinga say simply, *Aikorra lokora*, "The sun is above" (Rosato 1980, 128).

These sources confirmed what the young men told me about "pointing to the sun." To inquire in DiDinga "What time is it?" one asks *Ai korra ena?* that is, "Where is the sun?" In villages days are counted before or after the full or new moon, *nyelok*. The meaning of *nyelok* is similar to *moonath*, the Old English word for moon from which we get our English word "month." Likewise, *nyelok* means both "moon" and "month." Other references to the passing of time are more poetic in the DiDinga language: *Nyerkinit ci nyelogo*, "breaking open of the month," means the month begins with the new moon. After the new moon begins the counting of nights. Each month is divided into two parts. *Ortin*, "white moon," means the brightest night of the waxing moon. Waxing nights one through fourteen are counted; for example, *rama ci nyelogo*, "second night of the month," or *ortini omoto*, "tenth night of the white moon." *Mugur*, "dark moon," is the darkest night of the waning moon; nights during waning moon are called *tukul tang ngon*, "giving light to the cattle," and other descriptive phrases such as "home of the darkness" for the second night of the waning moon. *Adak nyeloki*, "the moon is dead," refers to the last night in the month. *Kebek kor* means "full moon," literally, "the sun observes the moon rising while the sun goes under."

I learned that although days are counted, the DiDinga do not keep track of months or years. A caseworker at the Refugee Settlement Services mentioned to me that this was a problem when answering questions on immigration applications. The DiDinga did not have birthdates or know their exact ages, so with the aid of relief workers, they approximated (Bixler 2005). Instead, although years are not counted, twelve "moons" make up *irkit* (a year). The year is divided into three main seasons: *lolo*, literally, "low grass," the rainy season; *lomotin*, the harvest season, and *tagis*, the dry season. During one interview, Simon explained to me that names for seasons were also the names of places in Sudan where certain agricultural activities took place in the same location.

In DiDinga, the traditional names of the months are Toposa loanwords. Although Rosato claims that these words are no longer used because they have been replaced by numerals (Rosato 1980, 21), the DiDinga in Syracuse sometimes used Toposa words when discussing seasonal activities with me. They also confirmed what I read in Kronenberg (1972b, 177–79): The DiDinga have adopted Toposa words which indicate seasons, not months such as *lomuk* or *madidil* (January); *lokwang-lodunge-lomaruk-titmaran* (mid-January to mid-May); *lochyoto-lolingacino-lomodohogec-lotyak* (mid-May to September); *loipo-kagor-cholong-tereheji* (September to December). In other written sources, Rosato includes *teregiji* for October, which means "rain- rich month." However, Kronenberg uses both *tereheji* and *tehereji* interchangeably. This confusion is probably due to an inconsistent orthography, but the latter may be a typographical error. For a non-DiDinga native speaker like me, the references remained ambiguous at best, and the young men were often at a loss as to how to help me understand the inconsistencies in these publications. They had never before encountered their language in written form.

I noticed when trying to inquire about dates for future performances, for example, whether July was an appropriate month for us to make arrangements for a proposed outdoor public program in Syracuse, one young man used Toposa words for the months or referred to the months as "time of harvest" or "the rainy season." Because of their transhumance in Sudan, the names of places represented occasions when a particular activity is held in those locations. In such cases, there would be no need to have a word for the season. To avoid confusion, I bought each of the men a small calendar, but I do not think they ever used them. Gradually, I inferred from the published sources I was slowly collecting that DiDinga is a topographical language.

At this writing, I continue to struggle with the language on a conceptual level because there are many complexities. For example, a different kind of relationship exists for words such as *bolohinit* (leaf). *Bolohinit* includes flower, for which there is no DiDinga word. However, the absence of a word does not necessarily indicate there is no category or concept (Berlin 1978). Instead, the verb *odoani* means "to flower" and the noun *doani* refers to the blossoming or flowering stage. In his research among the DiDinga-Murle, Arensen suggests that what may at first appear to be an "absence" is simply an alternative categorization (1998). Likewise, linguistic scholars have noted that the DiDinga-Murle worldview is quite different: "People of the West would tend to put all animals in a single category based on their appearance and various other criteria. The Murle has some animals in category 1 as prey, others appear in Category 2 as unusual animals or dangerous animals and yet others appear in Category 5 as animals that occur in large numbers" (Dimmendaal and Last 1998, 210). Similarly, Arensen notes that the DiDinga-Murle, who intermarry with the DiDinga, do not have single terms for things like "animal" or "plant" that can be defined as existing on the kingdom level (1998, 212). Other linguists have also found that neither DiDinga nor Murle people have an exact word for "flower" (Lokonobei and de Jong 1989). This proved to be true when one day, as Charles was riding in my car, I pointed to a flower and asked him for the DiDinga word. Then I pointed to a leafy plant with no flowers. He used the word *bolohinit* for both, which linguists have translated to mean "leaf" (Lokonobei and De Jong 1989, 81). However, on another occasion Joseph, who is the DiDinga-Longarim in the group, used the word *kavurenit* to indicate a flower and the others did not understand. When I asked why, Joseph explained that he spoke a "dialect." After checking published linguistic sources, I learned about the relationship of his Longarim dialect to DiDinga, and Murle lies squarely between the two. Thus, Joseph distinguishes "flower," *kavurenit*, from "leaf," *bolohinit*, but the DiDinga and the Murle do not.

DiDinga and Language Relatives

The conversations between Joseph and the other DiDinga about their relationships were intriguing. Language studies have indicated that Murle, DiDinga, and Longarim have probably been separated for over 100 years. At one time the two main groups, Murle and DiDinga, used the same vocabulary. According to folklore, the name *Murle* (sometimes spelled *Merille*) comes from the DiDinga words *muur* (mountain) and *lill* (valley) because the Murle are said to have migrated from the mountain to the valley. Although the languages today are very closely related, much of the vocabulary is different. According to the DiDinga in Syracuse, Murle is the "original" language because it is older than DiDinga and Longarim. However, the young men confirmed Arensen's opinion that "they are similar enough that a Murle or a DiDinga can still learn the other's language within a very few days" (1992, 65).

It was a folktale about soup, a traditional story told to me by the young men on several occasions, that demonstrated how closely related the Longarim, DiDinga, and Murle see themselves. The soup story is an oral tradition shared by all DiDinga, Murle, Longarim (who are sometimes called Larim or Boya) and Tenet (also Tennet) people. One day while I was driving Joseph to my home for a party for the young men, I was surprised when he began to narrate a version of this etiological tale in answer to my question about differences between DiDinga and Longarim vocabularies. When the young men gathered around my kitchen table, I asked Joseph if he would retell the story, so I could tape it while the others commented on it:

> Well, the origin of these different Murle, DiDinga, Boya, Tenet tribes. Actually, it's something like a history thing because younger generations born and people born and there are older people, granma and granpa, they just tell the younger people, the young children and teenagers. There was a very big group of people like one tribe, which included the DiDinga, Murle, Tenet, and these people. Then they went to the woods just for hunting. Then they killed this deerlike thing [gazelle]. It is kind of a very important animal. Its soup is really rich, they happened to kill it, and it died. While the others were in the woods hunting the other group came home and finished all the soup of this animal. The other group came over and say, "Where is this soup? What is all this meat here and where is the soup?" The people, who finished the soup, they were so happy because they had it, the soup. The people who didn't have the soup tried to separate to

go somewhere to hunt for this deerlike thing, you know. So separation started from that point. The Murle went a step forward and Tenet, they just went farther. But they speak the same like language and stuff. So that is Murle and DiDinga; we are speaking the same language and even Tenet. They know some words but it is all the same, you know. If they came today, it's our own people, you know.

Joseph "frames" his response by first summarizing the story: "Well, the origin of these different Murle, DiDinga, Boya, Tenet tribes," and he signals the end of his narrative with the explanation, "If they [Murle] came today, it's our own people, you know." He supports the "truth" of his narrative with the phrase, "Actually, it's something like a history thing." He validates the narrative by asserting, "younger generations born and people born and there are older people, granma and granpa, they just tell the younger people, the young children and teenagers." Later, after extensive library research, I was able to compare Joseph's version with a published folktale collected by Arensen, the only linguist who has recorded three versions of the soup story in Murle, DiDinga, and Tenet (the latter another DiDinga dialect). However, in order for the young men to read Arensen's written DiDinga, I adjusted Arensen's orthography (see below).[4] Arensen's English translation of the DiDinga version he recorded in Sudan some years before Joseph retold it in my kitchen along with Arensen's DiDinga-language transcription follow:

Soup of Oribi [Gazelle]

Long, long ago the DiDinga and Murle were one people. They lived together in the DiDinga Hills. They were one tribe.

One day people went hunting. They killed an oribi and brought it home. The oribi was cooked. Later people gathered to eat the oribi. It happened however, that some people here drank all the soup while the others were still away. So when the rest of the people arrived, they demanded it. They said, "Give us soup." The others replied, "There is no more soup. We have drunk all of it." The other group argues, "How is it that you drank and finished all the soup by yourselves. And why should you let us eat meat alone without any soup?"

These people who missed the soup became very angry and complained bitterly to those who completed the soup. "How can we live with people who disregard us in this way!" Thereupon they and their wives and children left the place and went away. They abandoned the country and went far and deep to some country there into the waters.

Now they are the people we hear they are there and called Murle and they speak the DiDinga language. And those who remained behind (those who completed the soup) at Haula in Zaracal the place where the people ate the oribi is located have stayed up until now. They are the people who are now inhabiting the DiDinga Hills.

People still think and say that the trees which were there then are still there today and standing. Zaracal is within Haula at Loudo in DiDinga.

Uuci Cik Maggɛɛrak

Ai baarkit baangaani ai baa gɔng arumi Didinga hi Murle odoyyii.
Aatik nɛɛg hɔdɛi Biyyaa ici Didinga. Ⱨin nɛɛg ggɔɔl hɔdɛɛzɔng. Nɛ ai kɔr
umwa ɔɔt eeta lika toroyooho. Ɔɔt uruhit mɛggɛɛr umwa ïca anyakta
olɔ. Ikia aahi mɛggɛɛri nicceeni. Ma baa hoti ho iita eeta
dahiita, iita adahit mɛggɛɛr nicci. Ⱨko nɛɛ occa ninga eeta ugɛɛgi aamito
uuci nɛɛ thuc.
Ma au ggoonoggya uruta ïca umuddyaak iding dyoo. Ijinit ggɔɔnɔgi
eneek ai, "Ityoontahetu uuci."
ɛdɛci ggoonoggya eneek ai, "Ittyɔɔ uuci tɔ. Iyya haamta naag uuci vɛlɛk
edeccya."
Ai, "Ɔgɔn hati hutuno aamit niig dyoo uuci edeccyak hï zï ho?
Nɛ utungteeketu ngagït hiita hadakta idinga haaga aitɔ uuci tɔ inni?"
Ⱨlïllɛɛcɔ mï ngaati eeta cik hɔllɔ amuda uuci ho gɛrrɛt udut.
Nɛ ma baa zɛk hoti ho ïtɔ nɛɛ, "Ma aai hi oho ho occa hɔllɔ
harumi hɔdɛi hi eet cik adimanneet bbuz hoti." Ningiti mï ningaata
ingaanni eeta nicceek hi ngaai ciggüng dɔhɔlɛɛni noho irimti ɔɔta.
Ulungatteek looc ngaaningita ɔɔt ittɔ many maamitɔ nüci. Ⱨhɔɔggɔ oko
eeta cik hazihi ai aatik ittɔɔtɔ nüci ai hai Murle ai ɔzɔɔz
Didingayyi ho. Nɛ eeta ugeegi cik idyongan uruta cik acuda uuci cik
mɛggɛɛrak Haulaa ngatü baa adahi eeta mɛggɛɛr Zaracala ho alattya
zɛk ningaata hï noho hɔllɔ ngaa ɔɔ umwaani. Ⱨhɔɔggɔ oko eeta cik
atiyyi bɛɛ ci Didinga.
Eeta ai ngaa zɛk aatik bɔɔbɔlɛɛna cik baa adahi eeta mɛggɛɛr
ci ɛngɛrrɔni nuhuta Loudotti. Ngaa zɛk abili hï kɔr hi nicceeni. Aai
Zaracali ngati hai Haula looccaa ici Louda Didingawa. (Arensen 1992, 304–06)

Here is my transliteration of Arensen's DiDinga-language transcription:

Uuci Cik Meggeerak

Ai baarkit baangaani ai baa gong arumi DiDinga hi Murle odoyii. Aatik neeg hodei Biyaa ici DiDinga. Iin neeg ggool hodeezong. Ne ai korumwa oot eeta lika toroyooho. Oot uruhit meggeer umwa iica anyakta olo. Ikia aahi meggeer nicceeni. Ma baa hoti ho iita eeta dahiita, iita adahit meggeeri nicci. Iko nee occa ninga eeta ugeegi aamito uuci nee thuc.

Ma au ggoonoggya uruta iica umuddyaak iding dyoo. Ojinit ggoonogi eneek ai, "Ityoontahetu uuci."

Edeci ggoonoggya eneek ai, "Ittyo ouuci to. Iyya haamta naag uuci velek edeccya."

Ai, "Ogon hati hutuno aamit niig dyoo uuci edeccyak hii zii ho? Ne utungteeketu ngagiit hiita hadakta idinga haaga aito uuci to inni?" Iliilleeco mii ngaati eeta cik hollo amuda uuci ho gerret udut.

Ne ma baa zek hoti ho iito nee, "Ma aai hi oho ho occa hollo harumi hodei hi eet cik adimanneet bbuz hoti." Ningiti mii ningaata ingaanni eeta nicceek hi ngaai ciggiing doholeeni noho irimiti oota. Ulungatteek looc ngaaningita oot itto many maamito niici. Ihooggo oko eeta cik hazihi ai aatik ittooto niici ai hai Murle ai ozooz DiDingayyi ho. Ne eeta ugeegi cik idyongan uruta cik acuda uuci cik meggeerak Haulaa ngatii baa adahi eeta meggeer Zaracala ho alattya zek ningaata hii noho hollo ngaa oo umwaani. Ihooggo oko eeta cik atiyyi bee ci DiDinga.

Eeta ai ngaa zek aatik booboleena cik ba adahi eeta neggeer ci engerooni nuhuta Loudotti. Ngaa zek abili hii kor hi nicceeni. Aai Zaracali ngati hai Haula looccaa ici Louda DiDingawa.

All DiDinga whom I met in ensuing months knew similar versions of this story. I never asked about the story; it was just told and retold to me by DiDinga whenever I inquired about DiDinga and Murle vocabularies. These variations of the soup story were consistent with earlier data collected by Fetterman for her doctoral dissertation. Fetterman associates the soup story with *kehngeromegeer*, a DiDinga word for "DiDinga-Murle people": "Today, this separation (over the soup) is referred to as *kehngeromeeger* (separated because of the gazelle) and is the same term the DiDinga use when referring to the Murle" (1992, 18). However, Fetterman's translation is an idiomatic one because all of my DiDinga informants translated the word to mean "dried meat," not "separated because of the gazelle." One evening while the DiDinga and I were eating pizza in a local restaurant in Tully, I struggled to clarify words from the few published sources on DiDinga and Murle language. Two of the performers who were visiting from Kentucky immediately recognized the word *kehngeromegeer* as the traditional word for the DiDinga-Murle people, "It means dried meat. It is a story. We used to be one tribe and so they kill a gazelle, the DiDinga people drink the soup. They keep the soup. They used to be one tribe but they gave them [Murle] only meat. And in DiDingaland, soup is very important. So they settled in a very different place. So the word for Murle, it means dried meat." This story is so widespread among the DiDinga groups in Sudan that yet another scholar reports hearing the soup story several times during her fieldwork with the Longarim. Her informants frequently remarked, "The Murle will come home," to indicate their belief that they had at one time been one group (Andretta 1989, 30). But although there are strong similarities among these Surmic speakers, the groups have been affected by geographical differences that are reflected in their vocabularies.

Further, the DiDinga claim that in Sudan their life is "nomadic," when, in fact, I read that the DiDinga are distinctive because, unlike the Murle, Longarim, and Tenet, their primary subsistence derives from gardening on their steep slopes. DiDinga women own these gardens, and they can raise their own goats and sometimes cattle, which gives them the opportunity to engage in trade. Pottery is a specialized activity of a few DiDinga families whose pottery is important for trade. DiDinga female potters trade for cattle and in this way become cattle owners within their own right (Driberg 1932c, 408). Compared to other neighboring groups such as the Dinka, a DiDinga female cattle owner is "a reversal of all accepted pastoralist norms and of a type with blacksmithing which is also associated with breaking the rules" (Mack and Robertshaw 1982, 126). The making of pottery for trade is unusual because, as Mack and Robertshaw have shown, pastoralist societies such as the DiDinga and the Murle "are not, on the whole, preservative ones" (1982, 126). The only exceptions are objects associated with ritual rainmaking and dance, and these are often repaired rather than merely discarded and replaced.[5] The DiDinga and Murle, who intermarry, are closely related culturally and linguistically, but the young men admitted that cattle raiding and resultant warfare is frequent between the groups and remains an activity common to all neighboring groups in southern Sudan. This interethnic warfare has continued to exacerbate the civil war. In their recontextualized performances for American audiences, the young men included songs which expressed this complexity in southern Sudan:

> *Ee uket nohoni*
> Why are you torturing us like this?
> *Ee longo cik gang dekererik i horoma ho*
> Yes, you guys on the hill?
> *Uket nohoni*
> Why are you torturing us?
> *Ee uki hati koruma iin meder*
> Yes, it will one day become a vendetta.

This is a song about the DiDinga oppression by the Arab Islamic majority in power. Although the groups are not named, one day, the DiDinga sing, the situation will be reversed. The "guys on the hill" is a reference to the police post built near Mount Lotukei, which is close to the Ugandan border. Most of the police stationed at the post were Arab Muslims from the north. The song is a protest about police brutality against the DiDinga, who were powerless to resist. They instead taunted their enemies with songs such as this one.

Songs such as this were recalled from their childhood by the young men in Syracuse. Unlike the other political songs, however, *Ee Uket Nohoni* is sung in the traditional DiDinga terse style; that is, the text is a symbolically dense narrative that relies heavily on contextual information in order to grasp its meaning. Like most traditional DiDinga songs, its specificity is only recognizable to DiDinga and, without an intimate knowledge of DiDinga oral history, the meaning would be entirely lost. I heard this song during the first *nyakorot* performed by the DiDinga in Auburn, New York, but the performers could provide little information about the meaning of the song or its references:

Charles: This is a song that mean there are minority people who are overpower by majority to do what they want. But one day it will turn verse verser [*sic*].

Simon: It's a political song.

Charles: It's like, before there are people coming to our area. And they mistreat us so we sing, why are you coming, mistreating us? But we will fight.

F: But who are the people who are coming, mistreating you?

Charles: There are many people, many tribes.

F: Is this a traditional song, an old song, or a new song?
Simon: I think it is an old song.

In taped interviews, Charles was not specific about the identity of the groups who were "mistreating" the DiDinga. In casual conversations, however, he admitted that, historically, the DiDinga engaged in conflict with nearby groups, including the Longarim, who were "Joseph's people." I read that traditional conflicts continued to plague the southern Sudanese because annual transhumance is central to the DiDinga and their enemies, the Toposa. The Longarim, however, are considered "one people" with the DiDinga, so to understand these conflicts outsiders must be aware that all groups must seek pastures during the dry season. The shared patterns of transhumance brought many differing groups in contact, and this is also one of the complexities that has contributed to the current conflict in Sudan.[6]

Experience with mutual cattle raiding among the groups is common during DiDinga childhood. To this day, neighbors such as the Toposa remain hostile to the DiDinga, but cultural exchange, in the form of language and customs, continues: "Actually, people grow with different language. As a generation grows, there is a lot of language change. If this generation of our grow, in Sudan right now, we will be in that high maybe middle-class of our people because we have already taken these initiation stuff of our people and we are all there, right. The language that we are supposed to speak at this stage for this, that language will never change. But it is already changing with people above us. So we are like growing, overlapping. It is very hard to understand but [pauses] that's it." In this taped interview, Joseph acknowledged that like language everywhere, DiDinga is not static. In fact, although they remain deadly enemies, the DiDinga have adopted many loanwords from the Toposa. These loan words, for the most part, have been incorporated into their expressive culture in the form of songs, dances, and material culture.

The most apparent example is the DiDinga's use of the Toposa word *nyalado*, the cattle fly whip used daily by cattle herders which also has an important symbolic function in ritual and dance. Further, Joseph indicated that within DiDinga villages, subgroups continually develop expressions and words that are not shared with younger members. Although I explained to Joseph that specialized in-group language is not unique to DiDinga, at the same time I was gradually introduced to many concepts that did not translate from DiDinga to English, such as the aforementioned relationship of place to a season and the fact that traditional names for people often relate to an event in the lives of those people. Yet it was never clear to me why Jacob was called Jima and sometimes Thomas.

I understood, however, that nicknames are frequently given by older relatives to children: one day at my house, the young men teased Charles, whose grandmother named him Lapopo, "little round thing," because he was a plump little boy. After that, whenever I wanted to tease Charles, I would call him by this nickname which inevitably reduced him to giggles. Laughingly, Benjamin explained, "Charles thinks he is too old for that name," but Fortunato shyly admitted that his friends still call him Lobolobi: "They called me Lobolobi. It's kind of the bull's name but not my real name. They chose it. It means really strong. Yes, they told me I was very strong little boy, like huge." Later, when I looked the word up in Rosato's dictionary, I learned that *lobolobyagit* means "glutton."

The young men told me that names play a very important role in the lives of DiDinga children, and, growing up, a child will have many nicknames because the way a child is viewed by his parents can differ. For example, Benjamin told me that when he was a very young child, his mother loved him the most, so she named him Lokwang (Loved One). His father, however, called him Lokringo (One Who Loves Meat) because Benjamin ate so much. All DiDinga children retain these names into adulthood. When I asked James what his mother called him, the others answered "Ippe." James translated his name as "He Who Will Be Known," explaining that his mother believed one day he would be famous. To this, the others laughed and translated "Ippe, He Who Knows Nothing." This exchange prompted James to demonstrate how much he did know: When I asked if any of them recalled stories told to them during their childhood, James immediately began narrating *Nakedo ki Idet* ("Hare and Chameleon"):

James: Hare and chameleon, they had like this competition. And then this man. . . .

Fortunato: He was hyena.

James: No, he was a real man.

Fortunato: Oh.

James: This man, he had the most beautiful daughter. He said the first to come to my house and to sit on the golden chair can marry my daughter. That was like the challenge so the hare is like the fastest animal and he can't compete with the chameleon because the chameleon is too small so you know, he had all this time and he just knew he'd plan everything. It was like, that is going to be my wife. So, the chameleon was like, alright, I'll just try my best and whatever time I reach, I'll just have to accept and the hare, you know, he just slept.

Fortunato: The lion, the lion.

James: No, it's the hare.

Fortunato: Oh.

James: So he said, you know, that's going to be my wife. He had to build everything. He was ready to bring the wife home. So that morning he was ready. So the hare woke up and he didn't have to worry about anything because he knew he would be the first one. So the hare saw the chameleon so the hare let the chameleon go so the chameleon knew the hare would get there before him so he jumped on the hare's tail. He's got a tail, right? The hare didn't know chameleon was on his tail so chameleon just ride on his behind. So he went to sit on the chair and the chameleon was the first one to sit on the chair. So the man was like, you, you are sitting on the chameleon. He was there before you [all laughing]. Wow, it was so funny [laughing]!

This story performance is embedded in an interview, but James keys his performance by introducing the title, "Hare and Chameleon," as a framing device. However, DiDinga folktales do not have titles. Fortunato attempts to undermine James's assertion that he does indeed "know something," but James successfully resists Fortunato's effort. In his conclusion, James reiterates that he is a good storyteller by saying, "Wow, it was so funny!" When we all laugh, James has effectively subverted Fortunato's attempt to undermine him.

DiDinga stories like "Hare and Chameleon" have didactic and entertainment functions, but cultural history is preserved in song rather than in narrative. If events are not within living memory, they are not preserved unless they concern the entire society. I was unaware of the extent of this song method for preserving DiDinga history until we reviewed a video made during one of the public performances. The song *Ichayo* (discussed in the introduction to this book) meant simply "Fighting" and refers to an historic DiDinga battle, while other songs such as *Sadik* are protest songs about the current Sudanese civil war. During their first *nyakorot* in the United States, the men sang both songs.

The song to Sadik Lugo is about the former Sudanese prime minister who was deposed in 1989 by Omar Beshir, the current military ruler. In the mid-1980s, John Garang, commander-in-chief of the SPLA, scored many military victories when he liberated strategic towns in southern Sudan from the control of Arabic soldiers. The song reflects the situation:

Enek Sadiq Lugo icia
Gerengi anyaha guwa ci hauna kicaya Kapuata ma kicaya Kapuata tel hotia
Tororita lahadi Juba ci ngati hengera huwanya iwir Sadiqi
uha Khatiba

Nakeng hichayo
Muksasa ereyo icia
Khatiba Ghazali nica anyaha guwa ci Sudani

Tell Sadik to leave [the south]. Garang is coming, bringing [military] force that we intend to bombard and liberate Kapoeta.
After we have liberated Kapoeta, we march on Torit until Juba [whereupon] we divide [munitions].
Nakeng Battalion, let us fight!
Broom Battalion, wait [for us]!
Gazelle Battalion is coming, bringing Sudan's force.

The words "Nakeng," "Muksasa," and "Ghazali" are the names of DiDinga warrior age-sets. The southern rebel soldiers warn Sadik to leave southern Sudan because Garang was bringing his military forces so that he could capture the cities of Torit and Juba and liberate them. One of the young dancers later explained, "We are telling Sadik to move out [of] that place [Kapoeta] and leave southerners alone to have peace as other people do. We will move from Kapoeta, Torit, and Juba if you [Sadik] will not move." The young men smiled broadly as they sang this military song, and the soloist later indicated that there was a positive "feel" to the song by adding: "This mean Sadik should move out of Kapoeta before the team come for reinforcement to overthrow," revealing the young men's boast that their DiDinga "team" will ultimately prevail.

The differences in DiDinga dialects became apparent when we listened to a solo sung by Joseph who spoke Boya (Longarim):

Nyelia koneyn
Nyetulia konyan nabura aremikori
Lotuliaki aremikori, lotulia kapanya
Nyababolionga adtuhothik chkaaca
Ahud babu narrac
Kuvachock tura aremikori lotulia
Aremikori lotulia, lotulia
Kapanya nyababolionga

All members of the chorus told me that I would have to wait for the translation because the "Boya singer" (Joseph) was not present at my home on the day we reviewed the videotape of this performance. It could not be translated fully because Joseph sang many "Toposa words" for aesthetic effect. This was confirmed later by Joseph, who admitted that it would be difficult for anyone else to translate his song:

> I am singing that one so I have to explain everything to you. It is a gun. A gun is there to take care of our goats and our lives of all the animals and stuff. If you take our goats and animals, we are like nomadic, going with cattle to get water and we are going to get food. To go to camp because we move with the camp, we get water, we decided to stay there for a moment. *Toboto* means going to camp with the cow. *Kuvachock*, give me more goats and cattle to take with me with the camp where the rest are. *Nyababolionga* doesn't mean anything. Just to connect the story together.

Although the others insisted that only Joseph could translate, they understood the gist of his "Boya song" because they had already told me that it was a song about a gun. Many of the "Toposa words" like *nyababolionga* were actually sounds without meaning. Inserted by the individual singer for stylistic reasons, such sounds constitute an important element in DiDinga song aesthetics. When I later had an opportunity to e-mail the song text to Paul Ejek Rwatamoi Atanya, he replied, "As for the first Boya song, I am still trying to find out the exact meaning from one of the elder Boya living here in Calgary. I believe the song is not a political song but a chanting bullsong-Chaali. There are lots of spellings that make it difficult for me to figure out its meaning. Usually Boya, like the DiDinga, tend to chant in Toposa language, the language I am quite fluent" (June 20, 2002). It appeared that older songs such as this, which are always more succinct, allow the lead singer to improvise. The translation is never identical because the text can be a reference to an older folktale or historical event. For nonnative speakers, many words could not be translated or were references only known to insiders or the members of a specific age-set. Until this realization, I was frustrated by their translations of DiDinga songs. Some of my difficulty was due to the topographical nature of DiDinga language, which is highly contextual. This was a common problem that confronted earlier researchers among the DiDinga-Murle, who wrote,

> [I]nevitable linguistic limitations made it difficult for me to understand the full range of symbolism in Murle thought, and much of the dualism in their philosophy; and the fact that for them words have associations, as well as meanings, proved a constant barrier in trying to unravel "hard" topics. In the Murle view

everything is "linked together," and all the various strands are so closely interwoven that it is almost impossible to start at the beginning in the study of a particular sphere of their life, and follow it through to its logical conclusion, and all too easy to miss the overtones of a particular definition. I believe, however, from my observations and contacts with the people, that this interweaving of different ideas into a coherent pattern is part of their very texture of thought and expression, particularly in their songs, which are so full of allusion, and association of words and ideas, that a few carefully chosen words naturally convey far more to a fellow tribesman who is well informed about their customs than a stranger trying to elucidate them. Their songs and sayings, which employ archaic words not understood by ordinary Murle—it was only the *gayok* who could explain them to me, and even then, not always as fully as I could have wished—are learnt by heart and transmitted from one generation to another, so providing a method of preserving tribal traditions and beliefs, and in turn, the continuity of their thought. To add to my own linguistic difficulties, my literate Murle assistants were too young, and their knowledge of English too restricted, for them to be of much assistance to me in this connection. (Lewis 1972, 126–27)

Fortunately for me, the young men spoke English, and they rapidly became acquainted with the American idiom. I was amazed that the DiDinga seemed to have no difficulty "code-switching" from a non-Western language to English, which was their fourth language after Arabic and Swahili. They had been forced to learn Arabic because, in Sudan, they were a small minority among dominant groups such as the Dinka, but, like the Dinka, they suffered oppression at the hands of the Islamic Khartoum government. However, in the United States they were again marginalized by their racial identity, though not as overtly: "The barriers facing racialized sojourners are often reinforced by socioeconomic constraints—particularly in North America—the development of a post-Fordian nonunion low-wage sector offering very limited opportunities for advancement" (Clifford 1997, 265). In the United States they faced tensions with urban African-American youth, who interpreted the DiDinga and Dinka's English as an attempt to accommodate white society. Before arriving in the United States, both groups had heard stories about African-American criminals and drug dealers, which they believed, and thus they unintentionally perpetuated these stereotypes. When the Lost Boys first arrived in the United States it appeared that Africans were being given preferential treatment, but a closer look at their daily lives revealed that this so-called "acceptance" by the dominant white society did not translate into greater access to economic or educational resources. Rather, their lack of transferable skills and credentials would confine the Sudanese to entry-level jobs for nonnative speakers of English.

Because they migrated from remote rural regions in Africa, they were also adjusting to a foreign environment which was urban. Nostalgic story songs about a rural countryside figured large in their repertoire, as well as the protest songs against the Sudanese war that they performed for American audiences. At this early point in our relationship, however, the young men did not feel at ease talking about their war experiences so I did not press them for explanations about these protest songs. Instead, we talked about *Lotim*, a favorite song about a baboon with "a black hand" who "eats up" the farm of Lonyume and Kulanga. The song, recorded here exactly the way that Charles wrote it, was one of the first songs the young men sang at Syracuse University on March 3, 2002:

Lotim holia thoti ahacaani ba ngani ngati holo akani ho
Lotim holia thoti ahacaani ba ngani ngati holo akani ho
Adak lotimi mana ci Lonyume
Lotim holia thoti ahacaani ba ngani ngati holo akani ho
Adak lotimi mana ci Kulanga
Lotim holia thoti ahacaani ba ngani ngati holo akani ho

The baboon, the black-footed. Who betrayed you from not being able to farm or cultivate?
The baboon, the black-footed. Who betrayed you from not being able to farm or cultivate?
The baboon ate Lonyume's farm produce. The baboon, the black footed. Who betrayed you from being able to farm?
The baboon ate Kulanga's farm produce.

When I asked Charles about the song's meaning, he provided a literal explanation about a lazy monkey: "You monkey, that you have a black hand. What make(s) you not to have (to) farm? Monkeys are eating Lonyume's farms. Monkeys are eating Kulanga's farms." Lonyume, the male owner of a farm, and Kulanga, his wife, were the names of actual people whom only Charles knew. As the soloist, he had authority to insert the names of people with whom he was acquainted. However, these names were incidental to the song's meaning. The other singers confirmed that this is an abuse song to chastise a lazy person. Monkeys and baboons are quite large and steal food from gardens. Like a monkey or baboon who eats but does not contribute, the unnamed person avoids doing his or her fair share of work:

> **James:** It is, like, about a mountainous area-that is, where they do a lot of farming and they have big farms and they have monkeys and other animals . . . and big cows.
> **Simon:** They come.
> **James:** They eat cows, so they sing, "You monkey, why you so lazy that you can't do your own farming." It's like a story. It is something kids like. Lotim is the name of a monkey.

When I asked if monkeys and baboons really eat cows, they all laughed and said, "It is something kids like to sing." Encapsulated in these songs were memories of helping parents to herd cattle and plant maize. By this time, I was truly humbled by the degree of their knowledge about the natural world, coupled with their adaptive ability to modern life in the United States. In dance-songs the young men would kill a number of birds with their public performances. They would have the opportunity to express a unique group identity in a prouder than usual way that resonated with an ancient identity. But just as their warrior songs would be only quasi-real because they were not initiated into manhood, they would display their wit before unsuspecting American audiences who would not know that they were only "fooling around" like children. In the following chapters, it will be shown how this dialectical tension between the individual and social agency contributes to their hybrid identity.

Surveying the
Landscape

Ololo Lobalu, Ololo Lobalu
Ololo Lobalu, Ololo Lobalu
Aitani cieth hutuno?
How do you think you are building the house?
Mumm Lobalu aitani cieth hutuno?
Mmm, Lobalu how are you building the house?
Aa iin cieth carret inni?
Why is the house [looking like] a porcupine?
Traditional DiDinga song

One afternoon the Lost Boys and I sat in my TV room to review their videotaped performances. James suddenly announced, "We come with riddles too. We got a lot of riddles." One of the other young men explained that "tricky stories" are told to DiDinga children by adults whenever the DiDinga community sits around a campfire. When I asked James to tell me a "tricky story," he said, "There's a house without a door." His simple statement initiated a lengthy riddle exchange during which I became both target and audience for their playfulness. I would no longer be a collaborator; I had unwittingly become their student, a DiDinga child who needed to be socialized:

F: I don't know. . . . What is it?
James: It's an egg.

F: Egg?

Fortunato: Yes.

Charles: Eggs!!

James: Because it is oval and it doesn't have a door. We got a lot of riddles. Some you can figure out. Some not.

F: Tell me some more.

Fortunato: Okay, you know monkeys? They sitting in some kind of tree? It is growing inside the sea. So, it's mango tree. And it gets ripe, you know? You really feel hungry. And you see the fruit to eat. The monkey's only eating there and you don't know how to get there from where you are to that tree. It is a sea. You cannot go across so how can you eat a mango from that tree.

James: And the monkey doesn't want to give it to you.

Fortunato: And you really need to eat.

F: What would I do?

Fortunato: Yes.

F: Sing to it?

All: No [much laughter]!

F: Swim to the tree?

All: No! You can be eaten by crocodiles [laughter].

F: Grab his tail?

All: [much laughter] No you can't move to get his tail!

F: I don't know! What's the answer? [All laugh loudly together.]

James: You have to get something like a stone and throw.

Fortunato: And the monkey will take a mango and throw to you.

F: Throw back! Oh! I throw something and the monkey throws something back!

James: He will pick a mango and throw back to you.

Fortunato: So you get to eat.

F: Well, I guess I wouldn't get a mango.

All: [laughing] No!

James: We got a lot of riddles. There's a flat, a valley. There's a lion, a goat, and you have to take the grain to the other side. [They start discussing.] Like a lion this side and a goat on that side and the grain on his head. He has to balance all this. It's kind of like a food chain. If you leave the grain with the goat, he will eat it. If you leave the man with the lion, he will be eaten. So whatever you do, they gotta be safe.

F: So how do you get everybody there?

Fortunato: What you do, you can take the lion and the grain together. Leave the goat on the other side. Leave the goat alone. Because lion cannot eat grain. Then you go for the goat and then it's okay.

Charles: But, you have to go twice because when you take lion first, then you come back and then get the lion to bring it back. Take the goat and leave the lion with the grain. Then you come back and take the grain and take the goat. Then you leave the goat this side and take the lion with the grain and then the goat.

James: There's a community. A big community. The older people will greet you first but younger ones are too fresh.

F: Oh, that's a riddle? What is the community? What is it?

James: They say, the seasons. In the fall, the old leaves fall to greet you but the young ones are too green. They stay on.

Fortunato: [Our] people like teaching, you know, for education.

Initially, I had waited for the riddler to ask, "What is it?" until I realized that this prompt is not part of traditional DiDinga riddling. My confusion only added to their humor. For a folklorist, this exchange provided rich data, but it also represented a very special kind of interpersonal communication in which I was able to simultaneously document their riddles and to participate as a player in the tradition. Public-sector work, like academic research, requires that "[w]e folklorists do not only study texts; we do not only study performances. We try to understand persons in performance generating texts and giving and finding meaning in their lives" (Titon 1995, 439). A reversal occurred as they taught me about DiDinga culture. What they knew was limited to the years before their childhoods were disrupted by war. Yet, because I could not do fieldwork in their homeland, I became their student.

Many African societies have contexts in which children or initiates are told riddles as a form of instruction. Although I did not recognize it immediately, throughout my work with the young men, we often entered into a play space; that is, a novel situation in which inversion was acceptable. This exchange had arisen spontaneously from conversation. They took on the role of riddlers, and I became the riddlee in a kind of status reversal. As folklorists have noted, in most societies in order for riddles to be effective, the riddles must be unfamiliar to the audience. It is also an accepted fact that riddles may disappear from circulation unless they can be told to newcomers. Likewise, for their dance-songs, an American audience would provide a conduit, enabling the Lost Boys to be active rather than passive bearers of the DiDinga traditions.

In addition to these riddling sessions through which I indirectly learned about traditional life in Sudan, I spent hours rereading published sources in order to grasp their country's complicated history and varied geography. It was frustrating that there were scant publications on DiDinga language and culture. Sudan is one-third the size of the continental United States, but in southern Sudan, where the DiDinga and Dinka were born, there are still only 17 miles of paved roads. There are even fewer lines of communication. Today, government officials in the south use Morse code messages to communicate with Khartoum, the capital city 1,000 miles to the north. Communication relies on Arabic language because there are more than 500 ethnic groups living in Sudan. The north, dominated by Islam, is called the "Arabized Sudan." Although many groups in the south have remained animistic, in recent years most southern groups have converted to Christianity. Although tribalism has always caused minor conflicts, the religious differences between the north and the south have further exacerbated a volatile situation that includes conflicts among the southern rebel armies.

The young men call the DiDinga Hill region by the name "DiDingaland" to contrast it with "Dinkaland." The former is a fertile mountain range in the southeastern region of Equatoria. The Dinka live along both sides of the Nile but their villages are concentrated in the Upper Nile Province, a swampy region fed by the headwaters of the Nile. The Dinka were pushed out from the east by the DiDinga-Murle, who raided their region. Historically, the DiDinga seldom, if ever, came into contact with the Dinka until they became refugees from the war. All groups, however, have words to express the "otherness" of their neighbors: In Dinka language, the DiDinga and other non-Dinka people who are not Arab are often called *nyamnyam* (*nyinyam*) or "cannibal." Throughout Africa, *nyamnyam,* used by many Sudanese ethnic groups, indicates a chewing sound. In turn, the DiDinga refer to Dinka people and other ethnic groups as *mirohit,* which has several meanings, one of which is "enemy."

Language is not the only major difference between the Dinka and DiDinga. Because they came from a remote mountain range in southern Sudan between Uganda and Kenya, traditionally the DiDinga do not rely entirely on cattle herding, as the Dinka and neighboring groups do. Instead, the DiDinga have a mixed agricultural and cattle economy, with smaller herds communally cared for by young men who take turns (Arensen 1983, 66). Thus, most of their food comes from small DiDinga gardens supplemented by hunting rather than the reverse.

Although the DiDinga commonly refer to their region as "DiDingaland," the official name is Budi County. Because of its geographical isolation, the young men describe their homeland as both fertile and sublime. In 1980 Marilyn Fetterman determined Budi County to be the most geographically remote district in southern Sudan since the era of colonial rule: "During the period of my research, it remained difficult to get to for a person who had anything more than a small parcel of goods" (1992, v). More than 20 years after Fetterman visited DiDingaland, the transportation system remains a remnant of the British colonial system, and the young men told me that roads have not been repaired since the British left the country in the 1950s. Further, since the arrival of war in DiDingaland in the 1990s, the roads have continued to deteriorate. Several of the DiDinga in Syracuse were born and raised in neighboring villages in Budi County, where they shared their childhood. After escaping from their villages and spending time in refugee camps, a fortunate few met in a missionary school in Nairobi, Kenya. It was only a coincidence that they were resettled together in our city. It was difficult, however, to elicit information about the region from the young men, who seemed more interested in singing songs than commenting on geography or history:

F: Are you from the same place?

Simon: Same place, but different villages.

F: What is your village?

Simon: Thunguro.

F: And your village is . . .

Charles: Nagichot.

F: Are they nearby?

Charles: Yes.

F: Did you know each other when you lived in your villages?

Simon: Yes.

F: How far away are your villages?

Simon: Not so far.

F: Can you walk there?

Charles: Ya.

F: Is there a road?

Simon: No [laughter], paths!

Interviews at this early period in our relationship were difficult, time-consuming, and limited by vocabulary. Language limitations extended to me as well as the young men. For example, in the above interview, a simple word and concept like "remote" posed problems. As the above interview revealed, there were connecting paths among villages but only one accessible road for the entire region. It was so badly in need of repair that they considered it an "indirect route" and preferred the "paths." Charles giggled uneasily when I showed him a library book that included DiDinga thatched huts with the caption "DiDinga family compounds." To defuse his uneasiness, I commented that DiDinga houses were "real houses" because, unlike Americans, DiDinga owners knew how to build houses from start to finish. I also told the young men my husband believed the ability to build one's own house demonstrated one's special knowledge and abilities. The photographs of the DiDinga houses made it possible to ask the men about their earlier lives, without talking directly about their war experiences, a topic which I sensed remained a painful one for all of them. Instead, I directed my line of inquiry to happier times. During the following interview, they studied the photographs for a long period of time before responding. They were so intent that I was not certain they were listening to my questions:

F: [pointing to a photograph of a traditional DiDinga house in Sudan, made of thatch] Is this an old photo or a recent one of a DiDinga house?

Simon: It is recent.

Charles: Yeah. These are the houses now but this [points to a small one]. . . . This is a granary. And this is corn.

F: And you hang it up to dry?

Charles: Yes! Exactly!

F: Is this an old picture [pointing to a different book]?

Simon: No, these are recent.

F: So, it looks cool inside the house.

Simon: Cool . . . you know, the grass makes the house cool.

F: Who built these houses? Did your parents build your house?

Simon and Charles: [in unison] Yes, they did.

F: Now, where did they get this grass? Is there woods nearby?

Charles: Yeah, first they get this one, this pole, my father is going for this pole and my mother is going for grass.

Simon: Yes, the grass.

F: Did you help?

Charles and Simon: [in unison] Yeah! Yes.

Charles: We went for the . . . the . . .

Simon: Poles.

Charles: Yes, the poles. And my sister is going with my mother for the brush.

Simon: So the work is divided . . . ladies going for the top, the brush and maybe the grass, for the roof.
Charles: When we make for the roof, the men put the brush, like . . .
Simon: Different styles.
Charles: When the women will make the, will plaster the walls with mud.

These interviews were tedious but nonthreatening. The young men became confident when they realized that I knew very little about DiDinga culture. Looking at photographs helped to establish that they would need to explain to me in detail how they had experienced a lifestyle far different from mine. While looking at the book, Simon associated my word "remote" with beauty:

Simon: Back in Sudan, there are no telephones. Maybe in the big city [Khartoum].
F: Do you mean, it is remote?
Simon: Yes [emphatic]! Very beautiful because we live in equatorial forest. There is no winter.
F: So, the weather is always good?
Simon: The weather is excellent—always sunny . . . but not everywhere in Sudan is like that, especially. . . . In the North, is desert.

They seemed delighted by this book of photographs of DiDinga houses: Where did I find such a book? They were amazed that it was available in our university library. When I asked again if the photographs were "too old," they insisted, "No, they are recent." As I pointed to other photographs, they accurately identified the houses of various neighboring groups such as the Toposa (Taposa, Topotha), which differ only because the roof is tiered. I read the description to them: "Each extended family builds its own homestead. Many of these are built on mountain peaks or cliff edges, so are extremely difficult to approach. This placement of homesteads helps keep them safe from attacks by peoples of the plains who are afraid of heights and of precarious approaches. Homesteads are sometimes surrounded by a heavy wood fence with a gate that can be closed at night to keep out intruders. When flying over the hills, it is intriguing to see some of these homesteads located in the most inaccessible and precarious places" (Arensen 1983, 67). To my confusion, the author had reported that many of the conical DiDinga houses have been replaced by squarer houses with rectangular walls made of interwoven bamboo, but none of my informants confirmed this.

Charles, who had lived in Sudan more recently than the author, said the information was "wrong" because the traditional conical building style had not been replaced.[1] His assertion underscored for me the importance of native confirmation of published academic sources. Dominic L., whose entire family had been killed as a result of the war, then described the appearance of his early home in detail and became animated as he recalled the role of children in the construction of his home:

> You know, in my village we got a lot of things going on—got the cattles, the goats, and the chickens. You have to fence in your house, the compound, really good. We can live something like four or five families together and like then we make a fence in the village and lock it at night. We raise some white ducks too to keep the compound safe and all these kinds of things [pause]. Just kind of, you have to clean first the ground and make the foundation. You take the rope and twist it, make like a circumference to make it round and then you put sticks all around and take the bamboo and then you pull all together and make a circle, just to make it hard [strong]. Then mix the mud and cow dung with water and then you splash it there to make it good. Then you build the rafters really good with bamboo, bamboo tree. Then you take the grass. You put grass there really nice. Children help take the rope and give it to their dad and big brothers. Sometimes you go inside the house kind of like a needle and you put the sticks where they [are] needed. They fix the rope inside there. You have it kind of off the wood and then you take it again [demonstrates with hands, rope over rafters] and pull [the rope] this side so you can hold it and tie it.

None of the young men expressed longing for their villages, but they complained about our city noise and lights: "Here you can't see the stars at night." As the newness of their life in an American city dimmed, a longing for the countryside became more obvious. After several ensuing conversations, I recognized nostalgia in cultural memory when the group sang *Lobalu*, a song that remained a permanent part of their recontextualized repertoire:

Ololo Lobalu, Ololo Lobalu
Ololo Lobalu, Ololo Lobalu
Aitani cieth hutuno?
How do think you are building the house?
Mumm Lobalu aitani cieth hutuno?
Mmm, Lobalu how are you building the house?

Aa iin cieth carret inni?
Why is the house [looking like] a porcupine?

The DiDinga commented that men take great pride in building their homes, houses, granaries, and other structures because building a house well affects men's marriageability. Women especially take note of this with respect to eligible single men as they approach the age of marriage because a marriageable man must be capable of designing a good house for his bride. The song is about an actual man named Lobalu who had poor architectural skills. Lobalu does not live up to the DiDinga's standards because he was an incompetent builder. During a public construction of a village house (a cooperative undertaking similar to building a Habitat for Humanity house), Lobalu's portion of thatched hut was rough. The grass was not smoothly applied; instead it stuck out like a porcupine's quills. The original song's composer wasted no time in exposing Lobalu's poor architectural skills to the whole village. Since there are no other means of communication, his failings were recorded in a song composed by one singer who memorialized Lobalu in DiDinga oral history. This example supports Neil Rosenberg's theory that a single singer can contribute to the larger group's repertoire (2002). If the group accepts it, it becomes tradition.

Lobalu's fate, Charles explained, was one to be avoided at all costs. To have their failures memorialized in song was a real concern for the young men, especially when I videotaped their performances. To me, it seemed unlikely that the videos could end up in DiDingaland, which has an elevation of 7,000 feet, a place which has only four miles of paved roads throughout its 320,000 square miles. But the young men assured me that "news travels" even to "remote" regions. I later learned that news does indeed travel: Eventually, I downloaded some of the dance-songs of the DiDinga singers in Syracuse and gave each young man his own CD on which I printed a simple label, "Traditional DiDinga Songs in Auburn, New York." When one of the young men mailed his CD to other DiDinga living in Canada, they responded favorably, sending word back to Syracuse: The CD was "very good."

These transnational information networks operated like the traditional methods for spreading news in Sudan. However, the lack of roads, electricity, and modern means of communication meant that it would have taken much longer in their homeland. This remoteness is something Americans can only imagine. Simon stressed the remarkable differences between north and south Sudan. DiDingaland was unlike the arid desert in the north which meant that the associated geographical problems did not exist for the DiDinga. When I asked the young men if our Syracuse weather with its heavy snowfall bothered them, Charles indicated his discomfort by answering evenly, "I have no choice." During our conversations, I spoke self-consciously as I avoided common expressions like "houses on your street" or references to "roads" between their villages. When I forgot, the DiDinga men patiently corrected me, "We have only paths," but defended the "remoteness" of their region by adding, "It is a most beautiful place." Their claims supported reports published by the few Western visitors to their region: "The homeland of the DiDinga is rich in vegetation, compared to the surrounding environments of the Topothaland" (Fetterman 1992). This in part explained the Toposa attacks on the DiDinga, whose land is so fertile that there is always plenty to eat. One DiDinga man explained, "We are still harvesting by hand. The U.N. brought in. . . . I don't know what you call it. It isn't a tractor, it is pulled by a bull. But most people are still working by hand." Similarly, Arensen, who visited the region in 1983, acknowledges that although severe drought is often problematic for groups living around the DiDinga, the DiDinga do not face this environmental problem in DiDingaland: "[T]here are rocky peaks and deep valleys surrounding a high plateau. The vegetation at the base of the hills is deciduous woodland and tall grass, but in gradually ascending altitudes, this gives way to bamboo and larger trees. The top of the range consists of large mountain forests and open fields of grass" (1983, 66). To this day, their natural environment, when not disturbed by the ravages of constant war, remains almost as idyllic as described by Jack Herbert Driberg, the first anthropologist to the region in 1927.[2] It surprised me that 75 years earlier, a more poetic Driberg wrote, "Shortly after the spring rains start a large variety of flowers burst into bloom, and the country is blue with a carpet of gentian, the forests become heavy with the scent of cyclamen, and the rhododendron colours the landscape with a profusion of blossom: then, while the grass is still short, and the days are cold and, as often happens, heavy with mist, and the bracken is green and dripping with moisture, one might easily forget that one was in tropical Africa and be transported in imagination to the enchanting hills above Edinburgh" (1927a, 388).

The close association between remoteness and beauty was repeated when we drove on country roads to my home in rural upstate New York: "It is very beautiful here"; "The hills are so green . . . the trees . . . it is like ours"; or simply, "It is so quiet, this is just like DiDingaland." The young men also noticed the dark night skies, commenting, "Here we can see the stars." During the summers of 2002 and 2003, the young men picked wild blackberries in my backyard, telling me, "We do this in DiDingaland." They taught me *hohomala* (DiDinga for blackberry).

Charles prepares traditional DiDinga food in his apartment, 2003. Photo: Felicia McMahon.

By the time Benjamin immigrated to Syracuse in December 2003, he had heard about my extensive blackberry patch. Looking from my kitchen window at the snow-covered landscape on December 25, he asked incredulously, "Do *hohomala* grow here?" To this day, we laugh when we say "hohomala."

The young men noted that, unlike the winter season, the rural upstate New York summer and spring were similar to seasons in DiDingaland. During the summer, James said simply, "I want to build my house here." Dominic R. later explained that DiDingaland was very different from the region of the Dinka and from the arid areas in the north. He explained how different groups came in contact with the DiDinga: "It is very fertile, so if we start harvesting, other tribes come to barter, they trade maybe a goat for our grain, maize, sorghum. They don't use money, only a very small percentage (do)." Dominic told me that DiDinga agriculture is unique because the DiDinga grow maize that is ground into a staple called *ahat* (Swahili *ugali*) and use it for trade. I replied that I think bartering is a better way to exchange goods than using money in the United States because then you know where your food comes from. Several of the men then admitted at first they did not like American food because it

Left to right: Jima, Simon, George, and Joseph celebrate with traditional food in their Syracuse apartment, 2003. Photo: Felicia McMahon.

was too "sweet," which meant that they were not used to salt as well as sugar in foods. The men also said they did not like the "chemicals" in American vegetables, adding, "The first week that we were here, all we ate was bread, nothing else. I don't know what you put into American food! No good!" Another commented, "We plant maize and sorghum or maybe vegetables, like cabbages around DiDinga houses, so you have your own. And when it is raining, you don't have to go far to get them."

One afternoon I offered to buy the ingredients for DiDinga food if they would teach me how to cook it. In the supermarket, they pointed to *weka* (okra), *haputh* (kale), *mango* (mango), *paipai* (papaya), and *naboloc* (banana). When we could not find *ahat,* we went to a local Mideastern store which carried ground maize. While we shared meals, they taught me basic vocabulary: *ubone* (bread), *mam* (water), and *kinyomoc* (fruit). I also noticed that the DiDinga always ate very small portions, and I never observed any of them overeating. As a matter of fact, they ate very slowly, appearing to carefully chew their food. Later, one caseworker explained that in the refugee camps the men were used to eating one meal a day. Although they later became accustomed to buying American food in supermarkets, none of the DiDinga were overweight. Benjamin later remarked that he believed overweight Americans "know how bad they look but they are addicted to food." And when Dominic R. returned for a visit from his new home in Salt Lake City, he told me, "Since last seeing you, my brother and I started cooking African food again. Now I just take my time cooking. No more pizza!"

A Unique Language, Common Customs

Although the DiDinga never mentioned it, they had had to adjust quickly to urban life, so very different from living in a pristine natural environment where their families grew the traditional food, which was prepared by traditional cooking methods by their mothers and sisters. Moreover, outside of the group of 10, the young men had no one in Syracuse with whom they could converse in their native tongue. Unlike the 70 Dinka Lost Boys in Syracuse living with a community of approximately 200 Dinka families in Syracuse, there were no DiDinga elders to provide a support system for this subgroup of Lost Boys. There were no cultural outlets for their spirited traditional dance-songs, through which their oral history is recounted. Paradoxically, in Syracuse, as in Sudan, the DiDinga remained a tiny minority. Further, the few Americans who knew about ethnic groups such as the Dinka and Nuer had never heard of the DiDinga and continued to confuse them with the Dinka.

At this writing, Syracuse remains one of the few American cities that has members from this Surmic-language group (exact number is unknown at this writing), whose language has no written or agreed upon alphabet. The Surma dialects of Sudan include DiDinga, DiDinga-Murle, Larim (Longarim), and Tenet (Tennet), and the groups intermarry when they come into contact through trade or when brides are taken after a cattle raid. For the first time in my career as a public folklorist, my public-sector work required that I become familiar with the complexities of an African tonal language because American audiences would need translated song texts. The published quasi-phonemic vocabulary used by linguistic scholars such as Jonathan Arensen and David Odden confused the young DiDinga because they were writing for me using an entirely phonemic system, albeit one on which they never quite agreed.[3] In spite of their differences, the Lost Boys could read other Lost Boys' written texts, unlike the orthographies created by nonnative linguists. With the exception of religious materials and Bibles translated by missionary groups, there were few examples written in DiDinga language for me to show them. These resources also tended to use a combination of English and idiosyncratic DiDinga writing systems, none of which adequately represented DiDinga sounds. As a matter of fact, every DiDinga whom I met used a different system. Charles explained,

"You see these letters. I cannot write in English. But when you write in English, maybe you'd put another [letter (makes sounds for DiDinga aloud as he writes)]. I write something about [like] this because we are like centralized for DiDinga."

The statement "we are like centralized for DiDinga" is a reference to the Tenet, Murle, and Longarim who intermarry with DiDinga and who speak languages classified as "DiDinga." A few linguists are currently working to develop a good orthography that fits DiDinga language (de Jong 2004), but the phonology (sound system) of DiDinga is not yet understood on an everyday basis.[4] There are features of DiDinga phonology which linguists recognize can not be adequately represented by our alphabet. Linguists working on DiDinga and other Surma languages note what is called ATR-harmony (Advanced Tongue Root versus Relaxed Tongue Root), tone, and a system of "heavy" and "light" consonants, which seems to manifest itself in a variety of ways. Because of these subtle distinctions, which do not occur in English, there are differences that are virtually impossible for an English speaker to hear. I experienced this when the DiDinga men corrected me for pronunciation errors which, to this day, my ear cannot detect. When I located two incomplete DiDinga-English lexicons, I was surprised that Driberg's list, published in 1930, was more accurate than the Rosato 1980 edition:

F: Tell me why these are funny.

Simon: "Someone is talking" . . . this one, this one, I've never heard of. "To kick" [laughs]!

F: Is this a dirty word?

Simon: No! But I've never heard it!

Dominic L.: I know this way is written in old time. Now the form of writing is different. For example, s [in Rosato]. They don't use it, they use th.

James: Instead of s, they use th. The dialects are changing.

Charles: Changing, yeah.

F: The pronunciation is different.

Charles: Yeah.

Rosato's publication is not only incomplete but so inaccurate that the DiDinga group laughed over many of the entries. They mentioned again "the soup story" (recounted in chapter 2) of the Murle-DiDinga as an example of how language can change. Initially, I had overlooked reference material on the Murle because I did not fully realize the close relationship to the DiDinga until the young men pointed me in this direction. Many scholars now believe that the DiDinga were part of the original Murle-DiDinga migrations from Ethiopia. The group broke off from the others and settled in the DiDinga Hills because it is similar to their land of origin. According to Arensen, "The history of migrations is complex, with one group pushing the next like a line of dominoes. Only during the British rule were these movements stopped. Even now, however, cattle raiding and fighting for territory take place in some of the more remote areas. . . . The jostling and fighting for land and territory has often resulted in shifting, dominant-subordinate relationships. . . . Captives are often adopted, well treated, and their beliefs given due respect" (1987, 8). The origins of the DiDinga remain conjectural but the DiDinga are certain that they were originally one people who migrated from Uganda. Although some scholars estimate that the DiDinga population is between 30,000 and 51,000 (Abeles and Peltier-Charrier 1979; Fetterman 1992), more inclusive figures which probably include Murle-DiDinga groups estimate up to 130,000 (African Institute of South Africa 1998).

Earlier, speakers of Surmic languages such as DiDinga were culturally grouped with the better known Nilotic-speakers such as the Dinka and Nuer, studied by many researchers (Huffman 1931; Evans-Pritchard 1940; Lienhardt 1961; F. M. Deng 1973). To represent a culturally similar grouping, anthropologists used the term "Nilo-Hamitic." "Nilotic" refers to peoples of the Nile basin; "Hamitic" is used for non-Semitic Afro-Asiatic languages, which includes Berber, Egyptian, and Cushite. In 1939 Driberg attempted to create cultural groupings of the major cultural differences between Hamito-Nilotics (Maasai and Nandi and others) and Nilo-Hamites (Lotuko, Topotha, DiDinga, Karamojong, DoDoth, Turkana, Murle, and others) predicated on traits from either a Nilotic or Hamitic ancestry. Driberg's attempt fails to adequately distinguish between "Nilo-Hamites" and "Hamito-Nilotics," and groups such as the Suk are placed in both categories:

Nilo-Hamites (DiDinga)	Hamito-Nilotics (Dinka, Maasai)
No circumcision	Circumcision
Weapons:	Weapons:
Throwing spears	Stabbing spears
Half-spears	Swords
Wrist-knives	Oval shields
Finger-knives	
Rectangular shields	
Metallurgy	No metallurgy
Labret	No labret
No friction drums	Friction drums

No bull-roarer	Bull-roarer
"Father of the soil"	No "father of the soil"
Hunters and eaters of game	Neither hunt nor eat game
Strong clan-system	Clan-system relatively weak
Rainmakers important	Rainmakers unimportant or absent
(1939, 21)	

There were other subtler differences, however, such as women's roles and gendered labor, which Driberg does not include in his groupings. The legal status of DiDinga women has always been greater than for other groups because they had relatively greater economic independence, and Driberg indicated his awareness of this distinction, "Among the Nilotics [Dinka] the cattle may only be milked by men, the herdsman of the day officiating if a cow's owner is absent, but among Nilo-Hamitics [DiDinga] this is one of the duties which women undertake" (1932c, 408). Driberg also observed that the Nilo-Hamitics (which he had begun calling Nilo-Hamites by 1939) do not recognize chiefs but share power among warriors and elders, equally an important distinction that is omitted from his categories. Driberg concludes that the DiDinga are "an interesting tribe which presents many abnormal features, suggesting a clash of cultures between possibly Semitic and Hamitic groups" (Driberg 1927a, 400). Although cultural differences may have contributed to the reason that Dinka and DiDinga do not intermarry, more importantly, the groups never lived in the same geographical region. In refugee camps in Kenya and again in cities in the United States, DiDinga and Dinka met for the first time. Most recently, cultural differences have been exacerbated by the clash between Dinka rebel soldiers and DiDinga civilians.

None of the Lost Boys recalled marriage between DiDinga and Dinka, yet both groups share the tradition of polygamy, still practiced in Sudan. It is not unusual for Christianized DiDinga and Dinka to have at least two wives. Several men in both groups held up at least two fingers when I asked if their fathers had more than one wife. However, this practice of "African Christianity" is usually not discussed, and the young men claimed that polygamy is accepted by Western Christian missionaries in Africa "as long as they [the wives] all get along [and] they still go to church as families, as long as everyone is happy."

In the United States, polygamy was a tradition that neither group would be allowed to continue, and most of the men claimed they did not plan to marry more than one wife: "It is too expensive." Traditional wedding ceremonies in Sudan take place as well as other associated marriage customs but within a Christian framework in which a priest officiates. For example, the DiDinga *thuan* is still practiced. One young DiDinga Lost Boy visiting from Kentucky went to great lengths to describe in an e-mail message the tradition as he remembered it from his childhood:

> *Thuan* is the time when the boy sees the girl and ask her to go out. In our culture, although the girl likes the boy, she can't just get up and say yes very soon. This may show that the girl is an easy girl. She can refuse from the first day even to one year. This gives the girl also to know wether [*sic*] this guy is really committed to her and no body alse [*sic*]. Within this period, the boy have to go to the girl's house and ask her there. When the boy come, the parent of the girl can stay outside while the boy and the girl are in the main house talking (*athuani*). This allow the girl's parents also to assess the kind of a person who want to marry their daughter. The girl also have to follow what her mom, sisters, brothers and other relatives suguess [suggest] about this guy. When the relatives doesn't like this guy, there will be a very big conflict in the time when the guy shows up in the girls house for "*thuan.*" So this will determined whether the boy is strong enough to resume *thuan* or give up. When the girl and the boy come to their agreement, then the boy will ask the girl to cook dinner/lunch (*rehinit*) so that he can invite some of his friend. This is where the village now know the girl for accepting the boy. So on the dinner, the girl will sloughter [*sic*] the cock [rooster] brew traditional beer and prepare so much food. Coming with the boy are his best friends (can be the girl's relatives), his sisters, mother, cousins, father and some old and responsible people. This shows that the boy ment [*sic*] business when he asked the girl out. Also on the other hand, the girl will ask the mother to let the neighbours know this and are very welcomed to visit. Even though *Rehinit* was for the boy, everybody had to celebrate and socialize with each other several times before wedding (*Nyahuta*). (2002)

I shared this e-mail message with the DiDinga group in Syracuse. At their next public performance, the group included *Lohaya Hitha Macuni*, a traditional DiDinga song about marriage. The song emphasizes the importance of the dowry over love in traditional DiDinga marriages. The bride is being questioned regarding the character of the man she is about to marry. His ability to pay the required dowry is also in question. The man's social class and economic standing are said to be objectionable and below the dignity of the family who is contemplating giving their daughter in marriage:

Lohaya hitha macuni
I have heard of your husband my cousin.

Ne thino tinati eto hithiha elemu borohena
I heard you have accepted to marry the lightning gods.
Lomagal Lopuk Kutur ne thino tinati eto
Lomagal Lobuk Kutur, what is it, daughter of man?

None of the young men were able to adequately explain the meaning of the reference to "the lightning gods." I contacted Paul Atanya, the DiDinga elder in Canada, who claimed it is "an archaic expression with a hidden meaning," but even he did not know the meaning. The song prompted me to ask the young men if they planned someday to marry an American woman. Simon said emphatically, "No! They are too bossy!" Although Simon told me that eventually he hoped to return to DiDingaland to marry a "DiDinga lady," it was not long afterwards that I began to see some of the DiDinga with African-American and European-American girlfriends. Eventually, however, the opportunity presented itself for one Lost Boy to be reunited with his DiDinga girlfriend, who had immigrated to a nearby state. When I asked what happened to the American girlfriend, the young man explained that she had never been his "real girlfriend."

Much later, another young man was reunited with his DiDinga girlfriend in the United States, and he became a father. Although the couple cared for their infant, both insisted they would not marry until the father could return to Sudan to pay a member of her surviving family a dowry of cattle. At this writing, it remains to be seen how the young man will negotiate between traditional views on marriage and his new situation. His life in the United States is not based on a cattle economy, and, therefore, the exchange of cattle and dowry and the associated cattle songs no longer play a role. Also, in order to marry a DiDinga woman, the young men needed adult status. Therefore, all of the Dinka and DiDinga fully expected one day to return to Sudan to be initiated into their respective bull groups, which would make them eligible marriage partners.

The bull has always been a leitmotiv for many groups such as the Dinka and DiDinga (Kronenberg 1972a). In Sudan, cattle still determine identity, wealth, status, marriage, and kinship. The longer I worked with this group, the more I puzzled over how the men were going to translate their African identity within an American context. It became obvious that in order to communicate a viable identity and to maintain a positive self-identity as young men, they would need to find acceptable cultural outlets that allowed them to practice their bull traditions, at least symbolically. Although none of the DiDinga young men in

Syracuse were given bull names before arriving in the United States, they, like the Dinka, recalled with fondness when each father gave his adolescent son his own young bull for which the son composed a distinct song. The bullsongs of adult warriors could then be sung during *nyakorot*, the community gathering after harvest or cattle tending.

The word *nyakorot* is a Toposa loanword, but the gathering tradition is said to be "really DiDinga." These ten hour or more dance celebrations are held on special occasions during prosperous times in every DiDinga village. During *nyakorot*, men, women, children, and especially, young male "warriors" fully participate by singing special dance-songs which are differentiated from the slower *umoya* of old people. The *nyakorot*, they said, must begin and end with *lilia*, the slow dance, that provides an opportunity for males to out-sing and out-dance other males so that they can attract the women of their choice. Status is expressed and displayed publicly through the performance of their songs and dances, and the best singer's ability is heralded even after his death. Since their escape from Sudan, the young men had not participated in any traditional dances. Therefore, I encouraged them to describe the dances they observed when they were children in Sudan:

F: So you mean that *lilia* is danced in a circle, and at the end of the evening after *nyakorot* the ladies can pick the men—but not the married ladies. And they might pick for fun the children, and they will go around with their arms around the men and they will sing and dance. The people are in the circle?

Charles: They are clapping. Those people who are not get a chance to go around, so they are clapping or there are ladies who are just singing, so the men are clapping.

F: Are the men also singing?

Charles: Yeah, everybody sings.

F: So married women can sing, they just cannot dance?

Charles: Yeah.

F: Tell me about *umoya*. Do they still do this?

Charles: Yeah, they are still doing this.

F: When?

Charles: They are mostly doing this like when I saw my father and my mother in a group. Mostly after . . . you know, they drink a lot [of beer] in a group. They go in the house to drink. Sometimes at night. Now they start now to sing this.

F: Is this only at harvest?

Charles: No, anytime that they are in a group.

Simon: Well, sometimes it is after cultivation and there is no work to do, and there is plenty of food to eat, and there is a lot of beer, *merti*, to drink. Anybody can cook beer in their place and invite the age group to come and dance and celebrate.

F: Is this dance held in the daytime or the night?

Simon: Anytime. Like from this night to the following day, when there is a lot of beer to drink.

F: What is the beer made from?

Simon: It is made from maize, wheat.

F: For *umoya*, are they in a circle or a line or doesn't it matter? Do they dance or do they just sing?

Charles: They aren't in a circle, they just start. They jump, they don't really jump up but they just jump. It's a bounce, like a bounce.

F: Is *nyakorot* always danced in a circle?

Charles: No, one song can be no line, then another song in like that [draws a semicircle] and then other song like *lilia* can just be so. It is not really a circle but it's just going around.

Dominic L.: It's a semicircle.

Charles: Yeah, but before we start, it is like a semicircle.

Simon: For the men, it is like, the men make a small arc on the other side.

F: The men make an arc on that side and the women make an arc on this side?

Simon: Yes. So you see the pattern [indicates a snakelike line]. For the *nyakorot* it is a complete circle with ladies in the center.

Charles: There is a man in the center with the drum and ladies.

F: But when you did this [here], there were no ladies.

Charles: And no drum.

The DiDinga are one of the few African societies that do not rely on the drum for percussion so I was surprised when Charles complained, "And no drum." However, like the recent introduction of the *lokembe* throughout Africa, this did not seem unusual; rather, it was another example of cultural syncretism, which often occurs when different groups engage in trade. During this conversation, I also learned that, unlike the Dinka, DiDinga require drinking *merti* (home-made beer) at celebrations. By contrast, a Dinka elder explained that among his people only men over 40 are permitted to drink alcoholic beverages. Among the

DiDinga, however, it is tradition to allow even very young DiDinga to drink during *nyakorot*:

> **F:** So how did you know how to sing *nyakorot* [in Auburn]? Did you make it up or had you danced in the mission school or did you [as] young boys in the villages dance? How did you know?
>
> **Charles:** These are like, it is in the blood because there is nothing you can practice.
>
> **Simon:** Every year there are new songs. But we were in Kenya. We didn't get a chance to hear the new songs.
>
> **F:** So the songs are always changing then?
>
> **Simon:** Yes.
>
> **F:** So, where did this song "Maria" come from?
>
> **Simon:** It just comes from Sudan, we knew it.
>
> **F:** Do you know this dance called *lokembe*?
>
> **Simon:** *Lokembe* is called disco sometimes.
>
> **F:** Do you do *lokembe* in Thunguro? In Nagichot?
>
> **Charles:** Yes.
>
> **F:** Do your parents dance *lokembe*?
>
> **Charles:** Sometime they do disco, you know like in their place, if his [points to Simon] parents want people to enjoy [themselves], so they send a report to my father to say I will come. I will bring my people for *lokembe* to the area so be ready and have beer for people from my village. So my father maybe will kill a bull and then make a beer and everything. So all everybody, they come to my father's house. And we give advice, "Do not go this way, do not go this way, go this way, go this way." My father is begging people, "Can you help me? The people are coming." So another house is making a beer free. So the people will visit from that place and we tell them, go to our house and enjoy yourselves. And visitors from this place, go to that place.

This interview contradicted Fetterman's published observation in 1980 that the DiDinga had not performed *umoya* and *lilia* for 20 or 30 years (Fetterman 1992, 75). Charles indicated that both traditions had been practiced when he was growing up in his village in the early 1990s. To understand the descriptions Charles provided, I read published research on the Dinka (F. M. Deng 1973) because the concept of the age-grade system is common among many East African groups. The DiDinga believe they borrowed the age-set system from the Toposa, whom scholars categorized in the same group with the DiDinga.

In fact, like the words for *nyalado* and *nyakorot*, the specialized names for the age groupings are also believed to be Toposa words.[5] Dimmendaal explains, "At a later stage, the common ancestor of the above-mentioned Surma languages came into contact with a language, which either was the common ancestor of the Teso group of languages within Eastern Nilotic, or an early descendent within this group. This interpretation is supported by the various words clearly borrowed in DiDinga and Murle, mostly referring to personal adornment. The process of borrowing from the Teso group (especially the Toposa) into DiDinga, Larim and also Murle probably still continues to the present day" (1982, 105). DiDinga language has incorporated numerous Toposa words such as *min* (love) in *kaminani, aminan,* (I love, I loved).

By adding the suffix *-an* to any foreign root, new DiDinga verbs are formed. For example, *kalimani, aliman,* (I teach, I taught) is from the Arabic *alimu* (to teach) (Rosato 1980, 21). This may in part be due to the fact that although the 100 distinct ethnic groups in southern Sudan are not all related linguistically, they do share some cultural traits, especially interdependence of cattle and humans. Published descriptions about the Nuer clearly demonstrate shared cultural similarities to DiDinga cattle traditions: "The attachment of a man to his cows and of boy to the bull with which his father presents him may be called almost religious. The one real sport for men is fighting, or cattle raiding, which is practically the same thing. These predatory expeditions are carried on wherever opportunity offers and are a cause of constant friction among the tribes. In their folk-lore tales a favourite subject is the story of cattle fights" (Huffman 1931, vii). According to many published academic sources, cattle raiding and intertribal warfare are at the core of male identity in all of the neighboring groups, and this played a significant role in cross-cultural exchanges. Because annual transhumance is common to the DiDinga, Larim, and Toposa, they must seek pastures during the dry season, and these shared patterns of transhumance also bring them into contact.

But according to my young informants, it is the institutionalized political war, not the traditional cattle raiding, which has disrupted traditional life to the greatest degree for all of the ethnic groups in Sudan. The civil war has escalated the violence through the introduction of guns, which now replace the traditional shields and spears. Political songs about war, brutality, and guns, often sung during *nyakorot*, replace the heroic songs about hunting and cattle raiding of early times. The *nyakorot* eventually performed by the DiDinga young men in the United States included several songs about the current civil war. When I asked the meaning of a particular song, one singer answered tersely, "It's a song about a gun." As Ken Bacon, head of the Refugees Institute, reported in a radio interview, "There is no reason that Sudan cannot be a prosperous country, but not as long as it continues this war" (*Weekend Edition*, NPR, February 28, 2004). On several occasions, the young men expressed appreciation for being allowed to live in the United States, often repeating during our conversations, "We are privileged to be in the United States," adding "There is no war here." To grasp their perspective on how the conflict with the Islamic north is affecting traditional cultures in southern Sudan, one must consider both the influence of and resistance to Arabic culture. For example, at a university program (discussed in detail in chapter 6), the Dinka wanted to sing the "new national song" of southern Sudan using English words and an Arabic tune. Some of the DiDinga, however, were reluctant to sing this song because they considered it the song of the SPLA, a military movement of mostly Dinka Bor sometimes in combat with DiDinga civilians.

Another language example of borrowing from Arabic is the DiDinga word for car, *toromile*, which is a loan word Rosato (1980) believes has its origins in Arabic but which may actually be derived from English as well.[6] *Bit toromilea* means "to go by car," even though there are no cars in DiDingland, because, as the young men expressed, "There are only paths through the woods. No cars, no roads." Arensen notes that when the automobile was first seen by the DiDinga-Murle people, they called it *kavool ci golu*, "canoe of the road," to differentiate it from a *kavool ci liilu*, "canoe of the river" (1992). The traditional vehicle of the DiDinga-Murle is a dugout canoe, used to cross a flooded river or to fish. Both expressions take the *-et* suffix in the plural and indicate the connection between a vehicle of the road and a vehicle of the river. Although the DiDinga-Murle language tends to be the most conservative dialect in the Surma group, this creation of a word made up of traditional words may represent resistance to adopting a loanword from Arabic. In other examples, creolization (Szwed 2003) is evident when the DiDinga incorporate Arabic as well as Toposa words in traditional songs. One of the songs by the DiDinga to conclude the traditional *nyakorot* is *Salamalekum Nadura*. According to one informant, "*Salamalekum* is derived from the Arabic language, that means 'greetings to all.' So the song says, 'Greetings to all who play and enjoy this part of *nadura*,' the conclusion part of *nyakorot*." The vocabulary associated with cattle, however, appears to have resisted any Arabic influence. For southern Sudanese, vocabulary related to cattle remains the most expansive and complex. The centrality of cattle for these cultures is shown in the extended meaning of the DiDinga-Murle word *otak* (mouth), which is the base meaning. *Tatok* is extended to mean "doorway" and also "family." If we analyze the DiDinga-Murle word *tiin* (cows), we find its extension in the word *tinkawin*, the DiDinga-Murle word for "marriage." Similarly, in both DiDinga and DiDinga-Murle dialects, *tena* is the nominative/accusative for cows; the DiDinga-Murle word *atenoc* means "there are cattle between us," indicating the cattle needed for the dowry which unites the families of husband and wife. In the words of one DiDinga Lost Boy, cattle is the basis of the traditional transaction that takes place in Sudan through a mediator:

The person who is the owner of the girl—the young girl's father—will choose someone else who can speak in his behalf and go to the girl's house to speak to her father, the mother and the girl's uncles (in order to get the message he should give to the boy about the amount of dowry). That person will be the mediator and will bring the thing the two people want, the dowry. And if there was a conflict in the families, then the conflict has to be solved before the marriage so everybody will be happy. And after that, they would start the wedding ceremony. Everything is prepared in the boy's home and when they are giving the wedding, the young man is there but the girl is not there. She can live around that place but she is not supposed to be shown there. That is one thing that we have never understood why. Maybe the girl is shy? The people will walk up to the girl's house and they will pay the dowry and this mediator person is the one who collects the dowry and gives it to the lady's parents and the lady's parents never pay anything. They return back, they invite their relatives to come to their party. They have their traditional beer which is already brewed in that house so they will dance *gyrikot* the whole night.

At this writing, all of the young men in Syracuse insist that the only acceptable dowry is cattle, adding some young men are already sending money from the United States to relatives in Sudan who purchase the cattle in their names. However, war has visited destruction on every village in southern Sudan, and there are often no cattle to purchase. This is one critical example of the way that the war has disrupted traditional life because traditions are interlocked, having a domino effect on the culture. As a whole the loss of one traditional element can affect an entire cultural system. This is true for both the Dinka and the DiDinga, which can have significant consequences. Some practices, such as cattle herding, not only regulate all of social life but ultimately remain integral to their sense of who they are. Others, such as belief in the DiDinga Rainmaker, already serve only a symbolic function for DiDinga identity. Prior

to the war, with the exception of the Rainmaker, the DiDinga cultural practices that Driberg listed in 1939 continue to be practiced today. Dominic R.
explained, "Those beliefs are still existing a bit. They are not used so much anymore, only when there is not much rain so someone will say that there is going
to be rain in ten days, and then it rains or if there is too much rain." Although
no DiDinga man was ever allowed to watch, Dominic R. recalled women singing special songs for rain.[7] As a young boy, he knew the singing was taking place
but males who came too near would be chased away. As he explained, "They
can be killed when those women gathered, it's as if they have to be naked, that
is the culture. They will sing for rain. The women gather and sing songs, and
if a man passes there they can remove [kill] him." All of the young men were
raised as Catholics, but their religion is a commingling of Western official belief
and DiDinga folk beliefs: "It's kind of real and sometimes I tend to believe it
because most of our community believe in these super, supernatural things,"
explained Benjamin in response to Dominic's comment that these beliefs are
"not used so much anymore." In Sudan most DiDinga have been Christianized,
but reverent stories about the Rainmaker are still told. On occasions, someone
will throw rainstones to affect the weather.

To the Western mind, rainmaking would be pejoratively labeled "magic," in
spite of widely accepted Western rituals such as baptism, which anthropologists
also classify as an example of imitative magic. However, the DiDinga young
men did not make such distinctions. For them, the Rainmaker was "just a person," and none had personally known a Rainmaker.[8] A few recognized the name
Alukileng, a famous Rainmaker of long ago whose memory is still respected.[9]
During informal conversations about the Rainmaker, I learned about other
animistic beliefs such as *mining*, the spirits who are known to kidnap people
from their villages. Belief in the *miningit* (singular for *mining*) is widespread in
DiDingaland, and the young men knew many stories about *mining*. Although
none experienced *mining* firsthand, they frequently heard stories about the dis-
appearance of people in their villages. In her dissertation, Fetterman included
a description: "*Mining* most commonly come up at night and dance in the
moonlight. It is impossible to tell a person from *mining* until a person gets close
to them and sees that they have no teeth. Only people have teeth; the mouths
of *mining* are described as being just red. As soon as a person discovers that a
person is not a person but a *mining* [*sic*], he or she tries to run away. People are
afraid of *mining* because no one wants to be captured and taken down to their
world" (Fetterman 1992, 217). *Mining* are emphatically real in Sudan because
as ancestor spirits *mining* must be appeased. In the United States, it was not

necessary to appease *mining* because the young men agreed that *mining*, along with witchcraft, "exist" only in Sudan. Their belief may reflect the relative ease of their lives in the United States, compared to former lives in rural villages in Sudan.

However, if the young men believed the *mining* are ancestors, it did not explain the contradiction. But contradiction is not unusual in a belief system. When I asked if *mining* were evil spirits or ancestors, the ontological uncertainty was not resolved for the young men: "The connection between misfortune and religion is salient the world over. This is one of the principal contexts in which people activate concepts of gods and spirits" (Boyer 2001, 169). In Sudan the *mining* are said to live under this world in a place called *lo hato* or *Giro* among the DiDinga-Murle (Kronenberg 1972b, 143). The DiDinga talked about the underground home of *mining*, but *lo hoto* was not a word with which they were familiar. Although *mining* have no bodies, one "can hear or see them" because *mining* are both in this world and not in this world:

Joseph: *Mining* is a belief that someone dies and rises again as a spirit and we call it *mining*.

F: Does it have a body, can you touch it?

All: No!

James: It's invisible.

Charles: But you can hear [it], and sometimes you can see it.

F: Like a ghost?

All: Yeah.

F: And is this good or bad?

All: Bad!

Joseph: I remember very well that there was a kid who was taken by *mining*, you know. It's like they take him, and people search for him and search for him over the mountains and down and all the kids [look] and all that . . . so after a while, two to three, no four to five months, they gave him up. They [*mining*] bring the kid where their home was and the people found him. And the kid was saying that he was taken by underground people.

James: A gnome.

Joseph: Yeah, something like that.

F: How old was the boy?

Joseph: He was like six.

F: When did this happen?

Joseph: It happened.

Charles: I was around when a guy was taken like 1990 and when that guy was taken, she say he was taken, by his wife, and where he was taken, I don't know but she said, and no one was seeing him but he was there . . . and when the wife brought the food, he was there, in the house. . . .

F: Did the *mining* ever come to the camps [in Kenya]?

All: No! This is in Sudan.

F: So the *mining* cannot travel to another country?

Simon: They can travel because they are spirits!

F: They could go to Kenya?

Simon: But this would happen, I think, if while my parents were alive, if I was not good to them, so then when they die, they come and tell you.

Joseph: When they die.

F: If you were in the United States, can a *mining* come and tell you?

All: Yeah, yeah they can come to you in the form of a dream.

James: That's more or less like a belief, you know.

Joseph: If you believe in that, it's gonna happen.

James: And if you don't [shrugs].

Charles: But this case [of the man], it is like I say.

The world of the dead is not entirely separate from the world of the living in many other cultures (Iwasaka and Toelken 1994, 15). Likewise, the young men told me that *mining* could "definitely travel," but they do not come to the United States. However, some DiDinga in Sudan believe otherwise: "*Mining* can travel around, just as we do up here [above the afterworld], and some *mining* have visited the cities of London and New York in their world" (Fetterman 1992, 218). The comment that if Simon were not good to his parents when they were alive they might come back as *mining* echoes a similar belief held by the DiDinga-Murle.[10] Arensen explains, "Even though *mining* are removed from the world of the living, it is obvious . . . that they are still thought to have a powerful effect on the living and, therefore, must be treated carefully. It is important at the time of a person's death the correct rituals be performed so that a person passes on to the world of the dead without anger or bitterness" (1992, 251).

The young DiDinga also believe in the power of the *buyak* (plural for *buyahit*), but as Benjamin explained, "If you believe it, it will come true. If you don't believe, it won't." According to Fetterman's data, one only becomes a *buyahit* if one is born into a *buyahit* family. The *buyahit* is an outcast. In Sudan, the penalty for being caught if you are identified as *buyahit* (witch) is death.

One young man told me about a *buyahit* who came to his family's compound in Sudan, but his father successfully rid his home of the evil man by hiding at night and then confronting the "witch." His father recognized that the man was *buyahit* because he came naked during the night and sprinkled blood around the family's house. His father chose not to have the *buyahit* killed when he promised never to come back. My informants were emphatic that the magic of a *buyahit* is used solely for evil purposes, in contrast to the power of the *ngare*, who predicts the future and heals.

When they said *buyahit* and *ngare* live in DiDingaland but not in the United States, I wanted to understand more about *tooto*, the divination with pebbles which Charles also mentioned. I read about a common DiDinga game, *pereaunai*, which also involves throwing pebbles. All of the young men played *pereaunai* and had used *tooto*, a DiDinga divination ritual based on the tossing of pebbles or sandals, to guide their lives in Sudan but not in United States. "Life is easy here," suggested James, who said that in the United States *tooto* was unnecessary. In DiDingaland, a person who is known to be good at *tooto* is called *aruk cawa* (Kronenberg 1972b, 15). Anyone who wants to divine the future can take the omens (*ruko tooto*). There are rigid distinctions between a diviner and a healer because *et ci aga hena* (healer) is a title which must be earned. The young men indicated that a respected oracle can also earn the name *ngare*, a separate distinction from *et ci aga hena* (Kronenberg 1972b, 159). Like the Rainmaker, in spite of their special abilities DiDinga diviners and healers remain "ordinary people" because religion is integrated with secular life. To demonstrate this, Charles "threw sandals" on two separate occasions:

Simon: It [*tooto*] is not a game! It is to tell the future.
F: Do they still tell the future?
All: Oh, yeah!
James: They still use *tooto*. They use beads or marbles.
F: Who can do that? Can you do that?
James: No, I can't. Sometimes they use their sandals too.
Simon: Two sandals.
F: If you had sandals, can you do it?
Charles: I can do it.
James: He can throw the sandals but his won't be that good.
F: Why?
James: He needs to do it a certain way. [Charles leaves room and returns with two sandals.]

Charles: You put it like this, on the ground [pounds the two sandals back to back and tosses them up to demonstrate].

F: What does that mean? [All laugh.]

Simon: You better postpone your journey [laughs]!

Charles: No good.

Simon: No, no something is wrong. [Charles throws again.]

James: Things are working better.

F: So this one is a game [*pereaunai*]. This one is not a game.

Simon: This is not a game. It is a serious matter.

James: It is not a game!

F: Do you ever do this here?

All: Noooo!

F: Why not here?

James: Everything is all right, everything is fine.

James: It doesn't work here.

Faye: Is there ever a time that you would do this in the United States?

James: [laughs] Noooo.

F: You have to be in Sudan?

James: You can do it [here], but if you are all right like now, you don't like to do anything. I used to do it in Kenya.

F: When did you do that in Kenya?

James: Like when I was in high school.

F: Like what kind of questions did you ask?

James: Things like . . . I had a girlfriend so you do that to know if she would be good to me. If it was a good day or a bad day.

F: And you were in Kenya, and it worked in Kenya?

James: Oh, yes!

F: So it can't work in the United States?

James: It can.

Simon: It can. Why do it in Sudan? Because everything is harsh, so you have to know, you have be cautious.

James: You have to be cautious all the time, things are moving.

Simon: In Sudan, if someone is going to attack you, you have to defend yourself . . . even if I want to get a girlfriend, I'll say, I want to get that girl, then I'll do it.

Simon's comment indicates that the young men believe *tooto* should be invoked for serious purposes only, such as "to defend oneself" or "to get a girlfriend."

Charles demonstrates *tooto* by throwing sandals, 2002. Photo: Felicia McMahon.

It is needed when "things are always moving," that is, when one has no control over elements in life.

The men clearly distinguished between divination and games, both of which are on the surface similar in form: I then asked them to differentiate divination from "*dae eth dae khon*" (give goat, give sheep), another African game in which pebbles are thrown like dice. In an early article on divination, Driberg reports, "The DiDinga also have a pebble game called *dae eth dae khon* which he [DiDinga informant] explains is a game played by children" (1933, 9). The young men continued to distinguish between *tooto* and *dae eth dae khon*, reiterating that the latter is definitely play and *tooto* is not because *tooto* is very "serious" and it "really works." The traditional belief in *tooto* demonstrated that some traditions cannot be recontextualized but remain intact even when the ritual is not performed. Before the DiDinga were Christianized, in 1933 Driberg documented *tooto*, which the young men accurately described:

Among the DiDinga, anyone may take the omens in this way, either for himself or for a friend, and they place implicit reliance on the correctness of the forecast, which the pebbles reveal. On one occasion, when I was proposing a journey on the following morning to a disturbed settlement, I threw the pebbles in the prescribed manner and three successive throws signified disaster. I then handed them to a DiDinga to throw on my behalf and again the omens were as bad as they could be. The men who were to accompany me were reluctant to do so, and everyone tried to dissuade me from my journey. Unfortunately, I refused to be dissuaded, and this method of divination received a gratuitous advertisement from the fact that three of my men were killed and two were wounded.

When I asked Charles to comment on this early published account, he nodded, "It's true, it's true." When I asked Charles if *tooto* could be used to predict my short drive home, he shook his head, indicating that certain traditions are not for recontextualized application.

Preserving Culture

This conversation demonstrated to me that the young men were fully cognizant of which traditions could be appropriately recontextualized. On the other hand, the issue of how to frame traditions in a way that would be meaningful for multiple audiences remained. The process would be similar to cultural code-switching among other immigrant groups. Their choices would indicate how they self-identified now and how they connected themselves to the past (Kirshenblatt-Gimblett 1983). For example, the young men insisted that songs about the Sudanese civil war have become "traditional." The south has been fighting for almost three decades to gain autonomy from the north, and the conflict in Sudan can be said to go back 150 years. This is accurate because during the nineteenth century, "Mahdi," Muhammad Ahmad, created Sudan's first theocratic government by establishing Islam after the uprising against Turko-Egyptian rule. The situation became complicated during British colonialism: "The British, in turn, during their subsequent half-century of colonial rule, cultivated Islamic sects as the basis for rival political parties. The longtime military dictator Jaafar Nimeiry, when his regime began to crumble in 1983, played the Islamic card, declaring *sharia*, the law based on the Koran. He thereby relegated Sudan's four million non-Muslim southerners to second-class status. That was the start of the current round of war" (Berkeley 2001, 200). The only African war longer than the Sudanese civil war is the Eritrean War in Ethiopia. It is a war in which both rebels and government officials are using food as a weapon. According to Jeff Drumtra, senior policy analyst for the U.S. Committee for

Refugees, "The people of Sudan have fled their homes in larger numbers than any other country on earth—4 million are internally displaced within the country, and 350,000 are refugees in neighboring countries" (1999, n.p.). Thus, modern conflict can be traced to 1955, and the situation remains dire.

Protest songs about mistreatment of civilians during the war were also considered traditional by the young men. The cause of the civil war in Sudan cannot be reduced to the simple explanation, and it is more than a civil war between the Arabic Muslim north and the animist and Christian south. Ethnic infighting among southern Sudanese rebel armies may have caused more deaths than the north-south conflict. Half of the deaths have been children. Famine and drought have only intensified the deaths and the war:

> In the last decade, the war, together with recurrent drought and prolonged economic crises, has destroyed the formal economy in southern Sudan. Major roads have been mined, bridges and railways destroyed, and water transport routes rendered inoperable. Large-scale manufacturing has ceased and local markets have largely disappeared. As soldiers besieged towns, razed villages and looted the countryside, villagers lost their livestock and stopped cultivating. State-run health, education and welfare programmes utterly vanished, leaving an entire generation of children without the basic necessities for their survival, protection and development. But in this land of suffering, no group has suffered as much as those children who have been separated from their parents and forced to fend for themselves, alone. (Zutt 1994, 5)

It would be my responsibility as a public folklorist to provide interpretation about the civil war to enable the audience to understand the scenario of intense personal suffering from which the performers escaped, without giving the impression that these grown adult men are helpless refugees. The DiDinga went about their busy American lives, attending a local community college, supporting themselves with service-industry night jobs, and sending money back to less fortunate Sudanese relatives and friends still in refugee camps in Kenya. Occasionally, a comment was made that a brother had been located, or worse, that a family member was dead. While I was writing this book, one DiDinga Lost Boy learned that his mother had been located in Kakuma, a refugee camp in Kenya. Five siblings were with her. His father, however, was still missing. Although his American foster family was paying for an apartment in Kenya so his mother did not have to remain in the camp, I could tell that the situation was confusing for him. I decided that any background information about the war should be relegated to program brochures that avoided rekindling painful memories.

Likewise, the young men insisted that the traditional joyful mood of *nyakorot* be emphasized because they saw this as a celebration of their new lives, not as a consequence of politics in Sudan.[11] I only had one direct conversation about this small group's political views, which was embedded in an early interview. After 9/11 occurred, I asked if the news caused them concern. They believed their arrival in the United States prompted the attack because most of the Lost Boys coincidentally had arrived in the United States just a few months earlier. Several of them wanted eventually to work for peace with the United Nations. I observed that the DiDinga kept their political views to themselves. While the larger group of Dinka young men were more outspoken about the need for U.S. military intervention in Sudan and in other parts of the world, my belief was that the DiDinga's reluctance to comment was due to their small numbers. In Sudan, the DiDinga are a small minority of 130,000 people, compared to the 3.5 million Dinka, and there were only 10 DiDinga Lost Boys in Syracuse compared to 69 Dinka in our city. To Americans, the cultural differences between the two groups were too subtle to recognize, but during our first interview, the DiDinga corrected me:

F: Is this DiDinga dance [pointing to photo]?

Simon: No [laughing], . . . they are from tribe of Dinka.

F: How do you know this dance is Dinka? What is different?

Simon: [laughs] Because there is a *big* difference! Every community has its own. This dance . . . when I went to different towns, sometimes the people come and in a group they perform their dance, and you can *see* the difference.

F: When I look at this picture, I don't know that this is Dinka. What should tell me that this is Dinka?

Charles: See the way they are putting their hands [indicates over head]? That is Dinka. For us [DiDinga] we are not putting our hands like that. See the way they are putting the chalk [points to faces covered with white paint]? The chalk we use, we put one [line].

F: Do DiDinga jump like this? High?

Charles: Yeah, but we jump straight but you see [points to arms held high]? For jumping, no [puts his arms at his sides].

F: Thank you for explaining this picture to me. If you hadn't explained it, I would not know that this is Dinka. No American could know that. I see how every detail is important.

Early exchanges such as this, in which I admitted my ignorance about DiDinga culture, enabled the performers to be self-reflexive about their traditions to help Americans distinguish between Dinka and DiDinga cultures. It would be important to acknowledge both groups as equal but distinct whenever they performed in public. Although both groups had been labeled as one, "Lost Boys of Sudan," they were not a unified group and disagreed frequently among themselves. Thus, I came to understand why at church gatherings or public events where both Dinka and DiDinga were present, they were mutually cordial but did not always interact. Since most Americans seldom interacted with them, a public folk arts program might be the only venue to help Americans to distinguish between the two ethnic groups.

A public-sector program, however, is never a one-way transaction: "The public-sector folklife festival or exhibition foregrounds this communication, since the tie between maker and audience is now defined as educational rather than commercial. . . . Of course such contacts can also create new relationships, with the practitioner acquiring a powerful identity as 'artist.' In this case the aesthetic and monetary value placed on the object in its new set of relationships will feed back to the network of origin and here too the object will gain new prestige and receive new elaboration" (Noyes 1995, 462). I would find out that when the young men performed, the American audience was not the primary venue for validation of DiDinga and Dinka cultures. During call and response, the chorus was a more important audience and the videotapes of their performances which were mailed throughout their dispersed community. It was not possible for the DiDinga to gather collectively, so they connected through technology. In a sense, the videotapes exchanged through the mail represented "vortices of behavior," the sites of memory (the marketplace, street, or gathering place) where audiences congregate and performers emerge (Roach 1996a, 25). For collective memory, these sites are important, enabling it to survive despite changes in the places where the original remembered events occurred. By mailing their videotaped performances to other DiDinga living in diaspora, the young men became the community's active tradition bearers, simultaneously preserving their past while creating a hybrid identity.

Entextualization and
Kinesthetic Communication

Adahit hodopuwana Lotiki likaibani
The vultures devoured Lotiki during his past hunting expedition.
Adahit hodopuwana Lotiki likaibani
The vultures devoured Lotiki during his past hunting expedition.
Likaiba Lotiki taminaro
Lotiki's great bushland.
Likaiba Lotika taminaro
Lotiki's great bushland.
Holo adahita
Oh, they devoured,
Adihit hotongutho heeni taminaro
They devoured until they slept on trees.
Traditional DiDinga warrior song

One afternoon as we sat around my kitchen table, I asked whether DiDinga men sang bullsongs, which I knew are common among East African societies.[1] The group affirmed that in DiDinga language, the word for this male tradition is *oli*.[2] Dominic R. stood, jumped up once, and, with a snort, began to sing. The others supported him by singing in chorus and clapping. This occurrence was remarkable because it demonstrated not only spontaneous composition by the singer but the chorus as well. According to Dominic, when he was a child, his father gave a bull to him. The bull was the calf of a cow which belonged to his uncle. Dominic's family paralleled the ancestry of the bull, and he had shared his family's history in his song. From the other room, my husband, John, who is a classicist, overheard Dominic's song and he recognized ancient pastoral patterns:

F: Do you have one? *Oli?*

Lino: Oh no, maybe if we would have stayed for some time we would have had one. If I had stayed there, I would have composed one, maybe. But it is not really hard.

F: I heard Andrew and Anthony sing their [Dinka] bullsongs once. It sounded very hard.

Lino: Oh yeah—being creative. You have your bull, and nobody can touch your bull. If it is dead, it is a matter of life and death. If someone comes, you defend it. Nobody should do anything to it.

F: Is this like your identity?

Lino: Oh yes, identity. Very important.

Dominic R.: Oh yes, very important.

F: If you went back to Sudan, after you have had an education—and not everyone has an education—would you still be able to have the bull and sing the bullsong?

Lino: Oh yes! It is our culture! It is our culture. You can't just say no, because it is your culture.

Dominic R.: I had my bull there. And when I was playing, it was still very very young. You know, I was really in love. So, I composed one of the songs to watch it. You guys, when we were talking here, it was something that I really remember.

John: Do you perform this song? Do you have it written down? Do you have it in your head?

Dominic R.: Yes, I created it and when I was with my friends, taking it to grazing, so I was just singing to soothe my young love, my bull. For example I can sing it:

Oli cani ci marini oo ci homina
Oo! Oli cani ci marini oo ci homina
Lochia eet, oli cani ci marini oo ci hamina
Ci ica aduot ci homina
Lochia eet, oli cani ci marini oo ci hamina
Illale, oli cani ci marini oo ci hamina
Lochia eet, oli cani ci marini oo ci hamina

I love my bull with its red head.

Oh, I love my bull with its red head.

Son of my uncle, I love my bull with its red head

Which no one will stone.

Son of my uncle, I love my bull with its red head.

Thank you, I love my bull with its red head.

Son of my uncle, I love my bull with its red head.

Dominic R.: That is why, when we were discussing this, in my head, I said, "Oh, I am very much happy to hear this and I had it in my heart." It is just something that is there.

John: It was very rhythmic. Is this a traditional rhythm or pattern of sound? Much of the Latin and Greek poetry from the ancient world derived from the kind of cultural things that you were just talking about. Pastoral poetry actually started from the songs of shepherds taking care of their sheep. The poems in Latin and Greek are highly developed as written down by poets but they come from the kind of tradition that you were singing, where someone would sing with or to the animals that they were taking care of, as shepherds. Later the poets developed this tradition into poetry. It is fascinating that you would have engaged with your bull in a poetic way, and the rest of you knew the kinds of traditional response.

Dominic R.: The song that I sung was about my bull's red head and black sides and that no one will touch it until it is gone bigger. That is brief about it.

Dominic L.: He liked the color of the bull, so that is why he sang about the color of the bull.

John: How long did you have this bull when you were young, and how long do people traditionally stay with one particular animal?

Dominic R.: You know, when I started getting that bull as mine personally, when . . . the mother give birth to it, then it was smooth and heavy and very beautiful and from that point, I was also very involved in taking care of it and taking it home with my friends and milking its mother. Suppose I was still in Sudan, I should love that bull until it's gone bigger and maybe I sell it and get money or maybe I [go to] someone to slaughter or do something in a special way . . . in a different way.

F: So you have a special relationship with this animal?

Dominic R.: Exactly.

F: Named? Do you have a name for it?

Dominic R.: Actually, I was supposed to come with a name for it but because of coming over here, that was the problem. In addition, it was still very young.

F: So you and this animal were kind of bound together?

Dominic R.: Yeah, because its mother was bought from my uncle, so my uncle brought its mother to the cattle I was taking care of, and from there its mother gave birth, then the young bull just came out very beautiful and I took from there.

The descriptive phrase "my bull with its red head" is characteristic of DiDinga bullsongs. Specific DiDinga words are typically used in bullsongs to convey the physical characteristics of a bull. The descriptive phrases are also traditional DiDinga names. Each DiDinga boy is given a "bull name," which is his middle name; it is also the name for his bull. When his first bull dies, the owner retains his bull name. For example, when I was introduced to Marino, he told me that his DiDinga name is Oroo, "Bull with a White Head." This was his bull name, but most of the others had been too young to have bull names:

holi ori chul	black with white tail
kari	dappled red and white
kodhori	dark shoulders and back
labaci	black with a white belly and back
mani	cream or yellow colored
mariki (marihi)	red head
mariki ori chul	red with white tail
olo	long-haired
ora	white
tarabal	gentle, tame
tongoleekou	baldheaded
tulki	striped

When Dominic R. finished his song, I asked the others, with whom he had never shared his bullsong, how they knew what and when to sing. Their explanation pointed to a traditional, improvisational technique of call and response which was an integral part of their informal education in Sudan. The DiDinga, like many other African cultures, have a tradition of improvisation that extends to all aspects of their culture, suggesting a flexibility that may extend to a greater cultural adaptive ability (discussed in more detail in chapter 7). Flexibility and creativity is a necessary part of survival, especially for nomadic groups. Unaccompanied young boys often run many miles from the village to distant grazing areas. During these long daily trips, they have to be adaptive and to improvise quickly. For the DiDinga, this vital improvisation, at the core of DiDinga cultural systems, is expressed in their music as well.

Similar call and response traditions of Dinka and Nuer people in south Sudan were noted by early anthropologists: "Many of their songs pertain to marriage, many of them laud cattle or persons and proclaim their praises. Sometimes they voice their disapproval of some individual in song so that all may hear. Some of their songs are of a vulgar type. In construction they are similar, consisting of a verse of one or more lines and a refrain. The verse is usually sung in a higher tone, the refrain being sung in lower tones. They seldom repeat any phrase over and over, but express the same meaning by the use of other words" (Huffman 1931, 68–69). Within the stable song text, the singer sometimes improvises by adding words to the song. During our 2002 e-mail exchanges, Paul Atanya described DiDinga music as "a newspaper" in which the singer not only transmits "news" but makes his or her opinion known. Paul's comments also underscored DiDinga music as more than a form of entertainment because it preserves the community's history and it regulates social life: "[S]ongs record the events of life as experienced by individuals, communities, and generations. Music in this form is equivalent to a newspaper." The chorus actually helps to ensure that the song becomes part of the group's collective memory. However, in addition to serving as a conduit for news and an historical record, the song transmits identity on individual and group levels. The song Dominic R. performed at my kitchen table was the *oli*, composed and performed when a father gives his son his first bull when he enters his first age grade. These age groups are divisions in a system known among anthropologists as the age-set system. A DiDinga young man celebrates himself by praising the characteristics of his bull in flowery verse while he is dancing or fighting: "Praising is an essential element of Longarim (and DiDinga) dance, hunt, and war. Anyone not praised is regarded as a 'nobody' and, upset, he will leave the place of dancing" (Kronenberg 1961, 265). An adult man often refers to his bull and his wives in the same song. Among men, the bullsong is composed by an individual, and usually no one else is allowed to sing the song except as part of the chorus. This is the reason that none of the young men offered to sing an example of an adult man's bullsong. Each song is as unique as a man and his bull. The identity of a DiDinga man is so intimately connected to his bull that when a wife is unfaithful, her lover will caress her deceived husband's bull: "Such an act under more normal conditions would be greatly appreciated by its owner, since 'if someone loves my beast, he loves me also' and often elicits a gift of a goat from an owner. But for the lover to caress the beast of the deceived husband only intensifies the humiliation" (Kronenberg 1961, 269). In retaliation, the deceived husband believes that his wife has been unfaithful because of the beauty of the bullsong of his rival, and he may steal or kill the rival's bull. Through descriptions of the attributes of the bull, a young man can also express his feelings and desire, and these verses can even include descriptions of his beloved bride and her attributes.

After extensive research, I found only two published bullsongs in the DiDinga language (Kronenberg 1961). For the most part, written song texts are nonexistent because DiDinga songs are never static and border on the ephemeral. Fortunately, in one published article, Kronenberg includes both the original DiDinga and English translation as well as this commentary, which provides a more detailed analysis of a mature bullsong:

> The 'bull'-song must be composed by the beast's 'father' and is usually sung in chorus. It usually consists of a short description of the beast, and often includes some remarks about the cow that gave it birth; further, the services rendered to the beast are related in song: what was killed on hunting parties for it, who shaped its horns (the singer indicates by raising his arms the form of the horns); who castrated it; who gave it the bell; what the best friend has done for it, etc. Sometimes also some verses relating to a girl with whom the owner is, or has been, in love are included. It is very important for a Longarim to compose an impressive 'bull'-song, because this is the surest way to make himself known and to attract the attention of girls. (1961, 265–66)

Kronenberg adds that prior to beginning the song, the singer jumps and stamps his feet once after he lands on the ground. This is the stance I observed when Dominic R. performed his bullsong for me in my kitchen. Although Kronenberg suggests that this arm motion is only used if the bull is *ikari* (uncastrated), none of the young DiDinga nor any adult DiDinga could confirm this tradition. Driberg's commentary on his English translation of a DiDinga bullsong mentions the call and response associated with bullsongs: "It is customary for the leader to intone a line or stanza . . . and then for the participants to repeat the last of the concluding sentence in a tense murmur of great impressiveness" (1932b, 2).

It was not until I played the tape I made of Dominic R.'s bullsong to several of the others who had not been in my kitchen that I learned bullsongs also have hidden meanings. This is a common characteristic of Dinka bullsongs: "The total experience in a particular situation being what counts for the purpose of a song, logically unconnected ideas are fused together in a way difficult for an outsider to comprehend. In some cases, external logic is totally ignored; but to the Dinka, the essential logic remains unaffected" (F. M. Deng 1973, 85). Francis Mading Deng, who is a scholar of Dinka heritage, continues, demonstrating this same element of inscrutability in one of his examples of a Dinka initiation song: "Among the Ngok (Dinka), nobody has fewer than fourteen initiation marks, with seven on each side. Far from thinking it an error, no Ngok would take the song as even attempting to give a correct figure. The figures are chosen for rhythmical purposes" (1973, 85):

> "My right forehead with five
> My left forehead with five
> My head will carry twelve." (F. M. Deng 1973, 86)

According to Deng, both singer and audience are aware that five plus five equals ten but twelve fits the rhythm better in the original language, and further, while listeners never have access to all of the coded language, there are criteria for judging the effectiveness of the song. Simply, an abuse song should amuse the listener; a dance-song should inspire listeners to dance, and so on. In other words, a good performance effects a culturally appropriate response in the listener.

The young men expressed their approval of Dominic R.'s bullsong by singing the choral refrain. But in order to fully appreciate a bullsinger's descriptive praises, the listener must know the symbolic meaning of the traditional system of horn taming and the associated aesthetics of the horn shapes. As the bull becomes older, its horns are often trained to grow in certain directions. These shaped horns are dictated by an ethnoaesthetic system, which is represented by a distinct vocabulary. Dominic R.'s bull was obviously still a calf, but he still held his arms over his head to represent a bull's horns, a stance typical for bullsingers. When the bull matures, its horns are tamed in one of the prescribed ways. Usually one of the prescribed terms is incorporated in the song:

iryeemani	crossed horns
chodoyi-otoni	one-horned
mariki oto	red horns
muguri-o	born without horns

nglec	one horn curved forward, one curved backward
nyadhogol	both horns upright
nyakododh	the horns are curved forward and downward
nyeluk	spreading or drooping horns
ori oto	white horned
tukula	curved or bent

Although he used arm motions to indicate a bull's horns, Dominic R. did not include a description of horns in his song because his calf had been too young. Places, people, and events named in the bullsong are not explained. Traditionally, the verse is a cryptic language known only to the members of the man's own age-set, thus making the complete meaning of the song accessible to a few insiders. This too became apparent when I found that some of the young men admitted that they could not translate many of the references in Dominic's song. Instead, they claimed that the words must be Toposa.

In a pastoral society with almost no material culture, a bullsong is a valuable artistic resource because it brings recognition to the composer and therefore attracts females. The succinctness of the bullsong ensures that it remains the "property" of its creator. The only published example of the complexity of DiDinga coded song language was recorded by Kronenberg:

Every day I must hunt for my bull, Lobakori.
The father of Lobakori kills something every day.
It was born of a hornless cow.
It will remain,
Its bell was given by Lounaryo Edvaringole.
Every day I hunt and kill many things for Lobakori.
Its mother gave birth to calves, all of which are hornless.
My father Cipangole was a good hunter, his speech was very long.
I lead it to Munaokori.
I cut its ears after the first hunt.
Nareboleteli killed many things for it.
I visited daily in Kanyangakapel the bull of Lormaloka. (1961, 267)

In this song, Lobakori, the bull, was born of a "hornless cow" (*muguro; ngolim*), mentioned in the bullsong because *muguro* are the most valued cows. Kronenberg tells us that the line, "it will remain" appears straightforward but it is contextually loaded because it indicates that the bull in the song is *ikari*, an uncastrated bull that is naturally tame. The young men in my kitchen thought that perhaps Kronenberg is referring to the castrated bull called *tomot*. According to Kronenberg, a boy can only have one *ikari*-bull during his life, and it is never killed or eaten. I found it odd that none of the DiDinga knew this tradition, but they did agree that an *ikari*-bull owner, "the father," must be a courageous warrior, a reference to the singer. The bell mentioned in Kronenberg's text refers to the cowbell, which is traditionally worn by the bull. In this song, it was given to the bull by the singer's best friend. The singer also praises his own father, whose speech during instruction of the age-set "was very long." "*Monaokori*" refers to a grazing place, and the singer indicates that he has taken constant care of his bull, and "Nareboleteli" is another name for the friend who "killed many things for it." This action represents his friend's regard not only for the bull but for him as a friend. The last line indicates that a mutual feeling of friendship exists between the singer and his best friend, Lounaryo Edvaringole, also called "Nareboleteli," because when their two bulls were grazing together in Kanyangakapel, the singer looked after Lormaloka, his friend's bull, while he was away. The relationships represented in bullsongs, however, are complex: "Often when praising the best friend his eldest brother will also be praised, especially if the best friend supplied the favourite beast. The eldest of full brothers is in charge of the family's herd, and if only the younger brother was praised he might feel neglected and demand the return of the animal" (Kronenberg 1961, 265). Lacking commentary by the singer concerning names and places in the song, almost all of the meaning is lost to the outsider. Kronenberg did not provide the text of this song in the original DiDinga language so my informants could not confirm the meaning nor discuss the musical aspects.

Fortunately, the second of the two existing published DiDinga bullsongs includes the original language:

maya kacini na Lonyangalim
maya kacini na Loyaylem
maya kacini na Nameripos
maya kacini na Lokiron
maya kacini nika Natilado
maya kacini gotoni nakamer ay zinin vatak
maya kacini gotoni Lonyailim
gerza kazi nana niko ay zinin mitidihinik
del kizeha na cikidik ay zinin mitidihinik
maya kizeha nana Lomaylim ay zinin bwa

maya kacini nika Nakamer ay zinin vatak
otodo maya kacini Lonyailim any zinin vatak

If I see Lonyangalim, my heart is open.

If I see Loyaylem, my heart is open.

If I see Nameripos, my heart is open.

If I see Lokiron, my heart is open.

If I see Natilado, my heart is open.

If I see the brother with asymmetrically shaped horns, my heart is open.

If I see the brother of Lonyailim, my heart is open.

If I hear something bad, my heart becomes angry.

If I hear whispering, my heart becomes angry.

If I hear Lomaylim, my heart laughs.

If I see Nakamer, my heart is open.

If I see Lonyailim with the diverging horns, my heart is open. (Kronenberg 1961, 275–76)

The mature bull in this song has eight names: Lonyangalim, Loyaylem, Nameripos, Lokiron, Natilado, Lomaylim, Nakamer, and Lonyailim. As with every bullsong, the singer provides the listener with a visual image of his bull; in this case, *otodo*, which indicates broken horns facing each other with diverging points. Kronenberg interprets this as a signal to the listener that the bull is not *ikari* because the *ikari*-bull's horns are never broken, and it is not castrated. Instead, it is described as *iwani* or "natural." The main refrain, *maya kacini na . . . ay zinin vatak*, "If I see my [bull], my heart opens," is an expression of the singer's intense love for his bull. It is also central to the song's poetic structure, exemplifying the intensification of "emergent parallelism." Emergent parallelism is not necessarily based on strict syntactical correspondence characteristic of canonical parallelism (Kratz 1990, 55). On the semantic level, the singer's love also extends to the bull's brother, and when he hears criticism of his bull, he becomes angry as an expression of his loyalty to his best friend. However, his loyalty extends beyond to his friendship with another boy for, if their bulls fight, it is considered "play." If, however, any other two *ikari*-bulls become engaged in a fight, their owners would be obligated to engage in a duel. The singer also expresses the enjoyment of spending time with his bull: when he hears his bull bellowing, "my heart laughs." Further, Kronenberg notes that a boy's relationship with his bull is used by other members of the tribe as a "diagnostic means to determine the way in which he will live up to his social obligations" (1961, 261).

In today's Sudan, bullsongs are still sung by DiDinga, Dinka, and other Nilo-Saharan pastoral groups in spite of the long-standing war which has disrupted the traditional way of cattle herding. It remains the same tradition recorded by Driberg in his book *Initiation: Translations from Poems of the DiDinga and Lango Tribe*s (1932b), but now I could assess how closely Driberg represented the DiDinga tradition:

The reedbuck calls to the roan like a young man, the reedbuck calls like a young man on the far side of the valley.
Gather ye together.
The rhinoceros stands silent at the foot of the acacia, watchful, head swaying from side to side.
Gather ye together.
The leopard crouches in the rocks, the black leopard of the forest crouches, eyes flaming, poised.
Gather ye together.
The buffalo swings his horns this way and that, scattering the mud in the river.
Gather ye together.
Ho! Akorikono of the spreading horns!
Ha! Akorikono of the spreading horns!
Ha! Akorikono, red, red as the blood which bought thee, the blood which hand-selled [*sic*] my manhood's spear.
As the red lightning art thou,
Akorikono, as the lightning which breaks over Taala
at the time of sowing. (Driberg 1932b, 7)

At this point, I realized the need for commentary by an adult bullsinger. Paul Atanya put me in contact via e-mail with Angelo Gola, a DiDinga adult in Tennessee whose name was familiar to all of the performers in Syracuse. Although they had never met Angelo, Lino confirmed his reputation: "He is known." At my request, Angelo e-mailed his bullsongs, which he had never written before. To my knowledge, the following are the first bullsongs written down by a DiDinga bullsinger:

Hodo hodo hodo. Ningiti mamu ho!

Manga hongi modung! Iyo Naita Riono
Manga hongi modung!

Manga hongi modung! Iyo Naita, Riono
Manga hongi modung!
(Ningiti mamu ho)

My! My! My! This place of water.

Stop sleeping on your stomach! Oh yes. Naita Riono.
Stop sleeping on your stomach!

Stop sleeping on your stomach! Yes, Naita Riono.
Stop sleeping on your stomach!
(This place of water.)

Ati Dololeco

Duha da nibuuk cugunik
Aito gi uma ci hanyaha na
Kai kedenano thong
Na Lolima, Awo Nyakori
Lolima, Awo Nyakori
Kamuhani na iyieni nganita

Mother of Child

You too tell your story.
There is nothing (no dowry) that I bring to you.
I am seeking a loan.
I Lolima, Awo Nyakori,
Lolima Awo Nyakori,
I was thinking of you today.

Manyi Doholeco

Duha da nibuuk cugunik
Aito gi uma ci hanyaha na
Kai kedenano thong
Na Lolima, Awo Nyakori
Lolima, Awo Nyakori
Kamuhani na iyieni nganita

Father of Child

You too tell your story.
There is nothing (no dowry) that I bring to you.
I am seeking a loan.
I Lolima, Awo Nyakori,
Lolima Awo Nyakori,
I was thinking of you today.

Arukan Oli Cani Hall

Arukan oli cani hal acina nganit manyi
Cin thida hulahaci tang ci baba

Arukan Lomagali hal ee acina nganit manyi
Cin thida hulahaci tang ci baba

My Bull roars all night.

My Bull roars all night. Because of me, (its) owner.
Observe, you poor man, the cow of my father.

Lomagal (Wide-horn) bull roars all night. Because of me, its owner.
Observe, you poor man, the cow of my father.

These vignettes can be repeated several times with pauses between, or they can be strung together so they form one lengthy bullsong. When I had the opportunity to observe Angelo performing, I noted, first, that he did not sing these particular

Angelo Gola kneels to perform his bullsong during *nyakorot* at Schweinfurth Memorial Art Center in Auburn, New York, 2003. Photo: Felicia McMahon.

vignettes but at the last minute decided to perform warrior songs known to the young men. He also used aggressive arm and hand motions to convey power. Sometimes he fell to his knees as he sang which was a strategy to motivate the audience.

This song was particularly emotional:

Etedia toliti
The tolit fruit has detached itself from the tolit tree.
Nalimaya tuhui hadim nak hasina bee shinang Nalimaya tuhui
We would like to see Mt. Nalimaya over turn.
Ero, ero, ero
Ero, ero, ero
Nalimaya tuhui hadim nak hasina bee shinang Nalimaya tuhui
We would really like to see Mt. Nalimaya turn over.

According to Angelo and the young men, *tolit* is DiDinga for a special kind of tree that is "very very big" and has very big "plums." When I later found *tolit* in Rosato's dictionary, I learned that *tolit* is DiDinga for the sausage tree (*kigelia pinnata*). It was no exaggeration when they said that the "plums" were very large. As a matter of fact, the fruit hangs on long ropelike stalks and looks like giant sausages. The *tolit*, which is in the bignonia family, has fruit that is two feet long and can weigh up to 15 pounds. I thought it was strange that a song about a sausage tree would be sung with such emotion until I learned about the song's "hidden meanings." The song is connected to a mythical belief about the rain serpent as well as to a historically verifiable event:

Benjamin: This song is like it happened one day. The SPLA, the SPLA, it's kind of weird. You know, there's a river in DiDinga, there's a mountain and in this mountain there's a river that was flowing down, the river was flowing down the mountain. And down the mountain there is this tree, tolit. Which they call it tolit, right? And these soldiers one day, you know, they came and there was a bush around the river and there was a big snake. There was a big snake. And I don't know, it's kind of [laughs] the community believe that this snake kind of was providing the water, the flow of water. I mean, the flow of water was . . . so the soldier just came and you know, they rested on the shade of the tolit so they saw this snake, big snake. Then they decided to shoot it. They decided to shoot that snake and this snake was kind of like a symbol of I don't know what [laughs], kind of a social belief that the snake allows the river to flow. Without that snake you, you know, it was kind of a social symbol. I don't really know much about it but they decided to shoot it. So they decided on the shade of the tree [lowers voice] while they were resting there under the shade these are you know just like lying there, resting and this biiiiiig tree is like bearing some big fruit, I don't know . . . the big ones. Like huge big ones and this tree according to the legend is like the Nature was annoyed with these soldiers of shooting the snake so it was like a curse [lowers voices] so while they were resting there fruit fell directly to one of the soldiers right there and he departed, he died there and it was like a curse because they shoot the snake. Now this is how the song was, this is what the song is all about. That is the meaning of the song. That is the literal meaning of that song. Yup. Nature was not pleased with the behavior of these. The Nature had to take its course and it's punishing these people, you know.

F: How did you know from these words?

Benjamin: That is just like, the people are singing literally but the real meaning of that song is what I am telling you.

F: And how did you learn this? Who told you?

Benjamin: Yeah, this thing, it just happened, you know. This song is not so old. It just happened. The Movement just started and it happened in the middle of like [19]80-something or [19]90-something.

F: And you were in Sudan?

Benjamin: No, I was living in Kenya and this is the real talk about the real story here. It is not some guys who are faking. It happened, it is something that happened. It's kind of real. Sometimes I tend to believe it [laughs]. Because most of our community believe in these super, supernatural things.

The location of this particular *tolit* tree represents a "vortex of behavior" (Roach 1996a). Vortices of behavior are sites of memory, like marketplaces, streets or any spot where audiences and performers emerge. These sites have powerful effects on collective memory, allowing it to survive despite changes in the places where the original remembered events occurred. "*Etedia toliti*" means "the sausage tree dropped its fruit," and the song is an ode to the tree in this particular locale where a group of invaders were killed when the *tolit* tree dropped its fruit while they sat under it. Therefore, Angelo was singing to the *tolit* to "do it again" and further, to invoke Mt. Nalimaya to "turn over" to evict the invaders. However, all of the DiDinga stressed that songs such as *Tolit* have "hidden meanings": "This song means the DiDinga are a hospitable people and the SPLA who are Dinka rebel soldiers came to our land but then they would not leave and we are asking the *tolit* tree to drop its fruit." Angelo and the young men believed that the song's composer must have seen the fruit drop on a visitor's head, which killed the visitor. Lino's explanation about a "hidden meaning" only confirmed that DiDinga songs are both old and new because traditional songs take on new meaning. Further, Angelo indicated that he improvised for "motivation" by adding words to the traditional text:

Etedia toliti
Guio, Lopu, Konyen
Nalimaya tuhui hadim nak hasina bee shinang Nalimaya tuhui
Ero, ero, ero
Naeimakon, metihari, natimahira
Nalimaya tuhui hadim nak hasina bee shinang Nalimaya tuhui

Literally, the names *Guio, Lopu, Konyen* mean "brawny one," "stocky one," and "big eyes." Angelo's improvised lines have no meaning in English because they are names of warriors whom he is calling because they represent "special qualities" recognized by the DiDinga community. The words "Naeimakon, metihari, natimahira" are Angelo's "favorite words" for the colors "black and white," "pink," and "multi-colored," which he used to describe the beauty of Mt. Nalimaya. When comparing Angelo's bullsongs to Driberg's translation, it becomes apparent that Driberg is using the English idiom to convey a feeling for DiDinga poetic verse. In Driberg's excerpt taken from a lengthy bullsong, the line "the black leopard of the forest crouches, eyes flaming, poised" differs a great deal stylistically from Angelo's succinct verse. Yet, Driberg claims that he has provided "translations in the strictist sense" (1932b, 1). It is, however, obvious that Driberg was attempting to communicate the poetic essence of DiDinga song rather than strict translation.

Driberg titles the first song "Bull-Song of Auranomi," who is the song's composer. The bull's name is Akorikono, which means "of the spreading horns" (see Appendix A). The difficulty with Driberg's text is that without the original DiDinga, the repetitions, which are central to the song aesthetics, are lost. Further, Driberg admits the song is a "compilation" of many bullsongs which he heard over a long period of time. It may be assumed from the length and the references in the song that it is not an accurate representative of a bullsong but rather demonstrates the extensiveness of a song belonging most probably to an older, high-ranking elder who composed vignettes over a period of time after performing it on many public occasions.

I had to wait until Angelo arrived to hear a mature DiDinga bullsong because the young men had not been "counted" (initiated) and therefore had composed only the first bullsongs of their youths. They had not entered the DiDinga age-grade hierarchy, so they had not yet composed group initiation songs, which are part of their bullsong tradition, and would not do so until they went through this ritual. I wondered if a recontexualized performance would inspire them to compose new songs or if they would adhere closely to the songs of their childhood. They chose the latter.

There is no published record of young men's DiDinga initiation songs except for the English version also published by Driberg, which he titled "The Ancient Gods: A Hymn of Initiation" (see Appendix A). Once again, Driberg's translation probably more accurately represents his familiarity with Western canonical parallelism than it accurately represents DiDinga parallel emergent structure. Rather, from Driberg's translation of the text, the reader gets only the suggestion of the kind of parallelism that must be evident in the original-language version: a rhythmic performance which, although a kind of dyadic composition, is not always predictable. This unpredictable parallelism contrasts with canonical parallelism, which is defined as regular pairing of semantically related words in syntactically related lines. It is important to recognize emergent parallelism in

African tradition "based on various semantic and syntactic correspondences that crisscross in complex ways and between types of lines. Furthermore, the absence of linear development is significant in the cultural understanding of these songs and their pragmatic effects. Emergent parallelism is created not by an individual performer, but through the sung exchanges and dialogues of a ceremonial assembly" (Kratz 1990, 44). When Angelo performed, the DiDinga young men took on the roles of chorus and audience. Angelo's improvisation, the "reading between the lines," was essential for the effectiveness of the song, which relies on the cultural literacy of the audience.

If members of the DiDinga audience are inspired, they spontaneously increase the effectiveness of the song by acting as the chorus and spontaneously embellishing it with *lilan* (shrilling in elation). Song is never separated from the corresponding body movement so dance accompanies every song. After several opportunities to hear harmonic coordination in the dance-songs of the DiDinga and to observe synchronization of body movement within the group, I recognized that these basic characteristics are the same for Dinka traditions, also

> . . . essentially a group activity in which co-ordination of action is of the utmost importance. The whole dancing group, and not the partners only, should be in full harmony. The dancers jump up and down or stamp the ground at exactly the same time, and, as the above song indicates, to be out of step is to degrade one's self as a dancer. This co-ordination, connected with the wide association of unity and harmony, is also observable in group singing. Choral singing is one of the most striking aspects of Dinka music. The power of a group song lies largely in the chorus although the role of the individual solo is a pivotal one, showing that the significance of the individual is not overshadowed by this group demonstration. . . . Even the group reference to 'I' indicates that group solidarity is fundamentally a construction of individual egos. (F. M. Deng 1973, 83)

A native East African scholar, Deng emphasizes the centrality of dance-song in Dinka society. As in most other African cultures, DiDinga and Dinka male initiation rituals are prestigious cultural events so it is during these rituals that the highest art is put on display. Deng documented and published Dinka song texts in his native language as well as English, for which he provides an insider's commentary.

All DiDinga with whom I spoke knew *Lotiki*, a traditional warrior song typically sung during *nyakorot*. The young men included *Lotiki* in every performance for American audiences. For a program brochure, I asked Charles, the soloist, to write the lyrics in DiDinga with a written translation. Patrick, a younger DiDinga from Kentucky visiting Charles in 2002, also offered to write the lyrics in English. I decided this was an opportune time to compare texts. However, there is still no official published orthography for DiDinga language, so inconsistencies are to be expected. Yet, the song texts, recorded in print for the first time here, are remarkably identical in spite of the fact that the men had not heard this adult song since early childhood:

Patrick's version: **Charles's version:**

1. Adohit kodobuana Lotiki liku bali   Adahit hodopuwana Lotiki likaibani
2. Adohit kodobuana Lotiki liku bali   Adahit hodopuwana Lotiki likaibani
3. Lika ba Lotiki tomiro   Likaiba Lotiki taminaro
4. Lika ba Lotiki tomiro   Likaiba Lotika taminaro
5. Holo adahita   Holo adahita
6. Adohit hotogutho heni tamiro   Adihit hotongutho heeni taminaro.
7. (Anek lo hirto gong ablahi tina buliohi)

1. The vultures devoured Lotiki during his past hunting expedition.
2. The vultures devoured Lotiki during his past hunting expedition.
3. Lotiki's great bushland, and the Savannah expedition.
4. Lotiki's great bushland and the Savannah expedition.
5. Oh, they devoured,
6. They devoured until they slept on trees.
(You have always been used to eating the cows.)

Lotiki is actually part of the warrior tradition of young men, found throughout East Africa. Songs are often associated with African age grades in hierarchical status systems. Charles insisted that the text concerns a hunter named Lotiki: "The vultures ate Lotiki during hunting time. Only men mostly sing it when they are hunting. Hyena kill Lotiki and then the vulture came and ate Lotiki's corpse. You hyena, one day they will come to eat you." During the second performance, he altered the text by omitting the final line, a reference to eating the cows. In order to confirm what I assumed was a chance omission, I reviewed several tapes of past performances with the other young DiDinga when Charles was not present. Their translation of the song was consistent with his, except they continued to refer to the omitted line:

Joseph: That is about a guy named Lotiki. Lotiki, he was like butchered somewhere. When people went hunting, he was butchered. You know, hyenas ate him up. Actually, all these songs are like stories.

Dominic L.: But they [we] don't sing it entirely. But they sing it in a proverb way.

James: The hyenas ate Lotiki. Then the vultures ate Lotiki. They could go and eat the cows. So, you could go and eat this meat and it is Lotiki. Tell hyena who eats animals at night to come and eat at daytime too. Vultures eat Lotiki and they sleep in trees like, like, I don't know the name for the word [*vultures*]. They are slow and lazy.

I asked Charles to write the song text a second time, and he continued to omit the reference to cows (*tina*). All of the young performers insisted that Lotiki was a hunter who was eaten by a hyena. Yet, when I asked Patrick and Peter, the two other DiDinga visitors from Kentucky, both of their versions included the final line, *Anek lohirto gong adahi tina baliohi* (Tell the hyena, you have always been in the habit of devouring the cows at night). After several e-mail exchanges with Paul Atanya in 2002, he explained that in DiDingaland, the hyena is one of the most despised animals because hyenas are the most frequent killers of livestock such as goats, sheep, and especially cattle, the basis of the DiDinga economic system: "The DiDinga word for hyena is *lohirto* but because of their dislike for this animal, the DiDinga call it Lotiki which means 'one with big ears.' Since he is a cunning as well as ruthless hunter, the hyena in this song is both admired and ridiculed; and at the end of the song, he is killed and eaten by vultures." When I asked Atanya to confirm the young men's orthography, he supplied yet a third way to represent DiDinga language:

Soloist: Adahit hodobwana Lotiki lika ibali
Chorus: Adahit hodobwana Lotiki lika ibali
Soloist: Lika ba Lotiki taminaro
Chorus: Lika ba Lotiki taminaro
Soloist: Holo adahita
Chorus: Adahit hotogutho heeni taminaro

Unlike Atanya, all of the young DiDinga translated the text to mean that Lotiki, a human hunter with big ears, was eaten by the vultures. Fortunato commented that it was "a kind of a warning": "The song means, they, the vulture, they eaten Lotiki because he was only one, and they sit on the trees. They fly and they get the man. If you go hunting you will be eaten like Lotiki, so don't go by yourself, go with your friends and avoid being eaten like Lotiki." None identified Lotiki as a hyena. Because no version identifies who killed Lotiki, the young singers said that the song implied that hyena was his killer. Finally, I asked Charles, the soloist for this song, why he deleted the last line; he declared, "for effect." It appears that Charles omitted the line because it fit the musical aesthetics of his immediate performance as well as the fact that cattle no longer are meaningful to his life here. Later, Emilio explained that his DiDinga name is Lotiki, and Lotiki is a common name given to infant boys. Emilio's explanation demonstrates an important part of the entextualization process: singer commentary which can reveal hidden meanings lost to researchers who rely solely on texts.

I accidentally learned about the *nyakereket*, the DiDinga male initiation ceremony, during which danced bullsongs demonstrate the centrality of the bull to initiation itself and to the men whose very identities are dependent on this interrelationship with cattle as well as with the age-set group. During a conversation with Fortunato, I mispronounced *nyakorot*, and he thought I was asking about *nyakereket*. For non-DiDinga speakers, it is difficult to hear the difference between *nyakorot* and *nyakereket*. Fortunato stressed that every aspect of a DiDinga man's life is connected to his advancement in order to participate in *nyakereket*, a part of their age-set system for which the DiDinga have no word: "We have senior, junior and we have old citizens. The old people, that's the senior, above us, you know. The old people have their names, like the high class, middle class. So, you have to sacrifice something to reach that. If you don't do that, you remain behind, no one knows you. You don't get recognized that you are somebody. You are child although you are big man, fifty years old. You don't be recognized that you are somebody unless you say that okay, I'll sacrifice to the old people that now I'm a man and high class. The first class is called giraffe. If my father was high class, I would be respected by people." Although there is no word for "age-set system," the process is known as *aut boloh* or "to stay on the leaves" (Fetterman 1992, 80). All men in every rank must participate in *nyakereket*.[3] *Nyakereket* is the word for a special male gathering held between harvest and the next year's planting. When I pointed to this word in Driberg's dictionary, the young men solemnly nodded, indicating the importance of this ranking ceremony. During *nyakereket*, the symbolic *nypio* takes place, which, they explained, are "thrashings."[4] The *nypio* is reminiscent of ritual hazing. In order to advance from the lowest rank in the hierarchy, each man was required to perform *thapaninit*, the ritual spearing of the bull.

None of the DiDinga in Syracuse had performed *thapaninit*, but during childhood they had been observers. They described in detail the ritual roasting of the speared bull's meat and how the initiates are required to jump over the bonfire. After the initiate makes three successful jumps over the fire, the young man is said to be *athapan* (cleansed). When I asked if they had not seen anyone jump too low, my informants laughed, although they admitted amazement that no one has ever failed because the fires are "really large." The words *nyakereket* and *nypio* are used by the DiDinga but are said to be Toposa words. This suggests that, as in *nyakorot*, the customs are syncretized and may have originated with the Toposa. However, the DiDinga Lost Boys claimed that *nyakorot*, *nypio*, as well as *nyakereket* are "really DiDinga." Further, Fetterman's informants claim that the origin of the ritual thrashing is described in a DiDinga folktale about an old man who is said to have asked some young boys to give him beer: "The young people refused and were rude to him so the old man thrashed them. The young people waited until they themselves were adults and then sought out and punished the children of these men, and over time the present age-grade ranking and punishments of *nypio* evolved" (1992, 85–86). Thus, the purpose for the age set system was to keep things orderly: "Without names, there would be confusion over which people you could punish and which people could punish you" (Fetterman 1992, 85–86). In another variation of the tale, two old men asked a boy to get some water. When he refused, one of the men went to get it and the boy drank it. This angered the old men, who beat him and made the boy go for honey. When the boy grew up, he inflicted a similar punishment on the sons of the old men and, thus, *nypio* became tradition.

Driberg mentions that a major portion of DiDinga initiation songs make reference to the gods of the tribal religion, an aspect that may or may not be relevant now because, since Driberg's early research in the 1930s, most DiDinga have been Christianized. Even so, it is considered a serious offense not to participate in these traditional initiation rituals. After the initiates have been baptized into the Catholic Church, a priest is called to attend and to bless the initiation. Because of the distances involved, the initiations are only held once a year or at times when the priest is available to attend. As Simon explained, "We would be jailed if we did not participate." In other words, refusal to participate is a grave offense, and the stigma follows a young man even if he leaves his village to avoid the ceremony: "The second, and ultimately far more important reason, is that a person who does not perform *thapaninit* will be light in everything, he will eat much but will never be satisfied (*uwawangi gena*)." And further, bad luck will follow him: "This means that he will grow up, get married and have cattle, but he will either not have any or many children and will definitely not become rich (in cattle)" (Fetterman 1992, 90). Thus, although *thapaninit* involves *nypio* by the elders, all of the young men told me that they wanted to be "counted" when they returned to Sudan.

This attitude toward *nypio* reflects the conservatism of this particular group of DiDinga men. In a study of the stages in the process of "urbanization" among the urban and tribal Xhosa of South Africa, Mayer found a major difference between urbanization versus conservatism in the urban emphasis on person-to-person friendships versus group friendships. Conservative migrants tended to isolate themselves in small close-knit networks based on their home villages. Similarly, at this writing, among Dinka and DiDinga in Syracuse, there still exists a "tribal" attitude, if we view tribalism as "a group's belief that a unique and exclusive relation must exist between itself and its institutions" (Mayer 1971, 293). Further, the young men's self-identity, even in urban Syracuse, remains tied to an age-set system. The DiDinga men believe they cannot avoid *nypio* because they will be cursed (*cinenit*).[5] *Cinenit* is so powerful that it follows the young men, and this is the reason for Charles's concern over the black feather, a tradition described by Kronenberg:

> *Ein jeder, der sich um die Angelegenheiten unseres napiyo nicht kümmert, soll blind auf Erden herumgehen. Wenn er seine Frau heiratet, soll sie ihn abweisen. Wenn eine Frau ihn aus Unwissenheit heiratet, so sollen seine Kinder sterben. Du sollst nur Mädchen verführen (ohne sie zu heiraten), und Deine Ronder sollen verschwinden (durch Busszahlungen für die Verführung). Deine Rinder sollen sterben, wenn Du dich nicht um unser napiyo kümmerst. Wenn Du ein Mann bist, der zu Blut gehört (d.h., wenn Du der Sohn jener bist, denen wir napiyo gezahlt haben), so sollst Du für immer weggehen und sterben. Du sollst zu den Karamojong gehen und dort sterben. Wir werden unsere Angelegenheit ohne Dich machen. Wir wissen um unsere Angelegenheiten. Du wirst gehen und allein nachdenken, und wenn Du zurückkommen willst und uns zahlst, so hängst dies nur von Dir ab, aber wenn Du fuer immer gehen solltest, so ist es Deine Sache. Wenn Du morgen denkst, dass Du am leben bleiben möchtest, und wenn Du Dir bewusst wirst, dass Du das Gesetz gebrochen hast, so kannst Du kommen, damit wir am Orte des Bullenessens auf Dich spucken (d.h. verzeihen). Du hast uns in unserem nyakereget beleidigt und hast uns das napiyo verweigert.* (Kronenberg 1972b, 102)

[Anyone who does not see to our *napiyo* will go around the earth blind. If he marries a woman, she should reject him. If a woman unknowingly marries him, his children will die. You will seduce girls without marrying them. Your cattle will die, if you do not see to our *napiyo*. If you are the son of a man who has been counted, you must go away and die. You must go to the Karamjong and die there. We will conduct our affairs without you. We know about our affairs. You will go and reflect alone, and if you want to return and (be) counted, it depends on you, but if you should go, that is your concern. If you decide tomorrow that you prefer to remain, and if you realize that you have broken the law, you can come to the place of the bull meal that you spit on. You have insulted us during our *nyakereket* and you have denied us the *napiyo*. (Translation by Felicia McMahon)]

This taboo is so strong that, although none of the DiDinga in Syracuse belong to an age-set and none had been initiated, they wanted to fulfill the traditional requirements of initiation when they eventually returned to Sudan. In Sudan, their age-set would have dictated the all-male dancing and songs associated with it.[6] In Syracuse, they created their own age-group identity, which included the shared experience of formal education in which educational grades replaced the classes in the traditional age-set system. The traditional age-set system, however, is more complex than this because in Sudan it is based on the classes (age groups) through which each of the boys' fathers progressed when they were counted. When I showed the age-set names listed by Driberg to Charles, he pointed to the highest class and identified it as his father's. He also claimed that his father was a chief. According to Driberg, in DiDingaland tribal leadership is not based on ancestry but on the number of cattle owned by a man, that is, how wealthy and influential he is. As Dominic R. demonstrated, during casual gatherings the DiDinga bullsongs are not limited to performances by elders, warriors, or initiates at ceremonial age-set rituals. Later, Fortunato told me that he too had composed a bullsong, but his was about a girl whom he favored when he attended the missionary school in Nairobi. When I asked him to sing it for me, he did so softly as the others sang the refrain:

Macineka buheyi gol ci oi huth
Please, have you seen my girl?
Hacini ya otholo thong
I saw the moisture of urine.
Hedebi ya oo thong
I follow her footsteps just here.
Kanuothi nga oo thong
I follow them while they are going.

This was the point at which I realized that bullsongs were about love as well as bulls and war. Although the young men translated the song for me, again there was no equivalent in DiDinga for the English word "imprint," which Fortunato translated literally "moisture of urine." Fortunato's bullsong is the story of a young man who hoped a certain girl would approach him. When she did, he did not notice but the others had. He then saw her still-moist footsteps retreating into the woods behind him, but she had disappeared:

Fortunato: [This is about] the footprint of the girl just went, right now. So I want to go after her.

James: Someone was coming to our trough and he is trying to ask this girl, and he could just see her footprints of this girl.

Fortunato: Oh, I missed her and I kind of wonder. I want to follow her! [Laughter.] Like that.

F: When you sing your songs about your animals, your bulls, there are other people with you? You mentioned bringing it to the grazing area?

Dominic R.: Actually, I sing alone when I take my cows in the morning, in the mornings still taking, very happy and sing and then, after grazing, I have to sing again, just praising it because after grazing it is very happy and I bring it back home now.

John: Are there times when someone like yourself who has another animal sings about which animal is better? In other words, have you ever had a competition, say, with someone else, singing my bull is better than your bull and the other person.

Dominic R.: [Laughs] Oh yeah! Exactly.

John: You know here in America, musicians try to compose their songs against somebody's. So it is just like that. It is just trying to draw attention from the audience to the singing that this bull or his song is better than theirs so that people come to his.

Dominic R.: Actually, I was not the only one to take care of the cattles because we have a lot of time. For example, when the cows get thirsty, you have to take them to the river, and have to get some water so they can drink so we have many of them so all of my friends have the same. Many not the young ones but the big ones. So they have to praise and show that they have [one] also so there is a bit of competition. Because I was still young, I came up with mine to show them that mine was the best.

John: The reason I bring that up is because some of the poetry we have from Greek and Roman culture there is this competition between shepherds who are taking care of their flocks and their sheep, and although it is not particularly about the animals, they do have a competition where they try to outdo one another in their songs or for love for a young lady. One would sing and the other would sing and a kind of back and forth.

Lino: When our people are performing, someone will perform, then someone else will perform. It is not just one singer.

The reference by my husband, John, to ancient pastoral poetry was duly noted. Lino confirmed that the competition was similar to the DiDinga bullsong tradition. Likewise, love, rather than bravery and war, appeared to be the focus of the young men's bullsongs. At another meeting, one of the teenager's brothers who was visiting from Canada, Joe N., told me that the previous evening the group performed *gyrikot* in Charles's apartment, and he also sang about a girl, Naboyele:

Naboyele namerirenga Limaluka
Naboyele, daughter of Limaluka
Ee Lomalachan
Oh, beautiful eyes
Nangoria
Who will marry her?
Nahomoli natihajokan
The person of good heart
Nahomoli natihajokan
The person of good heart
Nahomoli natihajokan
The person of good heart
Nahomoli natihajokan
The person of good heart
Ee Lomalachan
Oh, beautiful eyes
Ee Lomalachan
Oh, beautiful eyes
Ee Lomalachan
Oh, beautiful eyes
Ee Lomalachan
Oh, beautiful eyes.

The song is about a girl (*Naboyele*), the beautiful daughter of Limaluka. Naboyele has beautiful eyes. In the song, the soloist asks, "Who will marry her?" The chorus replies, "The person of good heart." *Gyrikot* often takes place from January to February when the work load is not heavy and people of all ages except for children participate in the this vigorous dance.[7] A gyrikot song like Naboyele is performed because it demonstrates the way that *gyrikot* can compliment a woman or chastise her behavior. On the other hand, it is also playfully used to embarrass community members who have committed certain offenses or who are lazy. Thus, *gyrikot* can take the form of an insult song, much like *Mariah*, the song which the young men first performed in my classroom, or it can be a song to attract women.[8]

However, *gyrikot*, *nyakorot*, and *lilia* represent only three of four living DiDinga musical traditions. I was eventually introduced to a newer, fifth form, *lokembe*.[9] According to Charles, *lokembe*, the pan-African word for the thumb piano, was adopted from Uganda in the 1970s. *Lokembe* is regarded by the DiDinga as a kind of tribal "disco" dance.[10] Therefore, *lokembe* is the most recent DiDinga tradition, while *umoya* (sometimes spelled *umya*) is the oldest dance, because it is performed mainly by elderly women and men. *Umoya* is uncommon today. As one singer explained, "It is a little bit still there," compared to *nyakorot*, the dance proper held during harvest season during which dancers take turns based on their places in the social hierarchy. The older males, females, and the aspiring warriors have center stage, the latter dancing with the women of their choice. In Sudan, musical instruments for *nyakorot* include ankle and wrist bells (*chugurena*), the wooden trumpet (*tooeri*), the whistle (*pelo*), and the shaker (*iyekanit*). The end of *nyakorot* is signaled by *lilia*, a slow dance. One young man explained the progression from *nyakorot* to *lilia*: "In the beginning of *nyakorot*, the dancing is very vigorous and then it goes down. It reacts like vigorous, then it settles down." During *lilia*, when girls are participating, the dancers hold hands, moving up and down, left and right, pushing the girl in one direction and then the other."

It was surprising to hear that the young men had observed *lilia* in their villages because I had read the DiDinga no longer perform *lilia*. In Sudan, it was danced to encourage men to enter into battle. However, my young DiDinga informants in Syracuse all insisted that the *lilia* is still danced in their villages today because it is embedded within *nyakorot* as the signal that *nyakorot* has ended. Eventually, they made it easy for me to interpret their traditions for Americans because they distinguished *gyrikot* from *nyakorot* by telling me that *gyrikot* is "percussion" and *nyakorot* is "jumping." The "jumping" to which they referred is called *ngothi*.

DiDinga "warrior" performs *ngothi* during *nyakorot* at Schweinfurth Memorial Art Center in Auburn, New York, 2003. Photo: Felicia McMahon.

One visiting elder told me, "In *nyakorot*, the soloist controls the dance," indicating the soloist must also initiate *ngothi*. This was significant because it was not apparent that Charles, the soloist, was always the one to begin *ngothi*. However, the most distinctive charateristic of *nyakorot* is *padan*, the slapping body movement of women against men which the young men had mentioned.

Padan is a dance movement unique to the DiDinga. With this rhythmic dance step, the women move forward and retreat after they have thumped their bodies against male dancers' bodies, thus producing a clapping sound. The DiDinga are very proud of their unusual dance movement: "Everyone [DiDinga], we dance that dance. It is like number one. Nobody else does this dance. Other African dancers have jumping but not this [*padan*]." Initially, the young men explained that traditionally their songs and dancing were regulated by the seasons and not performed until the work was done. In southern Sudan, when it is time for summer and winter grazing, the village routine changes. When the environment turns unfavorable, the village must move. When it is

DiDinga couple performs *padan* during *nyakorot* at Schweinfurth Memorial Art Center in Auburn, New York, 2003. Photo: Felicia McMahon.

planting time, there is a greater amount of activity, as when the crops have to be harvested before heavy rain: "Then we have a celebration." I recalled Driberg's explanation, written 70 years ago, of the economic connection between celebratory dance and work: "It certainly makes it difficult to hold communal dances and other social festivities, and accounts for the comfortable belief that dancing at this time [before harvesting] would cause the crops to wither away, a social necessity being, as usual, buttressed up by a religious sanction. A more mundane inducement is to be found in the fact that enough drink will not be available for a good party until after the harvest. Seasonal economic activities are therefore closely bound up with social activities, and a definite season for songs and dances, visiting and love-making is thus established by the interaction of environment and economics" (1932a, 204). After reading this, I saw clearly that all DiDinga traditions are performed within ritualized contexts. However, the performers had communicated successfully with American audiences at their first Syracuse University performance, demonstrating the power of their communication skills conveyed through kinesthetic imagination. They had made a connection without percussion instruments and without the audience's ability to understand DiDinga.

I witnessed this kinesthetic communicative ability when, one day at their apartment, the young men disappeared into their kitchen. I thought I heard the banging and clanging of pots and a debate in DiDinga occurring. Suddenly, they burst into the living room in single file, pots and aluminum pans in hand, on which they were striking with large spoons, forks, and knives. They formed a circle, initiating a string of songs which began with *Mariah* and followed with a series of others:

Soloist: *Ee aiir loholec beninit haga*
　　　Oh, the young woman is fleeing.
Chorus: *Naorekong*
　　　Naorekong
Soloist: *Mahati iiru vellek neitiha ne*
　　　You are afraid of the music?
Chours: *Gi ci airehi beninit haga Naorekong*
　　　Even if you flee what will you do Naorekong.

Naorekong is the victim in this song. Her name means "one with flying eyes" (a flirt). The young woman is planning to run away because she has been labeled a seductress which causes her shame. But the music follows her, and she cannot escape it. I was surprised by the vigor of this *gyrikot* performed out of context, in the young men's apartment. Like the repeated turning of a jump rope in a game, the repetitive lyrics motivate the chorus and the audience, which in turn lend variety in tone, rhythm, and motion. The music itself employs a pentatonic scale, with songs that are always antiphonal. As the song-leader sings one line, leading the group to follow, a stronger singer can take the lead. Among the young men, the jockeying for center stage never stopped. If the leader slipped for a brief moment, another performer would quickly move in and sing faster, louder, or change the direction of the dance itself. The competitive nature of DiDinga tradition was an aesthetic easily transmitted to audiences through kinesthetic communication, a kind of traditional body language. Comparisons of the young men's videotaped public performances became as important as entextualization for recognizing traditional DiDinga aesthetics.

Memory, Childhood, and Restored Behavior

Ee Limaluka ngani ci eheed warang
Hey, Limaluka. Who wrote the letter?
Nganita
It's me.
Ehedihi ngani
Whom did you write to?
Obote
Obete
Enehi ni neegi
What did you say to him?
Kenehi ne anya ripot hithiho ne au thinit lota
I told him, "Give me the report and my heart will be at peace."
Traditional DiDinga song

As we have seen, entextualization plays an important role in the recontextualization process. In this chapter, I consider the relationship between memory and "kinesthetic imagination" as an alternative by which the performers communicate a memory of home (Roach 1996a). Kinesthetic communication requires competency through learned body behaviors. When losses occur in a community, remaining members attempt to find satisfactory alternatives through "kinesthetic imagination" (Roach 1996a, 2). From this perspective, performance places high value on body learning and training, rather than linguistic communication. This orientation extends

Bauman's definition of "performance frame" as "an assumption of accountability to an audience for an authoritative display of communicative competence subject to evaluation for the relative skill and effectiveness with which the act of communication is accomplished, above and beyond its informational content" (Bauman, Sawin, and Carpenter 1992, 28) and Schechner's ideas about performance (1985; 2002).

Schechner's concept of performance as time-space sequence composed of proto-performance, performance, and aftermath provides a useful beginning framework for recontextualized traditions such as the DiDinga *nyakorot*. Before *nyakorot* took place, I questioned whether two culturally distinct cultures like DiDinga and American would interface meaningfully. Without a collaborative planning period supplemented with library research, it would have been impossible for me to grasp the significance of the young men's dance-songs. Prior to the first *nyakorot*, none of the young men had adequate facility with English, and none were at ease facilitating a staged performance. They had expressed concern that Americans would misinterpret their "warrior dances," demonstrating their self-awareness of cultural stereotypes about Africans:

Joseph: I remember the people who dance *nyakorot*, they are warriors. Right? And they are like not smiling and that. They are real serious. So maybe if we practice here, people will say, oh my god, why are these guys not smiling and all that? And they will say something is wrong. They won't know the culture.
James: It must be explained first before.
Joseph: Yes, explain that it is the culture and they used to jump and all that.
Charles: Yeah, before *nyakorot*, you [Felicia] have to tell them!
Joseph: Yeah, people will not understand, "What? What is going on?"

The young men also were aware our collaboration was necessary to adequately frame their performance for a low-context communicative situation (Hall 1976). In Africa they performed in high-context situations where listeners did not need background information. They understood that frames of reference differ from culture to culture so I suggested that we work on a written interpretative brochure with contextual information about DiDinga traditions. This in turn made me self-reflexive about my influence on their performance. Until the young men became adept at self-presenting, I would, by default, be the one to provide interpretation. Because the American frame of reference was so different from a DiDinga frame, I believed the appropriate audience for their first performance was an African–American community with whom I had worked in the past. I had reservations about whether it would be appropriate for me, a middle-aged European-American woman, to be the presenter for a young male African group at an AME church. Further, the performers had expressed reservations about performing for African Americans. They had heard many reports about gang-related violence in urban African–American neighborhoods. In dominant white American society, they recognized an unspoken double standard which favors recent African immigrants, thus creating a strain between the Lost Boys and African–American youth. James explained, "When I talk, black Americans ask me, 'Why are you talking that way?' and when I say I am from Africa, they say, 'Who do you think you are? You think you're something special?' But I try to say, 'No, no this is just how I speak English,' but they make fun of us." These anecdotes only underscore the long-term effects of colonialism and racism on both continents.

In spite of their reservations, the young men agreed to perform at an AME church in Auburn. The performance sequence of the recontextualized performance, however, did not entirely fit Schechner's ten-phase "whole performance sequence," which includes "training-workshop-rehearsal"; "warmup-performance-afterevents-cooldown," and "aftermath" (critical responses, archives, memories). Schechner writes, citing Arnold van Gennep, "Looking at the whole seven-phase performance sequence, I find a pattern analogous to initiation rites. A performance involves a separation, a transition, and an incorporation. In the original context each of these phases is carefully marked. In initiations people are transformed permanently, whereas in most performances the transformations are temporary (transportations). Like initiations, performances make one person into another" (1985, 20–21). Unlike in initiations, in performances the performer resumes his own self. Schechner interprets Van Gennep's categories as training, workshop, rehearsal, and warm-ups, which are preliminary rites of separation: "The performance itself is liminal, analogous to the rites of transition. Cool-down and aftermath are postliminal rites of incorporation" (1985, 20–21).

In Sudan, DiDinga children's games are performances which are imitations of adult behaviors, including fantasy games in which as children they perform the adult songs that they hear. Children's games are a form of informal education or training in many foraging societies, such as the DiDinga's, in which children's dramatic play is an accurate representation of adult ritual behavior and not just a replica. For example, sometimes this dramatic play includes *juhan*, traditional body painting, in which DiDinga children prepare and apply moist ground colored clay to decorate their bodies for rituals in order to indicate warrior age-sets: "The hunter–gatherer cultures set a very clear turning point from childhood into adulthood, thus separating the two cultural settings. Those two settings are not of the same nature; one is 'serious' and the other is 'not serious.' Because the 'not serious' culture often mimics the other, we might conclude that it is basically a 'school' in charge of training children for adult life" (Gosso et al. 2005, 242). From this perspective, young children's activities are both performance and play. According to Schechner, play is performative, and play is at the center of all ritual (2002). Thus, in their recontextualized dance, the young men performed historically verifiable adult DiDinga behavior for both DiDinga and American audiences because they have a real memory of the adults in their earlier lives as well as memory of acting out the behaviors of these adults. As in many African cultures, DiDinga children's games do not reflect a separate children's culture. Instead, their games are imitations of adult activities, including adult songs and adult dances because song and dance are not separate from African daily life (Shostak 1976, 267). This, in effect, creates a twofold or binary past which, when performed for DiDinga and American audiences, is hybrid.

In one interview, Marino described DiDinga children's play thus: "When it is evening and the moon comes up, the children go off somewhere to a playing ground and where the children go, they are playing [a] gourd and when others come, they are singing then. It is like a kind of practice about what they hear the adults singing. One of the ways to learn our culture is just to imitate it."[1] Hearing this remark, I compared Marino's explanation to an early anthropological account of south Sudanese children's games: "The best time for games is a clear moonlight night in the dry season. Parents do not encourage play during the rainy season, as there is work for the children to do the next day. . . . A song sung alone by one boy the day after is vastly different from the mass effect by moonlight, where every player's whole body enters into the rhythm. . . . The words of these songs count for little, often having nothing to do with the action of the games; some are mere eulogies on crops or cattle; sometimes a song is slurred out of recognition" (Tucker 1933a, 165–66). Marino's commentary proved significant because it substantiated that for almost a century DiDinga children's traditions remained consistent and remarkably stable. The young men's recontextualized performances were accurate representations of these childhood games. Like children's play in every African culture, DiDinga children's dance-song performances served a socialization function because they prepared children for participation in adult social life. Yet, in the United States they were also performing the same children's imitation games to communicate a new identity, a form of hybridization: "The richness in details with which indigenous children play the roles of the adults of their society is remarkable. The characteristic social straightforwardness of indigenous groups allows their children to gain a more complete social vision than that of children in industrialized societies" (Gosso et al. 2005, 236). However, the dancers had not participated in traditional village life since childhood. Therefore, memory of their children's games was the root of their recontextualized performances.

According to Schechner, training is an early stage in the performance process where known skills are transmitted. My collaboration began at the workshop-rehearsal stage, which Schechner views as two parts of the deconstruction and reconstruction of performance. He later termed this stage "proto-performance" to demonstrate that this stage is a "deconstruction process, whereby the ready mades of culture (accepted ways of using body, accepted texts, accepted feelings) are broken down and prepared to be 'inscribed' upon (to use Turner's word). Workshop is analogous to the liminal-transitional phase of rituals. Rehearsals are their opposite of workshops. In rehearsals longer and longer strips of restored behavior are arranged to make a unified whole: the performance" (1985, 99). In many non-Western societies, however, the training phase is not separate from the workshop-rehearsal phase. Among the DiDinga, young boys have grade-age levels which precede formal initiation and entry into the age-set system, in which they will advance until they gain the status of senior warriors. Within the age-set groups they create their own in-group expressions and warrior songs. Because of their forced migration, the Lost Boys had only briefly been exposed to age-set activities, but in a nomadic society such as the DiDinga's they had had a richer play community than other nonnomadic groups would (Gosso et al. 2005). This also means that they took their childhood play solidarity with them, which helps to explain their ability to go together on their perilous trek to eventual safety. Living communally in the United States, the young men continued their communal bond as an alternative to the age-set group. Prior to their performances, the young men engaged in a 'rehearsal' in which they recalled warrior dance-songs of adults as well as those that they had parodied as children. Because the young men were no longer children, this restored behavior was both ironic and paradoxical: "Restored behavior offers to both individuals and groups the chance to re-become what they once were—or even, and most often, to re-become what they never were but wish to have been or wish to become" (Conquergood 1994, 46). During this rehearsal stage, from which I would have been excluded in the original cultural context, I was allowed access. However, this may not be so remarkable because in adult DiDinga social hierarchy there is a strict gender segregation which does not apply to children's play. In addition, postmenopausal women are granted a degree of independence and respect in DiDinga society. When I had jokingly pointed to the wrinkles in my neck to indicate that I was no longer young, they emphatically insisted, "Those are lines of wisdom." Charles indicated my youthful demeanor by saying, "You are still good" even though we all knew that by DiDinga standards I was, in fact, elderly.

During this collaborative rehearsal period, I suggested that we review the videotape made by one of my students when the Lost Boys had visited my classroom. The DiDinga men watched their first public *gyrikot* with great interest, laughing at the do-rag worn by one of my African American students, commenting, "Look at that guy!" They laughed at Fortunato's rapid hip-rotation motions, and he laughed good-naturedly at his own enthusiastic dance. When the others noticed that Simon had not known all of the words to the "church songs," they mimicked his facial expressions. The group was ready to repeat their performance but commented that *nyakorot*, which is "really DiDinga," should be performed. I still did not understand completely the difference between *nyakorot* and *gyrikot*, so I asked if I could videotape some of the dance movements during an upcoming farewell party at the men's shared apartment. At my request, Dominic R., who was leaving to live with his brother in Salt Lake City, performed his bullsong, usually performed publicly during *nyakorot*. The group also sang a couple of other songs to give me an idea of the kind of performances involved in *nyakorot*.

The fact that I had never seen DiDinga dances in their natural context was both an obstacle and a benefit. My ignorance enabled the young men to recognize that the frame for their dances had changed. Only certain traditions and songs could be easily communicated to Americans. The young DiDinga had an almost endless repertoire of texts from which to choose. Imposing a limit on the number of songs was a concept foreign to the young men because the success of *nyakorot* was determined by its duration. I agreed with Charles, the soloist, that the inclusion of DiDinga "church songs" might bridge DiDinga and American cultures, followed by the informality of *gyrikot*, which would lead into the more formal *nyakorot*. The men explained that the duration of the lead soloist's song is determined by how "gifted" he is, and sometimes a competition among singers evolved. Later, I would learn that the degree of a singer's gift was determined by how well he moved the audience with his improvisational skill:

Benjamin: When you compare Angelo and Dominic L., Angelo is someone who is more experienced. He know much more about how to communicate about how a song can play, how a song can be made sweet, you know, how to add some words and Dominic is someone who is just a young boy without no experience, he doesn't know much about the songs. I mean, he just know the literal meaning of the songs, probably he doesn't know the real meaning, you know? He could not probably add some of the words that Angelo could add.

F: But you said he did a good job?

Benjamin: Yeah, that was a good start. He had that gift, he just need some time to polish up, to know something about it, you know?

Although a gifted singer is expected to improvise, at the same time he must conform to underlying lyrical patterns, which increase the duration of the song. It took some time for me to understand that the program "plan" had to be flexible enough to accommodate this improvisation and, at the same time, the men had to understand that a performance had to "fit" into a predetermined length of time. When I could find a published photo of traditional dances in south Sudan, I would show it to the men. It was time-consuming not only to explain the differences among DiDinga dances but for me to understand how these dances also differed from seemingly similar Dinka dances:

F: [pointing to Dinka dancing] Do you have a dance like that?

Joseph: No, that is Dinka.

F: But don't DiDinga have a dance where you jump?

All: Oh yes!! *Nyakorot* is jumping! (Joseph stands and demonstrates.)

F: Is this what you will do this summer . . . *nyakorot?*

Joseph: On yeah, I will do that! Is it me alone, I will dance? Because *nyakorot* is a lot of people.

I was still unclear about the difference between *gyrikot* and *nyakorot* songs, but the men insisted that they combine *gyrikot* and *nyakorot* in one cultural program. In the original context, *gyrikot* is not performed with *nyakorot* since the former is a casual dance and the latter is a large-scale celebratory dance. Much later, I realized that for young unmarried men, *gyrikot* represented a main interest of a young man—flirtation—while the *nyakorot* meant a display of male status which women found attractive. This was something that the young men had not yet achieved. Also, before coming to the United States, they had performed *gyrikot* for an international dance contest in Nairobi, where they won first place. Because *gyrikot* had brought them recognition, they felt confident that they could perform this traditional dance in an American context. James described *gyrikot* this way: "Like love songs, all songs in *gyrikot* are love songs, not performed by old people [laughs]. By young people, looking for wives. That's what it's supposed to be for, so that they get ladies."

The phrase, "so that they get the ladies," refers to premarital sex, which is not taboo for young DiDinga men and women if they follow kinship laws and if pregnancy does not result. If pregnancy does result, there must be an exchange of cattle: "Indeed, it may be said that DiDinga are nearly always lovers before marriage. A woman may have as many lovers as she likes, but it is considered incorrect to have more than one at a time" (Cerulli 1956, 76). Therefore, the point of *gyrikot* is sexual attraction. This cultural acceptance of premarital sex among young people contrasts with traditional mores of Dinka, for whom premarital sex was never acceptable. Driberg explains,

> Among the Nilo-Hamitics, and to a lesser extent among Nilotics, free love is socially encouraged, and so long as the marriage tabus [*sic*] relative to kinship are observed, the status neither of men nor of women is affected by pre-nuptial licence. There is really only one particular in which the scales are weighed against women [that is, if pregnancy ensues], and even in this respect the man suffers as much in some of the Nilo-Hamitic tribes. The status of the woman is definitely depreciated, but so in some cases is that of the man. For among the DiDinga he has to anticipate the date, which is recognized as fitting for marriage and is thus deprived of initiation into higher degrees, and has to pass the rest of his life in an equivocal position without any definite status at all. (1932c, 416)

Gyrikot, with its emphasis on flirtation, is a young people's dance. It was thus easily "recontextualized" because it can be performed informally anywhere and, with the exception of married women, by anyone. Participation requires no special status so there is no hierarchical sequence for the entrance of dancers nor are there rules about when or where the dance can be held:

F: This one is also danced during rainy seasons?

James: Yes, actually it is done during the rainy season, and the *gyrikot*, happy times, during harvest.

Gyrikot enables a man to show the "ladies" how well he can dance and sing. But the bullsong, which is central to *nyakorot*, can also be a love song "to attract the ladies." Therefore, *gyrikot* was only one tradition of great importance to the young men. It was important to include two parts in the recontextualized performance in order to accurately convey their identity as DiDinga males:

> **Fortunato:** Anyway, there are two types of [bull]songs, one is for a girl so you have to sing about her so she will get free with you. So that is part one. So when you want to get girls you have to sing so the girl will think you are a strong man and will be with you and will marry her.
>
> **F:** Do you know such a song?
>
> **Lino:** It is common everyplace in DiDinga. Whenever we have a dance, a performance just before the end of everything, before *lilia*, we do this. Someone who is old enough, he will compose his song and then after the most respected guy, then we finish with *lilia*.
>
> **Charles:** And when you sing the bullsong, and the girls come, you have to be in a group so that the guys can support you because if you are the only one, the others will start and those to support him, theirs will come up!

In his description, Charles refers to essential competitive male elements. I read about similar dance negotiations among the Yoruba. In Nigeria, Margaret Thompson Drewal noted that dancers negotiate rhythmically with each other; as the percussion increases, the rhythmic complexity of the music challenges the dancers to compete. In this way, the individual performers can either support, impede, or subvert other performers and even dominate the entire dance: "Improvisation can be parodic, that is, it can signal ironic difference from the conventional or the past, a past experience, their past performance" (Drewal 1992, 7). Although each performance is "generated anew" this kind of novelty or improvisation occurred during all performances. Drewal views improvisation as "moment-to-moment maneuvering based on acquired in-body techniques to achieve a particular effect and/or style of performance. In improvisation, each move is contingent on a previous move and in some measure influences the one that follows. Improvisation requires a mastery of the logic of action and in-body codes. . . . Most performers—maskers, dancers, diviners, singers and drummers alike—have been trained since childhood in particular techniques enabling them to play spontaneously with learned, in-body formulas. This kind of mastery distinguishes a brilliant performer from a merely competent one" (1992, 7). I discerned a similar kind of improvisation in the young men's songs, albeit to a lesser degree. Benjamin indicated that a single performance of a song did not represent one clear sense of musical structure because of the variables in performance. The stress on certain meanings coupled with the energy in the performance could

DiDinga *gyrikot* at Schweinfurth Memorial Art Center in Auburn, New York, 2003. Photo: Felicia McMahon.

affect the timing and emphasis as well as the meaning, but it did not alter the song structure itself. Unlike the rehearsed and assigned roles in a capella singing, which they had been taught in the missionary school, according to James, the songs of *gyrikot* were spontaneous:

> When you sing [in a choir], you kind of like float all of the voices and then you don't sing your own voice. You sing bass, sometimes you sing alto. You sing tenor. It takes a lot of voices. That's why it is so hard. In gospel and church songs, we got alto, tenor, bass [singers] and we come together with different voices. But with *gyrikot*, it is kind of random, it's like, you know, happy times, singing. You just gotta join in and sing any way you want. It's not specific like you gotta sing bass. It's kind of a group thing. It doesn't matter. In choir, you got to sit, and the choirmaster would teach us. You used for bass, you gotta sing bass; you used for tenor, you gotta sing tenor.

As James's comments indicate, the young men believed that *gyrikot* is creative, compared to singing in a church choir. Since there is also no separation between song and dance, good DiDinga dancers were those men who could synchronize their movements with the group, while jumping randomly into the dance without breaking the rhythm, while singing. During later public performances, the choreography was always so smooth that it was difficult to believe they had not secretly rehearsed.

Prior to the rehearsal stage, I asked if the experience at the university had been enjoyable for the young men before I continued to find other cultural outlets for their traditions. When the young men first arrived in my classroom, they had walked past the chairs I had reserved for them and sat on the floor in a corner. In retrospect, I realize that this would be the traditional location for DiDinga children at a village gathering. Not only were they shy but they were sitting on the floor in a secure play space, like children. In other words, they had assumed the position to which they were accustomed in Sudan. A colleague who observed this behavior asked, "How do you know they want to perform for outsiders?" This was a valid question, so after the university program, I held another meeting with the DiDinga. They responded enthusiastically. This was the first time that they performed *gyrikot* in the United States, and they preferred it to the stationary "church songs." However, they emphasized that they would like an opportunity to perform *nyakorot*. At the time, I did not understand that *nyakorot* meant a full-fledged celebratory dance, usually involving two or more villages. Warriors compete in groups to win the affections of women from whom they hope to receive an invitation for lovemaking. Once I realized that the *nyakorot* typically lasted until dawn, I raised the issue of time limits for the program. In response, they all laughed and then explained that without women, it would be a very short *nyakorot*.

In spite of this limitation, the men intended to wear the traditional markings of their age group and to wear "jingles" on their arms and ankles. I bought a few traditional African rattles so that they could use them instead of the pots and pans they had brought to my class the first time. They chose the pots and pans, along with the African instruments. I then realized that the pots had become "traditional instruments," used in the refugee camps and in their apartment on many occasions because they had never owned traditional instruments. And, like true musicians, what seemed to matter most to them was the sound that these items made, not their appearance. I was also instructed to find the appropriate red and white ostrich feathers. These colors, they explained, indicated that they had not yet reached adult manhood, when they would be allowed to wear the black feathers to signify this warrior status. Although I assumed that the young men had opted not to wear the black feathers as protest against warfare, the young men wanted to convey an accurate representation of their traditional status as uninitiates while simultaneously performing the dances of warriors. This signaled the emergence of their identity.

The tradition of the black feather has a long history. In 1922 Driberg included a description of hair ornamentation in which he noted that if a young man wore a black feather he had not earned yet, he would be penalized: "The natural hair is allowed to grow long and is worked into the shape of an inverted basin and often resembles a balmoral in appearance. This is called Temedik and on top of it is attached a holder (Chobechit) into which are inserted ostrich feathers (Kauri), white, black or dyed red. Black feathers however may only be worn by old men, and a young man observed wearing them has to pay a fine of beer and a bull or a goat" (1922, 221). During a televised interview on a community television program to publicize the upcoming event, Charles explained the taboo against wearing an "unauthorized" black feather: "If you videotape it [the performance] and send it back to Sudan and they put my name down [for initiation], no good!" Although the young men had already told me that the *temedik* is no longer worn by the DiDinga, they insisted on white and red feathers because these were still worn in Sudan. Finding the jingle bells was easy, but finding the ostrich feathers was not. I did locate *kahurii* (*kau'ri*), white ostrich feathers, at a local craft store (they were labeled ostrich feathers), which I purchased for the young men, and I found a few red feathers of undetermined bird species. The young men applauded my efforts and said that they were "good ones."

The Warm-Up

According to Schechner, every performance is preceded by a warm-up, which prepares the performer to advance from readiness to "performance" (2002, 205). In DiDinga culture, the entire community warms up with *lilia*.

There is no physical distinction between backstage and onstage because *lilia* prepares the community for the *nyakorot*. A soloist leads others in single file as they march slowly to the designated performance site. Therefore, as part of their first performance in the United States the Lost Boys wore red and white feathers of uninitiates and painted their bodies with their age-set motifs, having removed their T-shirts and wearing only summer shorts or jeans. During *lilia* the group squats and forms a semicircle formation, chanting *ngaria ngimoya*. These entrance words are sung in Toposa but are untranslatable even among the DiDinga. Although there are always words in every song that could not be translated because they were supposedly adopted from the Toposa, nonetheless the young men insisted that *ngaria ngimoya* had a special significance: "It's a

Joseph and Dominic L. wave *nyaladonya* to motivate the audience during *nyakorot* in parking lot of Thompson Memorial AME Church, 2002. Photo: Felicia McMahon.

kind of motivation." Schechner notes that the warm-up prepares performers "to make the leap to the other side," (2002, 205) and the effectiveness of this chant was apparent when the American audiences became subdued and readied for the performance.

It was a challenge to find an appropriate place and audience so the young men could perform outdoors. I also wanted to ensure that they were adequately reimbursed for their performance, since I knew that many of the young men had taken time off from their jobs. The Lost Boys' performance on July 21, 2002, took place in the church parking lot. It would be the first *nyakorot* ever performed in the United States, and it would be performed as part of an African cultural program funded by the New York State Council on the Arts during the annual folk-arts festival hosted by the Schweinfurth Memorial Art Center in Auburn, New York. The *nyakorot* was videotaped using two cameras, which enabled me to film the performance from a long angle while a professional videographer filmed from close up. At the time, I did not realize the extent to which these videotapes would affect the collective memory and critical response of this diasporic community. One of the refugee center's caseworkers had thought that a shared connection would be the struggle for freedom among peoples of African descent. Interestingly, this did not seem to interest the DiDinga. As a matter of fact, they just ignored the suggestion, even after the caseworker spent time with them so that he could explain in great detail the history of the church, which was founded by Harriet Tubman.

The Performance

On July 21, 2002, the day on which the performance took place, the weather in Auburn was hot, humid, and windy, with temperatures well over 90 degrees. With the help of the Refugee Resettlement Services staff, the small group of 10 young male DiDinga refugees living in Syracuse, New York, arrived at the Thompson Memorial AME Zion Church. Their host, the AME Church community, was behind schedule so microphones and chairs had not been carried outdoors from the basement, thus delaying the program by 45 minutes. The young men, showing remarkable patience, helped the minister to carry 50 chairs from the church's stuffy basement to the parched parking lot. Microphones were eventually set up in the middle of the parking lot but at a great distance from the audience. Although I urged the minister to move the microphones closer to the audience to encourage audience participation, he insisted that the equipment remain where it was. Because we were guests of this institution, I did not press the issue, but, just as I had anticipated, the distance hindered active interaction with the African–American audience.

The AME choir had agreed to begin the program with a few spirituals and gospel songs in order to welcome the young men. To avoid any possibility of dead time, I had also hired two Ghanaian drummers and a female dancer to perform during pauses in the performance. The DiDinga had known that the AME choir would sing first, so I suggested that they follow with their "traditional" church songs in DiDinga and Swahili, their third language. They had learned these songs in the refugee camp in Kenya and, having performed them before, felt comfortable singing them. Then *gyrikot* began as the young men tapped their feet in single file behind Charles. He led the men in. Each wore an American T-shirt and jeans. Each held a percussion instrument: a church tambourine removed at the last minute from a nearby picnic table or an aluminum pie tin beaten with a coat hanger or eggbeater. The remaining instruments were an assortment of handmade wooden clangers from Kenya and Senegal which I had given to them. They also wore small metal ankle and arm bells.

These traditional DiDinga percussion instruments were tied on their wrists, ankles, and thighs. The men formed a small revolving circle as they sang. They

The first "American" *gyrikot* in parking lot of Thompson Memorial AME Church, 2002. Photo: Felicia McMahon.

made hip-rotation movements to the 2/4 duple beat initiated by the soloist. He also initiated the hip-rotation movements of the dancers and sometimes held a paper over his head indicating to the others to do the same with their instruments. It was often hard to discern that he was the one initiating the movements because the others adeptly added syncopated percussion and hand clapping.

The *gyrikot* seemed like a medley of moving bodies. Without changing the rhythm, a series of songs were sung to the same melody with increasing percussion. Later, while watching the videotaped performance, Charles pointed to different songs: "That is another one, we connect songs, different songs." There had been the appearance of one continuous dance, coordinated to a melodic litany. Two distinct dance movements repeated throughout the songs involved a foot movement of repeated left and right taps and a hip-rotation movement that sometimes resembled the Charleston. The soloist indicated *gyrikot* had ended by slowing the rhythm with his body movements and singing more slowly as he led the group in a single file from the parking lot. The singing faded as they held their instruments above their heads.

During an intermission, the Ghanaian drummers performed. When the drumming performance ended, the DiDinga, who had removed their T-shirts, were wearing body paint and red and white feathers. They marched slowly to the

Left to right: Joseph and Dominic L. take on role of warriors during *lilia* in parking lot of Thompson Memorial AME Church, 2002. Photo: Felicia McMahon

center of the parking lot while humming softly. The humming became louder as they marched in a line formation called *lilia* to announce the opening of *nya-korot*, a warrior celebration which traditionally involves the entire community of adult male and female members. (At the time there were no DiDinga females living in Syracuse, but at later performances women who performed with the men were always at the end of the procession.) The soloist joined the other danc-ers, who were squatting in the middle of the parking lot. Two of the men stood up, ran out in front of the audience and feigned attacks by thrusting their sticks at the audience.

When the audience reacted, their movements were accompanied by a war-rior's song about his fierce ability to defend his bull. As they ran back, one war-rior waved a *nyalado*, a bull's tail, and joined the others who were still crouching together. All of the dancers followed the soloist by jumping and then moving counterclockwise in circle formation as they increased the tempo of the jump-ing. Percussion instruments are not traditionally used for *nyakorot* so they relied on clapping hands, which caused the jingle bells on their arms to rattle. At a certain point, the leader began to lead the group jumping one by one in a snake-like formation as others joined in. Images of African-American double-Dutch jump rope came to mind because the young men kept rhythm, concentrated as they rocked to and fro, and never missed a beat when they jumped into the line. Instead of a Western approach to thinking of rhythm in terms of counting beats and making fractions, as in most African music, this beat was expertly related to movement and vocal patterns of words and phrases, which motivated the musical rhythm of their performance (Drewal 1992).

The young men sang a litany of five songs. The key center for the songs alternated between an F-minor pentatonic and an A-flat major, which were modally related. Eventually, all of the dancers were jumping vigorously, and the soloist turned to his left as a signal for the circle to wheel. The first song in F minor emphasized a march in 6/8 meter. The others joined in, and when he began *ngothi* (jumping), so did the others. The soloist signaled an end to the song by humming a loud "HMMMMMMMMMMMMMM," which all the dancers repeated.

There was some discussion before one of the warriors began clapping and loudly singing a warrior song. When the warrior signaled the end of this song by humming, they all stopped, bent their heads into the center of the circle until he began to clap again. This time they sang and remained stationary until the warrior again started *ngothi*, and they began to jump counterclockwise until the leader signaled again to stop. This time they all leaned their heads toward the center of the circle. The warrior began another song, which was political in theme, and the dancers jumped two steps to the right and two steps to the left, repeating this movement several times.

To introduce the second song, the soloist moved to a tonal center of A-flat. The rhythm was similar to the 2/4 beat of *gyrikot*. The third song went back to F minor, with a melody descending from C. The fourth song in F minor was similar to the preceding song. Finally, the men formed a procession and sang the *lilia*. The key had shifted to a D dorian (also minor, but with seven notes), and the chorus ended humming in A-note, which in Western music is called "dominant." In this way, the performers had signaled the beginning, climax, and end of *nyakorot* by reversing the identity of the tonal center. At this final stage, the original soloist took over from the warrior and decreased the jumping and song tempo with the words, *ngaria ngimoya*.

The Cooldown

The original soloist had taken over from the warrior and decreased the jumping and song tempo with the words *ngaria ngimoya*. These words, which have no translation in English, signal *lilia*, both beginning and end of *nyakorot*. According to Schechner, cooldown always follows performance: "This transition between the show and the show-is-over is an often overlooked but extremely interesting and important phase. If warm-ups prepare people for the leap into performance, cool-down ushers them back to daily life" (2002, 211). The warriors marched in a single file in front of the audience, waving their arms out to signal that the performance had ended:

F: Then the *nyakorot* starts when Charles comes out the door.

Joseph: That song is to give you, to draw everybody's attention to be ready for *nyakorot* to start. So it is just to give people, what they are going to do. What I know, it is a song to open for the people to pay attention.

F: So the words, they are DiDinga words and if I saw those written down, I would know that those meant the start of the dance—words for the starting of the dance and you would never say them any other time?

Joseph: No.

Dominic L.: Or at the finish.

Joseph: Then they say the same thing [looking at video]. The *nyakorot* is now open for everyone to join in. So in Sudan, everyone will join in and we all jump.

F: How do you know when it is ending?

Joseph: It is a crescendo in the music, you can louder or lower. Aiiiiiii means I'm ending the tune and everyone says yaoooo or okayyyyyy [lowers voice]. Then we say we conclude the dancing. They will like hang out until all the dancers will go home.

Nyakorot is always framed with these formulaic words, which, although untranslatable, carry a special significance for the DiDinga community. Thus, although American audiences would not recognize the formulaic words used to signal "cooldown," the gradual slowing of the beat signaled the end of *nyakorot*. The American audience stood and clapped appreciatively for the "DiDinga warriors." Without the American audience's awareness, the fact that there were no women participating in this performance only underscored that the young men had in fact been parodying the adult DiDinga dance, which is a common child's game. On the other hand, the impact of this recontextualized performance was a powerful hybrid identity communicated by these young DiDinga warriors in a new land.

The Aftermath

In the traditional DiDinga context, the community comments about the *nyakorot* during the aftermath. According to Schechner, the aftermath continues in critical responses, archives, and memories: "The continuing life of a performance is its aftermath" (Schechner 2002, 211). Some of the songs composed by the singers would become part of the community's repertoire but not before careful scrutiny by the community:

> F: When someone makes a song and if the people don't think it is very good, what happens?
>
> Benjamin: That song will not be popular. Within a couple of days, within a short time, people tend to forget about it. People will not sing it in the village.
>
> F: If we were in the village in Sudan and someone got up during *nyakorot* and sang a song and it was bad and the DiDingas did not like it, what would happen?
>
> Benjamin: It would depend on the situation, where we are. People would just like try to understand the situation. People would not try to embarrass you right there but that is one thing about our community. They cannot embarrass you right there. They try to hide their feelings. They will just talk about it later. You can't just say it right there.
>
> F: Would they sing it?
>
> Benjamin: They would sing! They would sing the chorus. They would do all they can to make it lively but later on, they would talk about it and say, "That song [shakes his head]?"
>
> F: Would they make a song about me singing a bad song?
>
> Benjamin: Yeah, definitely! Somebody's going to compose something about you. Real quick [laughs]. But one thing they cannot embarrass you then. Later. Back in Sudan, they will always say something because the songs are talking about the community, the lazy people, about some who are lazy and has a duty but somebody in the community will sing something about his performance. Most of the time they don't mention their name but people really know who the people are talking about.

During the July 21 performance, the young men did not attempt to compose new songs but instead performed a repertoire of songs that they recalled from their childhood. There was very little improvisation. In the new performance situation, the aftermath for this group included validation of their new hybrid identity. This validation had depended on two distinct audiences, American and DiDinga. Videotapes of their performances were mailed to DiDinga refugees living in other parts of the United States and Canada. Because they had performed in a way that adhered to tradition, their performances were authentic in the eyes of the diasporic DiDinga community. However, in my home after the first recontextualized *nyakorot*, the young DiDinga men commented that by DiDinga standards it should be bigger: "This is a small one. It is not even a colorful one. It should be more colorful and more lovely." When I asked what would make the dance "more colorful and more lovely," they indicated women and more dancers. However, the lack of female performers had not affected the selection of songs for this occasion:

F: So the first one you sang was *Mariah*, then the political song and then one about someone wrote a letter and denied it. Why did you choose those songs to sing?

James: I think to have a balance, you know, a political song and *Mariah* song and then like a joke song. One guy wrote a letter to the other guy's girlfriend and so once he asked him, he was like really lied to.

F: Did it really happen?

All: It happens alot!

F: The guy wrote a letter and it was a love letter?

James: Yes, a love letter.

F: Did this happen in Kenya in the refugee camp?

All: In DiDingaland.

F: In DiDingaland, at home.

James: It happens alot.

All: Yes [laughing].

F: [watching video] Now we are back to the *Mariah* song.

All: Yes.

F: I get it. *Mariah*, political song, the letter, and back to *Mariah*.

Charles: That is how we finish it. Even at home, when you've done this, then you come [back] with one song, the entrance.

Simon: Most of these are performed during the happiest moments . . . joke song, political song, *Mariah* song [pauses], but women are supposed to be in the center of the circle.

Charles: To give motivation for us.

F: Who chooses the songs? How did you decide?

Simon: We've got so many songs.

F: But did you decide ahead of time which songs?

Charles: Everybody know, everybody know.

F: In Sudan, would you know ahead of time?

Charles: No, just going, just going but in Sudan many people know the songs so if this [one] is finished, another singer begins another. I'm the only one singing here that is why.

F: Because there is not another group.

Charles: Yeah.

F: That was a good idea to do it that way.

Although a big group and female dancers were two elements the performance lacked, the young men later mentioned *merti* (traditional DiDinga beer made from maize) as an important element to a successful *nyakorot*. I was fortunate to have my recorder when we reflected on the first *nyakorot* while eating pizza in a local café after the July 21 performance:

F: James said it should be more colorful. What else would make it better?

Charles: You have to have many. Good organization. Ladies. Ladies activate it. Traditional beer. People drink *merti*. It is fermented for one week. Men drink it before they dance. We drink for friendship. And then we go and dance.

James: Very badly! [All laugh.]

Charles: The ladies are allowed to drink too but not as much as the men.

Charles's response, "good organization," indicated that although there is the appearance of spontaneity, there is always an underlying structure to which the performance must conform. The ability to engage in spontaneous group synchronization is a culturally acquired skill.

Early anthropologists and dance scholars noted the differences between the structure of African and Western dance, but none adequately described the differences: "[It is] quite different from modern European dancing. . . . The component elements of the *gbere buda* [Zande dance] are music, song and muscular movement. Any of these elements without the others would be inconceivable in this dance, but it is difficult to understand the manner in which they are concerted" (Evans-Pritchard 1928, 446–47). An anthropologist writing about the associated dance-songs in Sudan commented, "The greatest difficulty lay in the rhythmic patterns—which are like and yet so unlike ours. The music intervals, too, were troublesome to record until I abandoned scientific precision on discovering that no one man sings exactly like his neighbor" (Tucker 1933b, v).

Since that time, modern ethnomusicologists have identified common elements intrinsic to African music: call and response, percussion, syllabic singing, short musical units which are repeated in small variations (Chernoff 1979). Further, A. P. Merriam identifies rhythm as the most significant aspect in African music. The four basic characteristics in an African rhythmic structure are equal pulse beat, a metric time arrangement, unity among a diverse array of simultaneous rhythmic patterning, and a specific beginning for rhythmic groupings (1982, 147). Thus, unlike Tucker and other early researchers, ethnomusicologists today note that improvisation within a unified song tradition enables both consistency and variety within the same song. Songs are not sung in exactly the same manner, even by the same singer. In addition, a gifted DiDinga singer is said to be a "good talker" if he communicates enthusiasm:

Benjamin: His voice is really outreaching and I bet you, his movement is also like real, he put spirit to motivate people with his own words in the song.

F: New words?

Benjamin: Yes, you know, add your own words in the song to make the song more and more lively.

F: If you were going to make a song, how do you decide what to use for the melody? How does it come to you?

Benjamin: You have to have it.

F: You have to have it already.

Benjamin: Yeah. In order for you to polish it, you have to have it already. I can't just decide, you know, I tried to fake that you can sing if you don't have that basic requirement of voice lifting because as hard as you may try to fake it you cannot. Because like Angelo, he's like gifted. You know, he has to be free in real communicating. In real life, he like talked fast as long as I known him, he talk fast. He can communicate with people freely. Like, what can I say?

F: A poet?

Benjamin: Not really a poetry. Someone who knows how to communicate with people. He can convince people. I think I should say someone who is so entertaining he can keep people busy. He's a good listener but he is a good talker. That is the main point of it. He's a talkative kind of person. He imagines things very fast. He doesn't have to think of some word to fix. The words are like just pop into his head.

F: You know American rappers? They talk really fast and they have this beat they don't really sing, but Angelo is singing. Is he a good talker first and then he sings or is he good with his voice first? Or are they the same?

Benjamin: No, I think he is a good talker first. He has to have that initial requirement of being a good talker and then comes the polishing of his voice. He has to have that initial requirement of being a good talker first. He's a good talkative person and his voice is like really high. That is the basic thing. You have to have that. They go hand in hand. You can't find someone who is a good singer and he is not a good talker. Same.

The relationship between improvisation and tradition is a paradoxical one: Like restored behavior, tradition is repetition in which the past is reenacted through stylized behaviors. At the same time improvisation is a deliberate creative move that celebrates cultural memory (Roach 1996a). Improvisation does not erase or negate tradition.

However, Schechner's explanation of performance as restored behavior needs some expansion. While the young men referred to their performance as a "flashback," what flashes back is a very strong repetition of powerful early traditions of their childhood but with the inclusion of the church songs and *gyrikot*. The overall structure of the performance is divided into three parts, with several songs and dances performed within each part. This combination results in a unified whole which communicates a paradoxical diasporic identity that is both traditional and not traditional.

Negotiating Tradition

Throughout my work with the DiDinga, it was Charles who organized the dancers, and it was Charles who explained when and what the group would perform. This did not mean that Charles was necessarily "a good talker" (gifted) but rather that "he can do it" (good organizer). I had observed an early meeting during which Joseph wanted to include a political song. Initially, Charles was against its inclusion, but surprisingly, on the day of the *nyakorot*, the group sang *Sadik*. In Kenya Charles had organized the group to form a choir. However, I noticed that Joseph and Dominic L. had stronger voices. Evans–Pritchard noted in his work among the Zande that the song-leader must have sufficient authority to make critical decisions related to organization of the dance: "The dance, like all joint activities, necessarily generates leadership, the function of which is to organize the activity. The problem of the allotment of roles in the dance is solved by the introduction of status. In the event of quarrels it is the song-leader who arbitrates" (1928, 454). Charles was at least four years older than Joseph, and his senior status was therefore accepted by the group. During another follow-up conversation, I asked Joseph about the "warrior song" he had chosen to sing for *nyakorot*. He claimed his selection had not been planned because he had composed it based on stories and ideas generally known among the people in his village. When the group never sang it again, the song did not become part of the group's repertoire. However, it had been Charles who signaled with his opening song that Joseph could begin with his bullsong:

F: When he [Charles] sang "Joseph," you were going to open it?

Joseph: Yes.

F: Did you know what you were going to say before you started singing or did it just come into your head?

Joseph: It just come into my head.

F: Right at that moment?

Joseph: Yes.

F: Did you have the idea?

Joseph: Yes. That one is just when in Sudan people take care of their bulls and stuff so that really is been to give message to people: "That bull I take care of it and no one will ever come and steal it from me." I am just trying to tell people, the audience . . . at first they told me to open the *nyakorot*. Then I have to open the *nyakorot* by telling the audience how brave I am—"He's a warrior, wooow." Actually, it's a challenge. No one will ever come or steal or do any harm to my livestock and my bull. It says that bull is still grazing in place call Chocagag [southern Sudan] while I am the owner taking care of it. I the owner of the bull, is drinking the mud water together, we will be sharing everything together. There is a repeating of "no" and "no" and "no one will ever unless he is finishing me."

Joseph was not considered a "good talker," although he did have a strong baritone voice. Unlike Joseph's bullsong, other songs for American audiences were sometimes parodies of earlier childhood parodies of adult "talkers." This playfulness inherent in these performances enabled the young men to disassociate themselves from the Western stereotypes of "primitive" cattle-herding African societies. At first, warlike stereotypes in Western popular culture had caused me some concern, especially when a visiting DiDinga elder reviewed the videotape of the young men's *nyakorot*. He suggested that next time they carry spears and shields. This would make the young men's performance "more real." From his perspective, these weapons did not necessarily represent a warlike attitude because, as has been noted by African scholars, "East African herding societies are not primarily oriented towards war, despite the titles born by warriors, the rewards gained by killing enemy tribesmen, the use of names which employ the symbolism of killing, the high status associated with bearing arms, the hero-worship of warriors by those youngsters next in line, the councils of elders, sometimes called 'war councils,' and the masculinity and virility with which warriors are associated. All these attributes are merely superficial and visible aspects that have contributed to the association of age systems with military functions" (Almagor 1977, 120–21).

During the aftermath I learned the extent to which the Lost Boys had injected playfulness into their "warrior" performances. The following summer a group of visiting adult DiDinga men and women from other parts of the United States performed *gyrikot* and *nyakorot* with the Lost Boys in Auburn, New York. The word had spread among DiDinga refugees throughout the United States and Canada that *nyakorot* could be held on American soil with no complaints about "noise." The young men were excited that there would be three "DiDinga ladies" to provide the missing women's participation for *gyrikot* and *nyakorot*. As I helped the young men make arrangements for older DiDinga bullsingers from Canada and other parts of the United States, Charles and Joseph became concerned about what their roles would be. According to the DiDinga hierarchy, the Lost Boys were at the bottom rung of the traditional ladder, with the children. Yet, they were young adult men, the leaders of this small group.

I wondered what effect the appearance of the elders would have on the Lost Boys' performance. Although it enriched their ensuing performances, it did not alter their repertoire. The young men, who had been playful during their performances before the elders arrived, continued engaging in parody and "play-fighting" after they left. Their recontextualized performances seemed to have been infused with vitality of another sort, which played out in the warrior tradition. Whatever earnestness or playfulness they performed in the original context in Sudan, their present playfulness was quite different in its diasporic framed targets. This playfulness would become increasingly prominent during a public performance: In lieu of the traditional body markings, across Simon's back another dancer had painted "CULTURE" in white paint.

Thus, the young men's performance was several things: (1) a projection of themselves as they were parodying a historically verifiable childish parody of the verifiable male initiations and (2) a parody that was now, however, projected into a novel diasporic parody for American audiences. Enacted through "kin-esthetic imagination," social memories are preserved and transmitted through body movements where associated social memories are real, remembered, residual, or imaginary (Roach 1996a, 27). The young men enacted a memory of home through movement because cultural memories are sedimented and reside in the body (Connerton 1989). In other words, dances played as children were authentic cultural memories, communicating authentic embodiments of the young men's childhood as a hybrid identity of what it meant to be a young DiDinga male in America.

6

Cultural Intervention
and Mediation

Kimaria ngimoi kimaria ngimoi
We fought over [defeating] the enemies. We fought over the enemies
Kimaria ngimoi kimaria Lowalangole
We fought over the enemies. We fought over [defeating] Lowalangole
Mmmmm, kimaria ngimoi
Mmm. We fought the enemies.
Traditional DiDinga warrior song

A few months after our first meeting, the Lost Boys expressed concern that the international community was ignoring the civil war in Sudan, the very reason for their immigration to the United States. As a research associate in the Program for the Analysis and Resolution of Conflicts at Syracuse University, I offered them an opportunity to bring their message to an American audience. My plan was to provide an open forum after a public program in which both the Dinka and DiDinga would share life stories to educate Americans about the uniqueness of their cultures as well as the political history of Sudan. The program was entitled, "The Wars of Our Fathers Are Not Ours," a quote from a conversation overheard between a young Dinka Lost Boy and a local news reporter.

In the previous two chapters, I demonstrated the importance of entextualization and kinesthetic imagination for defining diasporic identity. In this chapter, I demonstrate how tradition becomes politicized because it involves collective memory and community values. As a political act, recontextualizing tradition places the folklorist in the problematic role of cultural mediator, but "[w]hile such incidents feel like hell unfolding around the facilitator, they are the bread and butter of our craft. It is not usually the successes that hold the most valuable lessons. Those we must extract from our frequent failures" (Graves 2005, 173). The arts can demonstrate to groups involved in conflict that it is possible for both parties to work cooperatively to build peaceful, healthy societies. However, Joseph Montville, director of the Preventive Diplomacy Program at the Center for Strategic and International Studies warns that even the most brilliant mediator will fail unless identity conflicts sustained from generation to generation are given considerable time for discussion and healing during the mediation process (2002). Although most cultural facilitators know time is critical for effective mediation, the process is a complex one with all parties agreeing to full disclosure. Both Dinka and DiDinga Lost Boys had expressed interest in working in this public program, so I did not anticipate that a discussion period after a folk arts presentation would present problems. Further, both groups socialized and cooperated in many other ways, including regularly playing on the same teams in soccer games.

In the meantime, I read that a reconciliation and healing conference between the Dinka-Nuer rebel armies and the DiDinga had been held in Nakwaton, Kenya, during August 2002. At the conference, the two sides apologized to each other and pledged to unite to bring peace to their war-torn country. Since the Lost Boys were victims of the same war, I had not known that they were not in agreement about the nature of the rebel armies. Further, many Americans were unaware of interethnic violence occurring in refugee camps, including that between the Dinka and the DiDinga. It was much later before I read of Sudanese women's efforts to put a stop to these conflicts. One Dinka woman involved in the peace process who had experienced the violence wrote,

> We would like peace but do not have the power to bring it. You have to start at home with the way you stay [live] with your neighbors. You have to teach your neighbors how to stay with each other. Every fortnight all the women's groups meet as women to discuss our problems. Many women come. The DiDinga in the hills are treated as if they are separate from us. We would like to have unity with them. Currently, they are causing insecurity. They attack people on the road to Chukudum. They attack vehicles. Sometimes they loot. If you resist them, they kill you. We would like to talk with them so that there is freedom of movement in the area. This insecurity causes great problems because we cannot take children to the hospital. (Fitzgerald 2002, 120–21)

In the classroom, a university student asked Charles, "But aren't the differences between Dinka and DiDinga only small ones?" Charles enumerated differences which he regarded "not small": the Dinka practices of ritual cutting on the head, excision of teeth during initiation, male circumcision, none of which the DiDinga practiced—but he did not mention recent conflicts with the rebel armies. The young men evaded this issue with Americans. I began to hear that some Dinka young men objected to including the DiDinga in programs for the Lost Boys because the DiDinga had not been in the first large group of lost male children to reach the refugee camps. The DiDinga were perceived by some as getting a "benefit" to which they were not entitled. However, the U.S. State Department defined "Lost Boys" as all Sudanese boys "who arrived at Kakuma before 1995 and who lived in the camp without parents" (Bixler 2005, 89). DiDinga boys had also been forced to escape alone into dense forests and to survive for days without food or water. All of the DiDinga in Syracuse had suffered similar horrific experiences and had lived in Kakuma or other refugee camps in Kenya. Like the Dinka, a lucky few were selected to immigrate as parentless refugees to the United States where Americans greeted them as members of the "Lost Boys," an unfortunate simplification of their true ethnic differences.

I began to believe that similarities as well as differences in DiDinga and Dinka traditions affected the group's ability to perform together consistently in the public sphere. One of the similarities was the male warrior tradition which the two groups shared. None of the Dinka or DiDinga had been initiated into their respective age-set systems, a fact that prevented their entrance as warriors into the adult world, in which there is an inflexible hierarchy. All of them would remain the "kids" of their respective communities in the eyes of their elders, which had led me to believe that they could more easily view themselves as a cohesive group. Ironically, just the opposite proved true.

The warrior tradition in Africa has been called the "meeting point" of culture, war, and politics (Mazrui 1977b, 2). It is a male cultural formulation common to cattle-herding groups in East Africa. Through the symbolism of the warrior tradition, power and status are granted to men. Respect for such indigenous traditions as the warrior tradition can aid subjugated people to overcome self-contempt, a first step to making cultural decolonization a reality. Some Africanists believe "[m]ental and intellectual dependency, a lack of readiness to break loose from the metropolitan power, a compulsive urge to imitate and emulate what the west has produced, are factors which have on the whole had grave economic and political consequences for societies which are still unwilling to take drastic decisions for their own transformation, but they are also phenomena with deep cultural causes. The lack of a political will for an economic transformation might in part be due to a state of mental and cultural dependency" (Mazrui 1977b, 254). I observed how a shared tradition can pose problems. Although such symbolic behavior can promote positive self-image as a coping mechanism for change, the militarized language of warrior dance and songs can inspire an aggressive spirit in males. It was a tradition easily exploited during colonization by Europeans. Often equated with the "cattle-raiding complex" (Herskovits 1926), it has a dark side that has been easily co-opted by both the Islamic government and south Sudanese rebel armies.

Both sides in Sudan have attempted to mobilize ethnic groups to aid their respective military forces, and this has resulted in an escalation of violence as modern roles are assigned to a traditional tribal institution. In the past, for Dinka and DiDinga males the warrior status involved petty cattle raids and counter-raids with their respective neighbors over territorial conflicts involving water rights. The warrior tradition actually prevented the institutionalization of militarism because the warrior age-set is restricted. This is a system of checks and balances because each unit competes with the other units, and all are situated within the system as a whole: "The very nature of an age system, as a differentiated and hierarchical power structure prevents the military aspects associated with the grade of warriorhood from expanding and coming to dominate the other grades and hence disrupting the system" (Almagor 1977, 121).

Warrior status remained important to all of the young men because in both Dinka and DiDinga culture, warrior status had to be conferred before young men could marry. Becoming a warrior meant becoming an adult and could only be achieved by going through the age-set system, in which social groupings close and form units. In anthropological terms, both Dinka and DiDinga, who are relatively decentralized and egalitarian, have elaborate age grades, which constitute the age-set system. Membership in the age-set lasts for the duration of the members' lives because each age-set moves through the age grades as a unit. It is the age grade that provides the system of social stratification and political control, and it enables senior grades to oversee the junior ones. The DiDinga, though essentially egalitarian, nevertheless have a form of political structure, a "government" based on elders and judges in this rigid senior ranking.

There are approximately 10 grades in the DiDinga age-grade system. Although the DiDinga men in Syracuse ranged in age from 14 to 23 years of age, they were still considered in the *lotim* age grade. *Lotim* means baboon, and it was also the song that the young men performed on several occasions in the United States. The age grade of *lotim* is beneath *ngohit*, the first level in the system. During rituals, *ngohit* is allowed to sit on stones. Only the highest-ranking men were allowed to sit on ceremonial stools. Thus, the young men remained beneath the lowest level, which is normally for very young boys. They would remain there until they returned to Sudan to perform *thapaninit*, the ritual spearing of the bull.

It was not until the DiDinga told me about initiation that I realized how the song *Lotim* relates to memory and identity in their recontextualized performances. In Sudan, this song would be sung by children, not warriors. Like children, they, the uninitiated, were not allowed to sit on adult stools. Like children, they had had little experience tending cattle and for the most part had helped the women with their gardens. To rectify these cultural omissions, the young men insisted that they must one day return to Sudan to "be counted" in order to legitimatize their status as young men. The combination of songs such as *Lotim* with warrior songs resulted in strangely upbeat performances here in the United States. Although the warrior had become, for them, a nostalgic symbol, it remained both a powerful and yet romantic aspect of their hybrid group identity because the group's repertoire represented the totality of the group's unique shared life experiences.

Traditionally, a DiDinga age-set attains warrior status and the members serve as "junior warriors" for five years. Had the young men remained in their villages, they then would have gone through yet another initiation ceremony to become senior warriors. There would also be a requirement for all junior DiDinga warriors to form a lasting friendship (*gonohet*) with a senior warrior who acts like a mentor: "The primary object of this special friendship is military, not unreminiscent of the Spartan institution. It is the duty of the senior of the two friends to instruct the junior in all his military exercises and conduct" (Driberg 1935, 102). The duty to fight rests on these junior men, a status which would be appropriate for the DiDinga Lost Boys had they remained in their villages. Ironically, the same tradition was co-opted by Islamic and rebel armies in Sudan to force boys into the war which caused them to become refugees. Yet, it would remain a part of the recontextualized performances in which they protested the war. The modern armies in Sudan have claimed that the African tradition supports their use of children in armed conflict, resulting in "retribalization" in many cases. However, as M. A. Mohamed Salih has pointed out, there is a marked difference between conscripting children into an army and children defending themselves and their families from attack: "It is a process of putting new wine in old bottles. In other words, assigning modern values to traditional tribal institutions" (2001). Many of the Dinka and DiDinga in Syracuse had personally seen their own brothers' forced conscription into Sudanese armies, but they themselves had escaped from such a fate. In one videotaped interview,

Charles related how his father urged him to leave his DiDingaland home with the parting words, "It is better to die outside [the country] than to die in it."

Thus, in spite of the co-option of this warrior tradition, warrior songs and dances remained an integral part of the young DiDinga and Dinka's recontextualized performances. Prior to their first performance, Joseph had enthusiastically described the entrance of the warriors, which he had observed as a child during the DiDinga *nyakorot*: "And they are like not smiling and that. They are real serious." But Joseph also expressed reservations about performing this tradition for Americans: "People will not understand. So maybe if we practice here, people will say, 'Oh my god, who are these guys not smiling and all that?' And they will say, 'something is wrong.' They don't know the culture." In spite of the clearly serious nature of warrior expressions, African dance scholar Judith Hanna has suggested that there are distinctions because some differences can be seen in the actual dance formations. The distinctions may often overlap because "there are distinctions between warrior dances which are playful and those which are instrumental in violence. Among the Ga, for example, these were two distinct patterns in which the Nngawa Asafo military body grouped itself. One formation was used for going to war, to honor a new leader, or engage in public works. The other formation was created for what is called 'play'—drilling, training, dancing, singing and funerals. Such distinctions often become blurred. In Accra, many quarrels and fights derive from ancient rivalries and battle behavior boasted about in the play dance competitions" (Hanna 1977, 122). Within the original village context, the DiDinga men's warrior dances would be considered "serious play." Their expressive behaviors would reinforce the power and status of a society that might eventually call on them to engage in actual defense or warfare. In the United States, this would not be the case. While observing a videotaped performance of their warrior play, one visiting DiDinga elder smiled and called their performance "cute." His comments seemed to support the notion that even a recontextualized dance was both serious and not serious, and, like play, it was both "real" and not real when the symbolism linked to ideas about play

borrows or adopts patterns that appear in other contexts where they achieve immediate and obvious ends. The mimetic fight is divorced from the original motivation and is qualitatively distinct. There may be exaggerated uneconomical motor patterns, the sequence may be reordered with more repetition than usual, sequences may be fragmented, or not completed. The warrior dance is a playing with the body, ideas, and emotions. Play allows for distancing, safe examination of problems and the separation or merging of serious and nonserious.

Play, Schechner (1973) argues maintains a regular, crisis-oriented expenditure of kinetic energy which can be transformed from play energy into fight energy. The boundary between play and reality may, of course, dissolve. (Hanna 1977, 115)

In the United States the DiDinga's warrior songs focused, for the most part, on defending bulls. Lino explained the connection of the bullsong to the warrior tradition: "You have your bull and nobody can touch your bull. If it is dead, it is a matter of life and death. If someone comes, you defend it. Nobody should do anything to it." In spite of the seriousness with which the young men regarded the warrior tradition, they played with it during recontextualized performances in ways that may not have been permitted in a traditional context. For example, Joseph took the lead. He sang a bullsong in his DiDinga-Longarim dialect, which he later tried to explain:

That one [song] is just [sung] when in Sudan, people take care of their bulls and stuff, so that it really is to give message to people: "That bull I take care of it and no one will ever come and steal it from me." I am just trying to tell people, the audience. At first, they told me to open the *nyakorot*. Then I have to open the *nyakorot* by telling the audience how brave I am: "He's a warrior, wow." Actually, it's a challenge. No one will ever come or steal or do any harm to my livestock and my bull. It says, "that bull is still grazing in a place called Chukudum while I am the owner taking care of it. I, the owner of the bull is drinking the mud water together, we will be sharing everything together." There is a repeating of no, and no, and no one will ever [take it] unless he is finishing me.

None of the young men mentioned the cattle raiding, traditionally associated with the warrior tradition. Later, a visiting DiDinga elder repeated what I had already heard: "The DiDinga warrior tradition is a destructive one. It used to mean cattle-raiding but we do not do that any more. We are changing." Nor did the young men speak about mothers' roles in urging their warrior sons to carry out these raids. However, I had read that traditionally women's songs have been sung to encourage cattle raiding through praises to sons who are successful in these raids. In the recent past, cattle raiding has been at the root of intertribal conflicts among neighboring tribes. Today, it is frequent among tribal members of the DiDinga, Toposa, Turkana, Dongiro, and most recently with others with whom they now come in contact in the refugee camps. In the past, a son who returned with cattle stolen from a neighboring tribe would be blessed by his mother. She would gain status if she were the "mother of a tough warrior"

(Akabwai 2001, 6). Many of the battles over cattle are especially grisly: During one raid, a Toposa herdsman was shot and then disemboweled. Women too are victims and are often raped and maimed in such raids. In southern Sudan in April 2001, women from many neighboring tribes united for ending this tradition. They formed a traveling group, which went from village to village and replaced the praise songs for this warrior tradition with songs that bemoaned the consequences of cattle raiding:

> Toposa, Turkana, Dongiro, DiDinga,
> Fighting has become foolishness.
> What can we do to these cattle of ours?
> Cattle have run out while we scramble.
> They go to Toposa, they finish [kill];
> They go to Turkana, they finish;
> They go to DiDinga, they finish;
> They go to Dongiro, they finish;
> Men have died fighting,
> Fighting, fighting. (Akabwai 2001, 15)

However, by the time this women's effort was initiated, the DiDinga men of Syracuse had emigrated from Sudan. None of my informants was aware of this "emerging" women's tradition; and, for this group, warrior songs about the war, recalled from their childhood, remained an essential part of their recontextualized performances. Their bonding had become a substitute for the traditional unit of the age-set, but their repertoire consisted of children's songs, love songs, and warrior songs.

Dinka and DiDinga: The Issue of Cooperation

In the eyes of the Dinka and DiDinga men with whom I worked, to be regarded by Americans as one cultural group was a new experience because ethnic divisions had always existed in Sudan before the civil war. However, they themselves admitted that some traditions, like the warrior's bullsong, were similar: Dinka and DiDinga age-sets ritually stressed the young men's place within a hierarchy in which elders make up village councils and hold sway over even senior warriors. Dinka and DiDinga elders did not have military duties. Both Dinka and DiDinga age-sets engaged in ritualized antagonism and opposition (Meeker

1989, 122). In the United States, on the surface it seemed easier for the DiDinga group to come to consensus, but this may have been due to the small size of their group. I had invited the Dinka to participate in the university program to provide an equal opportunity for Dinka and DiDinga groups to educate Americans about the war in Sudan as well as the distinctiveness of their traditions. Ultimately, they made only a feeble attempt to perform "separately but together," which strengthened my suspicion that this was a consequence of several factors, including their ambiguous identity as "Lost Boys."[1]

The War for "The Wars of Our Fathers Are Not Ours"

In retrospect, I realize that neither group had been entirely forthcoming about interethnic violence in Sudan because they were fearful that it would detract from their cause. When I first offered to hold a Dinka-DiDinga public program at the university, the DiDinga men did not appear as enthusiastic as earlier when they had initially performed in my class without the Dinka. I invited Darius Oliha Makuja, a DiDinga priest living in St. Louis whom they had known in Sudan. Carl Oropallo, a volunteer sponsor of many Lost Boys, suggested Makuja might be a good moderator for the program. When I offered to invite a Dinka speaker, all except Charles voiced approval. I noted his hesitation, but when I asked him directly, he demurred.

I went forward with plans for the program, having secured funding to hold the event during State Humanities Month. The DiDinga priest was to fly from St. Louis, where he had been pursuing his doctoral degree. The other scheduled speaker was a prickly 74-year-old Dinka minister who had been granted safe haven in the United States as a political refugee. He was also the elder who, when I first invited the young men to my classroom, had expressed concern that the young men were not adequately familiar with their cultures. He believed that some of the views of the young Dinka men were too radical, to which the young Dinka men countered that this elder had not lived in the refugee camps. In the face of such growing complications, I realized that the program dynamics were more complicated than I had anticipated. As a consequence, I enlisted the help of the church choral director, who was the sponsor for most of the Lost Boys. We held an initial "planning" meeting at the choral director's home. I invited suggestions from both DiDinga and Dinka: What should the format of the program be? Which songs would be most appropriate for this occasion? Did they share any songs? Could they sing in each other's language?

Both groups wanted to sing a couple of songs in Swahili. In church, they had sung one song in DiDinga and one in Dinka, and they suggested that they would sing those. Although I did not voice it, the Dinka elder had expressed his opinion earlier to me, "Church songs should only be sung in church," so I knew this might be a potential problem. Suddenly, at the end of the meeting, one Dinka announced that they should sing the Sudanese national anthem, which is sung in English to an Arabic tune. When the DiDinga did not object, I asked them to think it over and to write the songs for our next meeting. I knew that this was asking a great deal of all concerned, and, by this time, I did not really expect that they would do any of it. They didn't.

In the meantime, a few of the DiDinga stopped by my house "on the way" to the state fair (five miles from their house but thirty miles from mine). They thought I might want to "sponsor" them so they could attend the fair. I agreed, but I also asked if they had time to review a video of their performance to decide about the songs for the upcoming performance. Two weeks later, we were to meet at the DiDinga leader's home, when Dinka and DiDinga would be present. This meeting did not materialize because everyone had a different work schedule, so the church choral director and I met with some of the Dinka singers after Sunday mass and then he and I drove to the DiDingas' home. In his kitchen, the DiDinga soloist finally disclosed that some of the DiDinga objected to the south Sudanese national anthem because it was a "political song" associated with the SPLA, the southern Sudanese rebel army. He offered the solution that the Dinka be allowed to sing "their song" but that the DiDinga would not.

I met later at the church with the Dinka men to explain that the DiDinga did not want to sing a political song. The Dinka argued that the song was *not* political, that it was not "from the SPLA," and further, it was really a "neutral" song. Any conflicts between the army and civilians had been a "misunderstanding," so the song had nothing to do with "sides" or "tribes." I asked if it would be better to sing a traditional Dinka song since the DiDinga would be performing DiDinga *gyrikot*. The Dinka were adamant about the SPLA song.

When I went back to the DiDinga, they still resisted performing the song, this time because it was in English. The DiDinga soloist offered again that those who wanted to sing should, but no one had to sing any song of which they did not approve. At a loss about how to mediate at this impasse, I asked the church choral director and a caseworker for advice. Neither had suggestions for a viable solution. As a last resort I spoke with the Dinka elder, asking him why the DiDinga were so opposed to a song which the Dinka insisted was "neutral." Further complicating the dilemma, he claimed the DiDinga are not "Nilotics" like the Dinka because they originally migrated from Uganda, adding, "They don't care about Sudan." My idea for a program already planned as "The Wars of Our Fathers Are Not Ours" seemed fated to reach a crisis level.

Eventually, we did reach a compromise: the two groups would sing a church song together in Swahili since all the young men were Christian and all knew it in Swahili. The DiDinga would perform their *gyrikot* and the Dinka would sing a song in Dinka. At the end of the program, anyone who wanted to stand to sing "Our Sudan" would do so. I thought we finally had a workable plan, but the Dinka could not agree among themselves about who would introduce their song or who should speak about their refugee experiences. One Dinka in particular insisted, "No Dinka speaks for another Dinka." He also insisted that the DiDinga must sing the final song. Because of his repeated insistence, I finally had to mediate by insisting that those who wanted to sing would do so and that the others could choose *not* to sing. The debate among the Dinka continued as the DiDinga diplomatically left the church hall.

What was becoming apparent to me was that issues related to identity on individual, ethnic, and national levels were simultaneously being negotiated before my eyes. Any discussion of a "Lost Boys performance" would have to be situated on the local level, but it also had to take into account that any member of a given group has several other groups with which he identifies. On a *national level*, the Dinka and DiDinga were "southern Sudanese," but, as in Sudan, in the United States the DiDinga remained a very small minority. Although Benjamin would later explain, "In Sudan, we [Dinka and DiDinga] are not even considered Sudanese citizens by the Khartoum government," among themselves, they remained distinctly Dinka or DiDinga. More importantly, these inherent and traditional differences had been exacerbated because of the rebel army's treatment of civilians, and opinions continued in new and foreign contexts. Yet at the same time, the war had caused both groups to become parentless refugee children who had shared similar life experiences for over a decade in refugee camps. Finally, as immigrants to the United States, they became recognized as one group, the Lost Boys, an unfortunate simplification of their true differences.

Resolution

The event took place as planned. Dinka and DiDinga participants spoke about their escapes on foot from their Dinka and DiDinga villages. They each performed their respective traditional dances.

DiDinga Lost Boys perform at Syracuse University program "The Wars of Our Fathers Are Not Ours," 2002. Photo: Felicia McMahon.

To my surprise all of the participants sang the contested song. Although I did not feel that the program I had envisioned reached its potential, in the following weeks I received several e-mail messages and telephone calls from both the Dinka and the DiDinga, thanking me profusely for providing this opportunity to "teach America." Indeed, a few months later, the Dinka initiated a Sudanese Community Program in Syracuse in which they invited the DiDinga to participate. And during the early part of 2003, on their own, the Dinka decided to formally establish a "Lost Boys Chapter" in which DiDinga were elected to hold offices. What had initially seemed a difficult situation had taken an auspicious turn toward resolution. Further, Charles and Dominic R., who had returned from Utah, had seized the opportunity to create a novel framing device for their performance: They sang *Jaluo* accompanied by thumb pianos. I had given Charles the thumb pianos when we first met because, although the *lokembe* is not a traditional DiDinga musical instrument, it is extremely portable, inexpensive, and played by youth throughout Africa. Without the knowledge of the other singers, Charles and Dominic secretly composed a song:

Uranga loholia jaluo
Uranga loholia jaluo
Uranga loholia chiagano
Uranga loholia jaluo

The young boys who are playing *jaluo*.
The young boys who are playing *jaluo*.
Our young boys are playing,
Our young boys are playing *jaluo*.

This act of keying their performance with an improvised frame required taking a risk. Representing a high degree of performance competence, their song resonated with both DiDinga and American audiences (Bauman 1978, 2004). The song consisted of only two lines, repeated several times to the same tune, strictly following the poetics of DiDinga tradition. To my knowledge, none of the DiDinga men had ever used a *lokembe* so I was surprised when they chose to do so. Their comments elucidate the emergence of a hybrid tradition:

Dominic R.: It is a song before the speech to at least let the people enjoy. You know, it's like opening. Opening of speech to let people, to get people to concentrate to what we will say. I told Charles we should at least use the *lokembe* to bring all people's attention, to attract people's attention. And Charles say, that sound good. Then we practice [playing the thumb piano duet] overnight and then practice in the morning [of the program] so we were ready and we didn't tell anyone.

F: They [the other DiDinga] didn't know?

Dominic: They didn't know. They just saw us with those things [thumb pianos] and then just kind of a trick between me and Charles [laughs]. That's why when I first started the speaking I came with the *lokembe* and said to Charles, you come now. So the song is really to get people to concentrate. It is like attention getter. The song really mean people should wait [to] listen to speech and get ready. We are very much happy. It is kind of short song. It doesn't take long to sing but with accompaniment of *lokembe* it make it so nice and bring people's attention.

In Sudan, the DiDinga frame "performance" when a high-ranking elder beats the ground with a bundle of brush. This is followed by a terse and formulaic song urging others to gather around the *arra* (courtyard). Musical instruments are not used, and lyrics are not necessarily in DiDinga language. Charles and Dominic focused on the word *jaluo*, which is not DiDinga. According to Dominic, "*Jaluo* is the name of a tribe in Uganda and Kenya, but it is also the name of a dance." This contrasts with the belief of Charles and Simon that *jaluo* is an "Arabic word" which they translated as "dance." However, according to an adult Dinka informant who speaks Arabic fluently, *jaluo* is also not Arabic. It is the word for a dance which probably originated in eastern Zaire among the Nagale people.

Regardless, in Sudan, the young men would not have the status to open a ceremony nor the opportunity to improvise *jaluo* as framing device for performance. However, in the new context they accurately assessed the need to communicate a new hybrid identity based in traditional DiDinga song aesthetics. According to Benjamin, "Our songs are not concerned with rhymes. It is like I told you before, it is like most of these songs are chorus. It's like first line and everything is chorus. That is our way of composing songs. It's like chorus. There is basic line that everyone repeats and then later on, the soloist tries to fix his own words to fix the chorus to make the song longer." Although the song *Jaluo* and the *lokembe* accompaniment were novel ideas, song techniques of improvisation with call and response are traditional among the DiDinga. In this recontextualized performance, a hybrid identity had emerged.

Nonetheless, this experience has become my cautionary tale about my own "cultural blindspot." I had made an assumption that did not hold up for this particular group (Graves 2005). In order for the young men to coperform effectively in an American context, they would need much more time to mediate the past and present in their new identity. For public-speaking purposes, they needed to arrive at consensus about how their traditions could be performed in a way that effectively conveyed a group identity. It also meant that the young men would need to take control of their traditions in order to recontextualize for an American audience. This required collaboration between the two groups, which a folklorist with sufficient mediation training might facilitate, but only after sufficient time for healing and discussion among the young men.

Gendered Performance

Atik Lodura caramac
Lodura had sex with an unmarried woman.
Atik Lodura caramac
Lodura had sex with an unmarried woman.
Atik Lodura caramac ci abuni ne inik goni eri ci abuna
Lodura had sex with a witch woman; he told his friend take one who is good.

Wi Lodura
Oh Lodura,
Lodura kere iye
Lodura, what is that all about?
Wi Lodura
Oh Lodura.
Song of the Lost Girls

As the traditions of the young men were emerging in new contexts, the group grew in size to include DiDinga women. Variables which acted on the emergence of the young men's traditions included nostalgia, childhood memory, race, politics, and eventually gender. Recontextualized performances provided new venues for identifying, affirming, and valuing the personal histories of both Lost Boys and the Lost Girls.

The epic march and tragic escape stories of the Lost Boys had finally captured the attention of the world (Ahial and Mills 2004; Bixler 2005; B. Deng et al. 2005; Eggers 2004), but few inquired about the fate of Sudanese girls. For all intents and purposes, they were forgotten. When I first met the DiDinga in Syracuse, I had asked why there were no women in their group. Many of the men told me, "Ladies are not allowed to travel alone" or "Ladies have to stay with the family." Some believed that the girls had not survived the ordeal. Others were said to have been adopted by relatives. Traditionally, if a girl loses both her parents, she will be taken in by relatives. However, as I began to read reports on the internet, I learned that poverty among refugees in southern Sudan was so dire that relatives were taking bride price for the girls who were then married to Sudanese men.[1] At the same time, refugee agencies had assumed that the girls were in the safe hands of foster parents, and therefore, girls did not meet the criteria for resettlement in the United States. Technically, they were not orphans because, traditionally, the girls are protected by their relatives. Many foster parents, it seems, did not have the girls' welfare at heart. In a place where poverty is rampant, young women are a valuable commodity. They can be sold off for a good bride price. When international attention focused on the Lost Boys, the Sudanese community kept the girls away from the limelight. Sudanese leader Gideon Kenyi says, "The issue of dowries had become a priority to the people who are owning the girls. They see the girls as a way of generating wealth, by marrying them or giving them to someone rich. Refugee workers from international agencies assumed that the girls were safe, because they were being sheltered by their own people. That assumption has turned out to be wide of the mark. But the head of the UN refugee agency in Kakuma, Kofi Mable, is doubtful that the girls can be helped now" (quoted in Matheson 2002, 1).

In December 2003, as an answer to my inquiry about the Lost Girls, Charles handed me a sheet of paper on which there were several "ladies songs" typed in DiDinga. He then announced, "There are three DiDinga ladies here." At first, I thought he meant the adult married DiDinga women settled in Sioux Falls, South Dakota, had returned to Syracuse, but he said emphatically, "No! They are living here, from Sudan." I was understandably surprised because I had read about the controversy over the Lost Girls. I waited for Charles to arrange my meeting with the women, but apparently he did not think it was urgent. After two months, I called the caseworker who then told the young women about my interest in DiDinga culture. The caseworker suggested that I call and make arrangements to meet them separately from the young men because, in the presence of the men, the women were less talkative. For DiDinga women, this is customary behavior, something I would observe later.

I dialed the number given to me by the caseworker, and a melodic voice answered hesitantly, "Hello?" I introduced myself and explained who I was. Her name was Ursula, and she lived with her sister Sabina, her cousin Elizabeth, and her brothers Emilio and Benjamin. Her English was impeccable. I noticed immediately that, unlike the young men, she did not have a distinctive DiDinga accent. Ursula readily accepted my invitation for lunch and told me that Mary, another DiDinga young woman, had just arrived from Sudan that day with her male cousins Marino and his younger brother Michael. In the evening, I called Fortunato because I was looking for Charles to tell him that I had contacted Ursula. When I told Fortunato that I had invited the DiDinga women to lunch that day, he said simply, "Mary is my girlfriend." They had known each other for seven years and had met at the missionary school. Recalling that Fortunato had sung a love song in my kitchen two years earlier, I asked him if Mary was the girl in his song. He giggled and softly replied, "Yes." I was as elated as he at their good fortune. Mary, who was 17, had known Fortunato since she was 10 years old. In an impossible coincidence, she had been allowed to immigrate to Syracuse because she had male cousins who could accompany her. In Salt Lake City, Dominic R., having heard the news that Fortunato's girlfriend was coincidentally sent to Syracuse, commented to me, "It means it was meant to be." Moreover, "The Children Are Reuniting," one of the songs Charles gave to me, seemed an appropriate description of their reunion:

Chorus: *Homotohatinak loholia holohoruma ikanyani*
Homotohatinak loholia holohoruma ikanyani
We shall reunite in some years to come, children.
We shall reunite in some years to come, children.

Soloist: *Ayaaya loholia holohoruma elee*
Ayaaya loholia holohoruna elee
Hey children one day we will meet.
Hey children one day we will meet.

Chorus (refrain): *Ayaay loholia holohoruma elee*
Ayaay loholia holohoruma elee
Hey children we will meet.
Hey children we will meet.

Soloist: *Thala oyu Canada holohoruma elee, hehedakung katina waraga*
Thala oyu Canada holohoruma elee, hehedakung katina waraga
Even if you go to Canada, I will write you a letter.
Even if you go to Canada, I will write you a letter.

Chorus: [Refrain]

Soloist: *Thala oyu America holohoruma elee hithowakung katiaraga*
Thala oyu America holohoruma elee hithowakung katiaraga

Even if you go to America, I will send you a letter.
Even if you go to America, I will send you a letter.
Chorus: [Refrain repeated twice]
Soloist: *Ayaaya gurubi holohoruma elee*
Ayaaya gurubi holohoruma elee
Hey age-mates one time we will meet.
Hey age-mates one time we will meet.

After Charles sang this song for me, he translated: "This song means as many people depart to different countries in the world, the group gap and age gap come together." He then wrote a proverb: Men do meet but mountains do not meet. Joe N. explained the song another way: "The meaning is, the world is small, have many friends because you don't know maybe we will meet them on the other face of the world." Finally, Mary's cousin, Marino, explained the relationship of the proverb to the song: "The song teaches us that we are not mountains, which do not meet, but rather we are men who can always meet—that's way its talking of the meeting in the near future and the constant letters they keep on writing and sending."

Coincidentally, some of the young men had been altar boys for the DiDinga priest who visited the refugee camps in Kenya years ago. They had not seen him for over 10 years. In yet another stroke of luck that year, he was granted a fellowship at a local college in Syracuse. His apartment was around the corner from the young men's apartments. When I called Dominic R. again to tell him how happy I was about the DiDinga reunions, he replied, "It is all coming together," but I was saddened when Dominic told me his younger sister was still in a refugee camp. Yet he remained optimistic that one day he could save enough money to bring her to the United States because it was his "responsibility" as her brother.

When I visited Ursula's apartment, the first thing I noticed just inside the door were the many pairs of shoes arranged in a neat row. They belonged to the five people who shared this tiny apartment. I was introduced to Ursula's family. The members of this small family were related to Charles and James through marriage, but I was never quite sure to what degree, since polygamy is still practiced in Sudan. Mary, a Longarim (Boya), was from Joseph's village, and she lived in an upstairs apartment with her male cousins Marino and Michael. I immediately noticed the serious nature of the young women. Their chronological age was approximately 17 years old, but they were extremely poised, and their English far surpassed that of some of DiDinga men who had been living in Syracuse for three years. Ursula and her sisters had arrived in Syracuse in the middle of a December blizzard, which they described as "scary." Marino explained that they had never seen snow before except on high mountains in Kenya. I asked Marino where he had lived in Kenya, and he replied, first in Kakuma refugee camp after they escaped from the war and later, the Dominican Missionary School in Nairobi with the others: "We have had it hard but we are here now in this country and we want to get a job and an education so we can make a contribution to this country and maybe someday I can also help my country to be at peace."

During lunch with Mary and Ursula at a local restaurant, I told Ursula about an upcoming program I had arranged for the DiDinga at the nearby art center. I asked if the women would like to sing a DiDinga women's song as part of the program. Mary and Ursula readily agreed. When they had first arrived, Charles had played the video of the previous year's *nyakorot* at the art center. They knew the songs Charles had given me, but Ursula immediately added a song that was not humorous:

> *Nalele haina jaho*
> Nalele, I say, keep quiet!
> *Nalele haina jaho*
> Nalele, I say, keep quiet!
> *Nalele ma anyaii bondoro na aratati eeta haino jaho*
> Nalele, you have a *bondoro*, people will molest you, I say, keep quiet.
> *Tinati Bulani jaho*
> Daughter of Bulani, keep quiet!
> *Tinati ma anyaii bondoro na aratati eeta haino jaho*
> Daughter, because of the *bondoro*, people will molest you, I say, keep quiet.

Ursula believed that the song was also "tradition," commenting, "The *bondoro* is like a gun but not a gun"; a handgun rather than a rifle or machine gun. The singer tells the daughter of the Bulani clan to remain silent because her clan is involved in the dangerous ammunition trade. Although Ursula explained that the song is sung to reassure the daughter, a male DiDinga later told me, "The song deals with encouragement for the youth to defend themselves and their home." This prompted me to ask about Ursula's family, and the whereabouts of her parents, which I immediately regretted. Both women became very quiet as Ursula said, "You know, it is a hard life." The following day I learned from caseworkers that she had not seen or heard from her parents since she was a young child. According to the caseworker, when the war reached their villages, the boys had run off to escape forced enlistment in the rebel armies. The parents, however, had kept the girls with them until they could protect them no more. The boys returned to the village undetected and, when they had been able to escort each girl in safety to a refugee camp, had done so. It had taken a long time because they had had to escort the girls through the forest one at a time. Eventually, the girls had been taken in by a missionary boarding school, where they had lived with Dominican nuns in Nairobi until their immigration to Syracuse.

To avoid discomforting them, I never asked again about their parents, Kakuma refugee camp, or their war experiences. Instead, I asked about songs they recalled from their childhood. Ursula said she would talk with the other women, and they would write their songs for the program brochure, although Ursula admitted that this would be the first time that she had written in DiDinga. Then she asked if I would be able to get the animal skins they needed for women's dance attire. James had told me about *ceremi*, the leopard- and goat-skin skirts that women wore for *nyakorot* to make them "beautiful." I told Ursula and Mary I would do my best, but I knew I wouldn't be able to find *rika*, the chipped ostrich eggshell used for girls' aprons. The girls laughed, telling me these belts are now made of beads. I began the search for the appropriate animal-print cloth and some beads, which I hoped would suffice for the folk-arts program. Back at Ursula's apartment, I announced the women's desire to participate in the upcoming program to the men present. Since the young men would be paid as a group, I suggested the women would receive a separate check in Ursula's name, which she would then divide among the women. The women smiled, and I sensed that this pleased them. I showed everyone the women's songs that Charles had given me, and I was surprised that the men were familiar with them. When I asked how this was possible, Marino explained that, as children, boys sing in a chorus to support the girls' singing when they play. Unlike adults, boys and girls sing together, and their play is not segregated by gender. The group continued to laugh as we discussed the women's songs, most of which were humorous.

One young DiDinga man described the women's songs as "shallow" to indicate the humor in the songs. He offered as an example *Tuluhu*, a reference to a girl's fiancé who hides in her family's indoor goat pen. The refrain, "*Tuluhu naya tuluhu lochoro naya eee naya*," consists of the noun *tuluhu* (squirrel), the nonsense sounds, "naya eee naya," and *lochoro*, which Joe N. translated as "hall." At first, I thought Joe N.'s translation was incorrect because it seemed unlikely that DiDinga compounds would have halls. However, according to Driberg, *logur* (*lochur*) is DiDinga for the indoor goat pen that is common in DiDinga houses. Although the genitive is usually preceded by *ci*, to denote intimate connection between nouns, it can be omitted (1931, 141). Hence, in the song, "*tuluhu ci lochoro*" is shortened to "*tuluhu lochoro*," literally, "squirrel of the goat pens":

Maku gotona naya henechi aito naya eee naya
When my brother comes, I tell him he [fiancé] is not here, naya eee naya.
Tuluhu naya tuluhu lochoro naya eee naya
Squirrel naya squirrel who-lives-in–the-hall, naya eee naya.

Maku ngona naya henechi nicheni naya eee naya
When my sister comes, I tell her he is here, naya eee naya.
Tuluhu naya tuluhu lochoro naya eee naya
Squirrel naya squirrel who-lives-in–the-hall, naya eee naya.

Maku baba naya henechi aito naya eee naya
When my daddy comes, I tell him he is not here, naya eee naya.
Tuluhu naya tuluhu lochoro naya eee naya
Squirrel naya squirrel who-lives-in–the-hall, naya eee naya.

Maku mama naya henehi nicheni naya eee naya
When my mama comes, I tell her he is here, naya eee naya.
Tuluhu naya tuluhu lochoro naya eee nay
Squirrel naya squirrel who-lives-in–the-hall, naya eee naya.

Maku mara naya henehi aito naya eee naya
When my maternal uncle comes, I tell him he is not here, naya eee naya.
Tuluhu naya tuluhu lochoro naya eee naya
Squirrel naya squirrel who-lives-in–the-hall, naya eee naya.

Maku inna naya henehi nicheni naya eee naya
When my maternal aunt comes, I tell her he is here, naya eee naya.
Tuluhu naya tuluhu lochoro naya eee naya
Squirrel naya squirrel who-lives-in–the-hall, naya eee naya.

The song provides important cultural information about kinship because it reinforces the way that females subvert male authority. A young woman brings her "squirrel" home, but he appears only when the female relatives are at home. Like a squirrel, he darts in and out of the compounds where the female family members live: When she was asked by her brothers if he was there, she said he was not there. When asked by her sisters, she said he was there. So she only shows her fiancé to her mother, sisters, and aunt, and not to her father, brothers, and uncle. She calls her fiancé *Tuluhu Lochoro*, "Squirrel Who-Lives-in-the-Hall." The line "*Tuluhu naya tuluhu lochoro naya eee naya*" was difficult for the DiDinga to translate because there is no English equivalent for this phrase in which the genitive is implied. I then learned that this song is *apiti*:

Benjamin: This *apiti* song. *Apiti* is like women sing it during when women are really happy like after a great harvest. Basically like when we are happy they will come.

F: Is it like *gyrikot*?

Benjamin: *Gyrikot* is not a DiDinga dance. It came from Uganda. *Apiti* is like real DiDinga. *Apiti* is for women.

F: But the men sing to support them?

Benjamin: No, no we like tried to fake it but typical thing is for women. Men are not even supposed to participate in it.

F: So how do you know this song, *Tuluhu*?

Benjamin: You know *tuluhu* is like squirrel, a cunning animal, so cunning. You know what I mean by cunning? Like if someone tries to stop it, the squirrel will find a way to get what it needs, you know? When someone is like trying to shoo it out, the squirrel will like make him miss it because the squirrel is like a real cunning animal. What the song is all about is squirrel is like used in so many songs. In this song, this is like a love song. Sometimes they sing it after *nyakorot* by the young girls. Here they praising, they are talking about their boyfriends. The girl is like talking when the dad is coming first, asking about her boyfriend, the girl will like to try to hide the boyfriend under the bed and say I don't know nothing, there's nobody here. The same case with the mom is coming and all these other people. What she is trying to say here is since mom is more understanding, she tells her he is hiding. You see? For the uncle, he is not here. Most of the women are understanding, since she is a girl.

F: Is it a funny song?

Benjamin: It is a real fun song like after *nyakorot* when everyone is leaving and is exhausted, they just sing that song to enjoy. You feel like really great.

F: Will the women stand in a circle and clap?

Benjamin: They combine and like mix and the soloist is a girl at the center and she'll be like singing. It is a fun song.

When *apiti* songs are performed during children's imitation play of *nyakorot*, Benjamin indicates that this is not traditional behavior ("we like tried to fake it").

In a new context, like children's play, it would be performed "for fun" because adult male performance is exclusive and privileged in DiDinga society. *Apiti* is performed separately by women but during childhood girls learn these songs, which they sing during unsegregated play with the boys. Although the children know the lyrics, they do not entirely understand the adult meanings.

A second song, *Nathuka*, was difficult for the group to translate because they had learned this song as children and, since an early age, have been separated from adults. When I pointed to the word *nathuka*, Marino said, "It is like a sheet." When I asked Ursula if it meant cloth, she said, "Yes, but it is worn by women and folded." She indicated her waist. As I tried to understand what *nathuka* implied, I asked about the DiDinga women's decorative metal belt, *nataka*, but was told the *nathuka* was "not the same thing":

Hapelingiro kumanekani ele kumaneka nathuka
Hapelingiro, prepare for me, prepare the *nathuka* [bedsheet tied around waist].
Otta doholia otta loholia hoko moroto inganit doni kumaneka nathuka
They are gone; the children are gone; they are gone to the bush and I am alone; prepare the *nathuka*.

Loholecieni kumanekani kumaneka nathuka
You child, prepare for me, prepare the *nathuka*.
Otta doholia otta loholia hoko moroto inganit doni kumaneka nathuka
They are gone; the children are gone; they are gone to the bush and I am alone; prepare the *nathuka*.

Loholecieni kumanekani kumaneka nathuka
You child, prepare for me, prepare the *nathuka*.
Otta doholia otta loholia hoko moroto inganit doni kumaneka nathuka
They are gone; the children are gone; they are gone to the bush and I am alone; prepare the *nathuka*.

Gotona kumanekani kumaneka nathuka
Brother, prepare for me, prepare the *nathuka*.
Otta doholia otta loholia hoko moroto inganit doni kumaneka nathuka
They are gone; the children are gone; they are gone to the bush and I am alone; prepare the *nathuka*.

Homonec kumanekani kumaneka nathuka
In-law, prepare for me, prepare the *nathuka*.

Otta doholia otta loholia hoko moroto inganit doni kumaneka nathuka
They are gone; the children are gone; they are gone to the bush and I am alone; prepare the *nathuka*.

After our conversation, I noticed Lino, who was listening carefully and who commented, "You know, I had forgotten about the *nathuka*. I was very young when I left my home and your questions about our culture made me remember and I thank you for that." Moreover, this song seemed particularly meaningful for the young women. It refers to women who must remain in DiDingaland because traditionally women are not allowed to travel beyond the village. Hapelingiro is the name of the man to whom the song is addressed. He decides to stay in the village after the young men leave to live in other countries. He tells all the women that they must now do whatever he commands. The women sing to him *"Hapelingiro kumanekani ele kumaneka nathuka"* (Hapelingiro, prepare for me, prepare the *nathuka*). The line refers to the cloth that the women wear folded around their waists, which is removed for lovemaking. The young men and women agreed that there are no words in English for many of the DiDinga words in the song. However, there were gendered opinions about who was singing the song to whom:

Benjamin: It is a recent song. It is sung to tell the girls, come tie this thing around my waist, make me [laughs]. It is a funny song.

F: Are they flirting?

Benjamin: Yes. Just like the *tuluhu* song, after *nyakorot*. When I was in Kenya and new people were coming, I heard this song and I really tried to get the meaning. It is like a new word, a slang word. Because it is not a DiDinga word. They tried to fake it and make it like a DiDinga word.

F: Where did this word come from?

Benjamin: I don't really understand where it got this meaning from, but they made it like DiDinga. This is a new song. I just heard it when I was in Kenya.

F: Who is the composer?

Benjamin: You can never know who the composer is. The song just pops out and you don't know who the composer is.

F: Could the composer be a woman?

Benjamin: No, no a man is talking here.

Although Benjamin did not know the origin of the word *nathuka*, in an e-mail message of February 26, 2004, Joe N. wrote, "*Nathuka* is a derivative word from

Turkana warriors of Kenya. *Nyathuka* refers to the bedsheet tied around the waist for lovemaking." Unlike DiDinga women in Sudan, the young women singing the song in Syracuse were living independently, undominated by males. In the new context, the song challenges a reading of the past in which women are under male control. From the women's perspective, Hapelingiro is under their control thus subverting the original meaning. In response to my question Who wrote the song? Benjamin replied, "The song just pops out," implying that an individual's creation can increase a community's repertoire if it is accepted (see Rosenberg 2002).

By contrast, in the song *Ngitagira*, it is the young men who are granted license to travel. Like *Nathuka*, the song has an unusual structure, divided into three parts sung by three different soloists. Benjamin believed it was a modern song, not tied to a community function: "Actually, it is not like *apiti* and not like *gyrikot*. It's like entertaining. It is a youthsong, sung by girls":

Otta ngitagira
Otta ngitagira
Hegereny moro hicuu odolan
Lohotha Lohichokio hatal mum hithalak
The traders [businessmen] have left.
The traders have left
Walking fearlessly through the forest [bush] in the morning
In Lohichokio where their faces become smooth.

Otta doholia
Otta doholia
Hegereny moro hicuu odolan
Lohotha Lohichokio hatal mum hithalak
The children have left.
The children have left
Walking fearlessly through the forest in the morning
In Lohichokio where their faces become smooth.

Otta nyekothowa
Otta nyekothowa
Hegereny moro hicuu odolan
Lohotha Lohichokio hatal mum hithalak
The warriors have left.

The warriors have left
Walking fearlessly through the forest in the morning
In Lohichokio where their faces become smooth.

The song refers to the DiDinga traders who carry their goods on their heads and walk to Lohichokio, Kenya, the first border town where goods are commonly traded with the Turkana. The distance from Sudan to this crossroads is about "four days walking." The unusual structure and the irony of female singers living unchaperoned is a clear example of an emerging song tradition which subverts a male-dominated reading of the past. This recent song enigmatically refers to the underground sale of arms, a common occurrence in Sudan. We had a humorous exchange as I tried to interpret the English translation, "their faces become smooth." Charles translated, "their faces shine," and I responded with "their faces brightened." Eventually, Benjamin clarified the metaphor by explaining that this is a descriptive phrase for people who encounter new experiences:

Benjamin: This basic meaning of it, this song is like you know the border between Kenya and Sudan where the DiDinga traded—these traders? They just like walk, walk across the country and to buy these cheap, cheap thing, you know like clothing and so it's like praising their work, their business, encouraging them. Go, walk to Lohichokio. It is like a meetingplace.

F: A marketplace?

Benjamin: Yes, a marketplace at the Kenya border.

F: A border town.

Benjamin: Yes, the last one, the first town in Kenya.

F: Who do you trade with?

Benjamin: Sudan tribes come. It's like everybody who comes to Kenya has to come to this town, from Sudan to Kenya is the first town. It is where the border military. I mean like the DiDinga community come, it is like busy, to get all these things, like cloth. So the call is let's go, let's go, let's go get these things, you know?

F: And what do the DiDinga bring to trade?

Benjamin: It's like, long time before, it's like bring the ammunition.

F: Ammunition? For the war?

Benjamin: Yes, ammunition. Sometimes they carry tobacco, trade with them.

F: Who do the DiDinga trade with?

Benjamin: Turkana.

F: Anyone else?

Benjamin: These are the main tribe they meet at the border.

F: What do the Turkana give them?

Benjamin: Sometimes they get money and the money they get they go for these basics like household stuff and clothing. These words, *"Lohotha Lohichokio hatal mum hithalak."* In Lohichokio everything is new and bright, a complete metamorphosis, a real change.

The "metamorphosis, a real change" is also represented in this particular song's structure. Because of its unusual structure, as compared with the other DiDinga song texts I collected, it appeared to be a form of cultural syncretism, but the DiDinga could give me no more information about the song. While we continued to discuss the translations, the women discussed the details of the public performance, especially their traditional dress. I realized that this would be the first time that they had control of a public space, which in Sudan was male domain.

In the new context, the women would transform the space into an arena where they could contest male dominance by giving the aura of a "traditional" performance. Therefore, animal skins would frame their recontextualized performance in terms of an African past. I attempted to explain that in the United States it probably was impossible, if not illegal, for me to buy leopard or tiger skins or even goat skins. After calling several stores in Syracuse, all of which had sold out of "animal" cloth during African-American history month, I eventually found a fabric store in Auburn which had leopard-print polar fleece. I bought several yards and hoped it would be acceptable. In addition, the DiDinga priest had urged me to find large dried gourds so the young men would not have to use the pots and pans. He was concerned that their performance was not "authentic." I sensed some generational dissonance, but I hoped it would not interfere with our program planned for April 25, 2004, when the DiDinga women would dance for the first time in the United States with the DiDinga men.

This was the first time that I would speak with DiDinga women about their role in the dances. The young men had told me earlier that women were there to "support the men," but Ursula explained that, in addition to supporting the men's singing, the role of women is to keep the men "from going too far." Although I had read that traditionally DiDinga women's songs praised the cattle raiding of men, these young women were telling me that their role was to reduce aggressive behavior. Thus, although men controlled public ceremonial space, there were gendered dimensions of evocation and provocation (Feld 1982, 264). These gender differences would be played out before new audiences in the United States. As I talked with Marino, Ursula, and Sabina about our plans to hold this program in Auburn, I asked if they understood the word "audience," but they said no. I explained that people would sit and watch them dance, to which they laughed and shook their heads. I then decided that it would be a good idea to show the newcomers all the videos in sequence of the young men's past public performances. Lino, who had participated in most of the programs, also joined us because we needed to use his VCR. We viewed the video of the first occasion when the young men had visited my university class singing church songs and then *gyrikot*. The viewers agreed that the young men looked uncertain about performing before Americans: "They do not know what to do." The trio enjoyed immensely the second videotape, which had captured the teasing exchange between Fortunato and Lino during the initial performance in Auburn. Talking excitedly among themselves in DiDinga, they laughed at the young men's antics. When we finally viewed the following year's *nyakorot* with the elders, they watched intently. During *Tolit*, Lino commented, "This song is very emotional."

During the video, I asked the young women about the arm gestures of the DiDinga adult women visitors the previous summer. Each woman had bent one arm up and one arm down while trilling. Sometimes they motioned with both arms upward. Ursula explained that the women were signaling to the men, "Calm down." The women's movements assuaged the provocation of the warrior's thrusts, thus emphasizing gendered difference. I wondered how the presence of these four young single women would affect the young men's next performance, especially their warrior songs and their playful antics.

Analysis: Performance as Music Event

To elucidate the process of recontexualization, I considered the linguistic notion of "speech act" as an interpretive method for a music event such as DiDinga *gyrikot* and *nyakorot* (Campbell and Eastman 1984). By mapping out the formal features of *gyrikot*, a casual event, against *nyakorot*, which requires full community participation, I found it easier to determine how closely the young men and women adhered to tradition. Arranging the formal characteristics according to Hymes's notion of "speech act" ([1975] 1981) revealed how song symbolism interacts with traditional DiDinga society:

type	*gyrikot*	*nyakorot*
setting	informal gathering	formal celebration in *arra* [courtyard]
participants	adult men and women, youth	entire adult community (youth, adults)
ends	ensures proper social conduct	transmits social history; attracts marriage partners; displays male prowess; preserves social hierarchy
act sequence	spontaneous; soloist initiates song; chorus sings refrain; all play percussion, swaying left and right in unison	formal ceremonial opening with *lilia* in strict line formation; antiphonal (call and response while clapping); formal exit with *lilia*
key	percussion; swaying; female hip rotation	male and female padan; male *ngothi*; handclapping; age-set markings; distinctive male/female attire; males sing *oli*
instruments	percussion	ankle bells, flutes
musical features	melody/texts set by soloist; litany (one or two phrases repeated several times); improvisation in melody; songs strung together, no break; order set by soloist; limited melodies	antiphonal; improvisation foremost; additive form (new parts are added which require no reference to preceding parts); many melodies; pauses between songs; wide melodic range
rhythm	2/4 duple to 6/8; progressively faster	slower than *gyrikot*; 2/4 duple (march)
interaction	alternating slow and fast	entrance/exit line formation; dignified entrance; competitive dancing
genre (physical configuration)	separate lines for men and women	concentric moving; loosely structured semicircles

Hymes's schema elucidates how *gyrikot* and *nyakorot* symbolically communicate traditional social values and history to solidify the community. Each music event has its distinctive purpose: *Gyrikot* expresses DiDinga values related to appropriate behavior and mores; *nyakorot* provides men with a sense of team spirit while they simultaneously compete for women's attention by displaying their dancing and singing abilities. In the original context and in recontextualized performance, the music events are highly gendered, but *nyakorot* is more so. Translations of some of the associated songs reinforce the connection of *nyakorot* to lovemaking and marriage:

Akhaca loholec loci
Akhaca loholec loci

Loremaa
Loremaa
It is so unfortunate for this girl.
It is so unfortunate for this girl
From Lorema,
From Lorema.

Haiita nan ngakhumudaa buhec ci antak nyapala nyigitee
Since ancient time we have never seen a girl with a *panga* in her mouth.

Arita ngania umwa ci ongoli heng muuna
Arita ngania umwa ci ongoli heng butubut
Arita ngania umwa ci aburi heng heron
Some are born with rotten hearts.
Some are born with rudeness in their blood.
Some are born with unsocial hearts.

The lyrics are sung by men to ensure women "cooperate" after *nyakorot*. At the culmination of *nyakorot*, it is expected all men and women will celebrate privately as couples. *Akhaca Loholec Loci* is "an old school song" sung by young men "to alert women of their bad behaviors when approached by men." *Panga* is Swahili for a kind of machete and is used metaphorically in this humorous song to chastise women who resist warriors' advances. Benjamin's translation, however, is idiomatic because in the original DiDinga, comparisons of the girl's mouth are made with *muuna*, which is the waste product of a local fermented beer, and *butubut*, a plant: "It has a kind of flower, sort of leafy but smells so bad. The plant is good but the smell is what sucks." Like the other young men, he recalled singing songs like *Akhaca Loholec Loci* when the children observed adults making love after *nyakorot*:

> **Benjamin:** We just go there and hear people talking about you know [laughs], try to, this is when you get to know these songs because children, as children, let me say, really in our community, little childrens most of the time are not allowed to *nyakorot*. But you always hear these songs in the village, the boys and girls go at night, the couple inside, you always find couples at *nyakorot* [laughs]. I don't know if it is a good thing or bad thing [laughs, shakes head]. People always have these affairs. Children are always like playing songs. They are like singing game.

Ursula leads women's *apiti* with Lost Boys chorus at Schweinfurth Memorial Art Center in Auburn, New York, 2004. Photo: Felicia McMahon.

On April 25, 2004, the DiDinga recalled their own forms of girlhood play by performing the *apiti* dance. Sometimes pairs of little girls perform *padan*, the traditional body movement between male and female dancers during *nyakorot*. The young men and women insisted that *apiti* means "father's dance," which seemed ironic since no men were even allowed to watch this women's dance. According to a DiDinga elder, *apiti* is not a DiDinga word because the dance originated in Uganda. In Rosato's dictionary (1980), I found that *apa* is the DiDinga vocative used only by children for "father," which the young DiDinga confirmed. This was another example of the way that the Lost Boys and Lost Girls were performing traditions from the perspective of DiDinga children. It was also an important observation for understanding how the young performers interpreted recontextualized traditions such as *apiti*. For the new audiences, the young women performed serious songs such as *Nalele* (above), but most of their songs were humorous, like *Lodura*, a song about a man who had an affair with a "witch woman":

> *Atik Lodura caramac*
> Lodura had sex with an unmarried woman.
> *Atik Lodura caramac*

172

Lodura had sex with an unmarried woman.
Atik Lodura caramac ci abuni ne inik goni eri ci abuna
Lodura had sex with a witch woman; he told his friend take one who is good.
Wi Lodura
Oh Lodura,
Lodura kere iye
Lodura kere iye.
Wi Lodura
Oh Lodura.

The women chastise Lodura who, in turn, warns his friend, "Take one who is good" (not a witch). The song reinforces the community's taboo against premarital sex as well as adultery. In DiDingaland *buyagit* (a witch) is despised. Women who are witches use *egero* (poison), said to be used by some women in the refugee camps. Today there may be little witchcraft left in Christianized DiDingaland, but talk about it continues to frame the way that the DiDinga think about misfortune. Lodura warns his friend to stay away from witches, suggesting that such women cause misfortune. In Auburn, the young women decided to sing the song to their soloist, whose DiDinga name is Lodura. At the last minute, he chose to visit friends in another city instead of participating in our program. Thus, the meaning of the song was recontextualized in a way that indicated hybridization.

In DiDingaland, the significance of the music event is always connected to its social milieu; for women *apiti* gives voice to their opinions and criticism, but it also ensures women recognize privileged male performance. In the new context, the song challenged male dominance. The young women's *apiti* conforms to DiDinga song aesthetics with emphasis on repetition based in call and response with the chorus. The text also incorporates the syllables "kere iye," which are not words but rather sounds that increase the aesthetic effect. As in all DiDinga music events, the song message and dance form are a united genre (dance-songs), with no instrumentation and melody playing a less important role. However, as recontextualized tradition, the event for the young performers evoked a traditional African past while simultaneously creating a new identity.

For the young DiDinga, an important part of this process became the videotapes of their recontextualized performances, which were mailed to DiDinga friends who had relocated to other parts of the United States and Canada. In these performances, traditional behaviors by which members express identities were selected and reformulated by the group for presentation of a lived bifocal experience. Earlier, without the participation of the young women, the significance of

George and Sabina during Lost Boys' and Lost Girls' Emerging Traditions Folk Arts Program at Schweinfurth Memorial Art Center in Auburn, New York, 2004. Photo: Felicia McMahon.

gyrikot and *nyakorot* had been incomplete, and the lack of females only underscored the exclusively male nature of a public space where they parodied warriors. With the reintroduction of DiDinga women into their performance, they no longer played warriors; they became warriors in a new land.

The addition of the young women dancing flirtatiously with the young men charmed the American audience, but in doing so, the women also carved out their own new identity in this shared public space. The self-reflexivity of the young performers was evident in their comments, "We were wonderful!" Audience members also acknowledged their competency in performing and communicating a new identity; "I think I really understand who they are after seeing them like this. I knew them but now I feel that I really know who they are now," commented the foster mother of three of the young men. It was apparent that the women had improved the performance in the eyes of the young men. "It was very colorful," said James.

A few months after this performance, a second peace accord was reached in south Sudan, but the war spread to Darfur in the western region. In the United States, the young men and women faced challenges with limited educational resources and personal relationships and slow advancement from entry-level jobs. In spite of their playful performances, concerns for those left behind were always paramount: "Basically, these kind of songs are sang by [for] the fellow youth whom we left them back. They sing these songs to remember their friends who are displace all over the world and some who have passed away and left them back. Some of these songs are so emotional in a way that one can either be courageous to do the best of his/her life, or just be forever depressed especially when they know that one of the dearest friend has died and will never be seen again.—yours, Joe N." (personal communication 2003).

This concern inevitably made their performances different from the danced play of their childhood. At the same time, many of their dance-songs appeared to be reflective of a premature age that would not have been experienced if they had performed the dances ritually as adults. In short, preadolescent play life required more humor than adult society and may be the reason that, in spite of serious concerns, these now-grown young men's performances were more jocular. During the 2005 staged performance of *gyrikot* for a mixed audience of Africans and Americans, the young men replaced drums with large plastic bowls. The bowls substituted for drums which they struck with metal kitchen utensils. The bowls were also used to tease the young women dancers. From behind, the men would quickly place the bowls on the women's heads. This forced the women to continue dancing as if they were unaware of the bowls on their heads. An emerging reflexivity was apparent in this strategy as it was articulated in the performance. Paradoxically, the young men maintained a connection to their childhood in a performance that defied strict categorization because it was both "not children's play" and "not not children's play" (Bateson 1955; Schechner 1988). Other instances of excessive jocularity among the men demonstrated characteristics of playfighting typical among male children in many cultures. The dancers lampooned their performances at the same time that they proudly manifested their own male identity because they may actually have been ambivalent about aggression and trust. They also performed a counterhegemonic image that challenged the image of the refugee as a "poor, desperate, exhausted, deprived person" (Hrvatin and Senk 2004, 77). Although this behavior called attention to the distance between performers and audience, as kinesthetic communication it doubled back and signaled solidarity when audiences responded enthusiastically to the performance. Thus, the contested arena of the public domain provided a metaphorical playground in which heightened artistic behaviors revised and reconstituted the young performers' status in more than one society, enabling them to "enter into dialogue with the past, performing their parts in cultural scripts wherein emergence tracks in the future" (Kapchan 1995, 500). The addition of the young women did not eliminate playfulness but the ambience of the performance was transformed.

8

Conclusion: "I Carried It in My Heart"

Dominic R.'s words "I carried it in my heart" underscore the nostalgia for childhood play that is at the root of the emerging traditions documented in the preceding chapters. Until the second *nyakorot*, there were no DiDinga women with whom the young men could dance, and the traditional gendered competition for winning women's approval had been replaced by playfulness and parody. At the first *nyakorot*, I heard one DiDinga call to another who had walked away from the circle, "Hey, where's my girl?" The other dancers immediately broke into laughter. When reviewing the videotape of the song *Limalukai*, the young men revealed adolescent joking behaviors. Lino was the good-natured "target" of the performance because his name, Lino Ariloka, was similar to Limalukai, the cuckolded husband in the song. This playful behavior served as a bonding mechanism for the group:

Simon: This [song] is about a woman who left her husband and went to another man.

James: They are like kidding him that his wife left him and went to another man . . . [bursts into laughter]. That was funny!

F: Why is this funny? Why are you all laughing so much?

James [still laughing]: He [Fortunato] is mentioning somebody's name . . . he is mentioning someone's name instead of the real man, Fortunato in mentioning Lino's name [all laughing].

Simon [still laughing]: He's saying, what's wrong with him?

James: Yeah, he just picked Lino's name instead of it.

DiDinga Lost Boys and Lost Girls relax after a performance at lakeside home of Rob and Barb Rogers, Otisco, New York, 2004. Photo: Felicia McMahon.

Playful behavior had substituted for the motivation that women generally provide during adult *nyakorot*, revealed in the videotapes. Without careful entextualization (Cashman 2000), the playfulness that made the tradition unique to this group of young men may have gone unnoticed. In his work with refugees in Australia, Greg Gow also noted the usefulness of the videotape for dislocated people: "By suggesting continuity between past and present, the video-recorded event articulates historical tragedy, political objectives and collective identities within a grand nationalist narrative" (2002, 94). In Syracuse, the dancers asked for multiple copies of their videotaped performances to mail to other DiDinga relatives and friends in the United States and Canada, establishing a connection among scattered diasporic DiDinga. In performance, the young men created their own counterdiscourse that resisted characterization of their identities as victims; they became "found," rather than "lost," boys.

During the current academic discussion about globalization, what strikes me as a folklorist is that expressive culture can still be distinct from everything else. These young men pay rent, buy videos, communicate by e-mail, drive fast cars. Economics and politics can be integrated and globalized but their traditional dance is central to individual identity and the culture's sense of self. Why should the expressive culture be where identity is preserved? It seems that at the site of the performance, collectivity is continued. The collectively performed dance

DiDinga Lost Boys perform warrior dance at 2003 New York State Fair in Syracuse, New York. Photo: Felicia McMahon.

allows preservation of that "other" identity that is not Western, even though the young men frame it with the use of microphones and camcorders, just as they have acculturated to using money, driving cars, paying rent, reading books, and other aspects of modern life. The ability to reexperience what the young men had only been remembering from their childhood demonstrated the endurance of the shared cultural identity in the performance, the ritual itself. It connected them to their ancestors. Instead of feeling alone and cut off from their ancestral homeland, having lost all contact with their families and relatives, in performance they saw themselves as the preservers of DiDinga culture, both preserving culture and simultaneously forging a hybrid identity: The young men used their traditions to make themselves the preservers of DiDinga culture, for example, like a flag standing for freedom or something other than just a flag. The recontextualized performance itself became an icon for their culture.

At the same time, each young man had the opportunity to compete to display his own individual talent through improvisation within accepted boundaries. The staging of playfighting enabled the young men to bond as a collective unit. For most of the young men, their small group of 10 (now 18) necessarily took the place of the age-set: "The performance of the songs mediated the journey from the present to the past, marking the stages of people's lives leading up to the present. Many of the audience had no photographs and certainly no books

178

from the past, but all had songs to recall. The songs recalled the intricacies of their past lives: the sounds, the smells and noises of life back home" (Gow 2002, 80). Critical for recontextualization of their past, the dancers enacted nostalgia in song parodies and in imitation play. Hampton points out that "while music and dance are constantly changing [at home], artists who have been geographically displaced and deterritorialized tend to cling to the traditions they retain or can acquire from the homeland" (2004, 15). However, by combining two dance forms and by giving prominence to women's tradition, they have changed tradition in significant ways that reflect new functions in the new context. In these recontextualized performances, they re-present childhood dances to reconstruct paradigms of meaning that employ traditional DiDinga imagery. In a sense, the young men became both the kids again of the community, and at the same time, they proudly portrayed themselves as African warriors. Their dance-songs subverted the social reality of being uninitiated boys. This would most likely remain integral to their group identity because it represents the early stage at which they had been separated from their families.

There were boundaries, however, such as the taboo of wearing the black feather reserved for *ngikothowa* (warriors), which they respected. This combination of factors contributed to a hybrid identity which also became an important resource for coping with the stresses and demands of a new culture (Nesdale et al. 1997; Zhou and Bankston 1994). Globalization has created many global commons, resulting in the creation of new performance spaces where there are few guidelines to help facilitate mutual imbrication: "In the end, globalization cannot be thought of simply as a westernizing affair, nor can it be viewed solely as a homogenizing one. It must be read instead as a complex process that brings the west to rest and the rest to the West" (Inda and Rosaldo 2002, 22–23). In recontextualized performances, the "Lost Boys" reacted to labels of displacement by asserting the power to name themselves, to communicate a powerful new identity as warriors, not refugees. In this new global commons, public folklorists are in a position to make valuable contributions with long-term and far-reaching effects at a time when "other narratives and victimization remain hidden to the view of folklorists: stories collected in combat zones, refugee encampments, prisoner-of-war zones, prisons, detention centers, concentration camps, resettlement zones, whatever they are called. Here the casualties of war or territorial pride are tucked away. Questions of how to represent relocated and dispersed peoples encourage us to confront even more dark and important subjects, leading ethnographers and other social scientists into subjects of great moral and political importance" (Abrahams 2005, 206). However, when told to or performed for new audiences, traditions risk being essentialized and misinterpreted if there is no mediation to ensure that folklore is adequately and appropriately recontextualized (Rynearson 1996). For this reason, "folk artists should be adequately prepared in order to appropriately and effectively adapt their repertories and performance styles and rhetoric of performance" (Baron 1999, 192).

According to Baron, the responsibility of introducing traditional performers to new frames falls squarely on the shoulders of the presenting folklorist. I left decisions about program content in the hands of the performers, but I knew their unfamiliarity with American staged performances left them unprepared for audience expectations. In fact, they had little or no concept of "audience." At times, a few of the young men made half-hearted attempts to self-present at performances. However, until one of the young men felt comfortable in the role of cultural interlocutor, they continued to rely on me to interpret their traditions for American audiences:

> While folklorists recede as mediators by encouraging self-presentation by folk artists, they nevertheless continue to intervene in the (re)presentation of traditions. . . . Folklorists thus retain a measure of authority in the construction of interpretation. They are increasingly conscious of the need to negotiate and share authority with tradition bearers and recognize the value of adopting dialogical approaches to interpretation. Presentations must be developed in collaboration with the artists, traditions, and communities whose traditions are represented. Nevertheless, we should have no illusions about our interventionist and mediative role, regardless of how explicit or covert. (Baron 1999, 195)

My collaboration with the young men introduced the concept of framing (Hall 1976; Bauman 1986). In the original context, *nyakorot* and *gyrikot* would have occurred spontaneously. Dance-songs were an everyday part of daily life, with participation by the entire community. The change from a spontaneously performed dance to a danced performance is not small and is further complicated by the Western tradition of payment for musical events. From the young men's perspective, payment for cultural performance was potentially unethical. This dilemma was resolved when they understood musicians in the United States *expect* to be paid for entertaining audiences unless it is volunteer work: "It is the American way," said James. After a few months, the young men told me that they were prepared to accept the honoraria offered to them by U.S. institutions, with the understanding that back in Africa, "We would never accept money for our culture." Eventually, the money which they earned from their performances was sent to relatives in refugee camps in Africa. Because they viewed their performances as a play form, the performers resisted commodification by the West.

On August 17, 2003, I had the good fortune to coordinate the program with Paul Atanya, the DiDinga musician living in Canada, who had agreed to travel to New York State to assume the role of presenter for the Lost Boys' upcoming performance. His interpretive talk demonstrated to them the way that an experienced insider frames tradition for new audiences. After his participation, the young men assumed this role, and we collaborated as to how traditions might be meaningfully decontextualized and recontextualized for both DiDinga and American audiences. The young men shared a wide traditional song repertoire recalled from their childhoods. After coming to consensus about which traditions could be decontextualized, they sometimes talked these over with me to see whether I "got" it. For example, I had not understood how *nyakorot* differed from *gyrikot* so the young men decided they would embed both music events in their performance. This combination created a unified whole which resulted in a hybrid music event, both traditional and not traditional. Synthesis of Hymes's notion of speech act applied to their music events, and analysis of a performance through the lens of Schechner's restored behavior revealed that these were hybrid traditions. They emerged from nostalgia for earlier childhood games, which were stylistically accurate representations of adult expressive behaviors. The following diagram conveys the dynamics of this process, which is not a passive act:

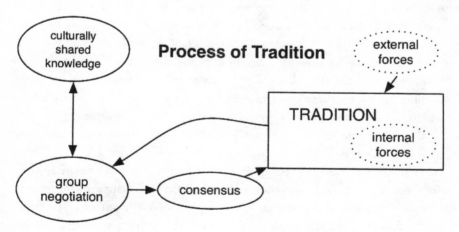

In an earlier work on tradition, Hermann Bausinger (1992) notes that in industrialized countries there is the tendency to "freeze forms" selected from the past in order to make claims for tradition. In preindustrial societies, festivals are improvised each year, demonstrating the way that tradition within a cultural system is an organic process involving constant decision making. However, continual negotiation among these dancers demonstrated how tradition remains dynamic, not frozen, in a recontextualized performance. Selection from their song repertoire is like behavior in any social interaction in which one chooses a certain course of action from several possibilities. Recontextualizing a selection did not mean that ensuing performances were essentialized but actively renegotiated from a myriad of combinations.

Further, in the new context where DiDinga *gyrikot* and *nyakorot* are performed, relationships are egalitarian and inclusive, and herein lie new meanings. This process is intricately connected with identity because, like tradition, identity is constantly being renegotiated, with emergence the key to identity formation. The process is never "complete" unless the tradition (or the individual) is no longer living. Because performance communicates identity, I listened to what performers said about their performances, that is, their intentionality, and their reasons why they performed certain traditions and not others. The review of the videotaped performances placed the performers in a reflexive position, aware that Americans were looking at them. It was the performers who then decided what was both appropriate for outsider display and what was most meaningful for them. On occasions when the outward appearance or form of the dance remained the same, nonetheless, it took on new meaning and purpose, for example, communicating a new identity to other groups: "The act of musiking establishes in the place where it is happening a set of relationships, and it is in these relationships that the meaning of the act lies" (Small 1998, 13). Coupled with the adoption of a temporal perspective in the documentation of performances of the same dances by the same men in different contexts, it was possible for me to locate the dances within a larger body of performances, as well as in history and society, to reveal an authentic diasporic identity.

But the question remains: In public folklore, who decides which "emerging traditions" adequately represent a diasporic community since issues of identity are at stake? We know that public folklore is informed by all sorts of assumptions about things such as agency and what is culturally appropriate for presentation to audiences. These questions beg for development of a systematic way to find the middle ground, a public presentation that does not essentialize tradition or impose destructive changes on a group's traditional identity. The solution lies in cocreation of identity where power is evenly distributed during the negotiation process. In everyday life, the performance of identity itself is an abstract, complex, and fluid process, and people have multiple identities. Since cultural identity is fluid, one's cultural identity is always emerging: "Identity [has] to do not with being but with becoming" (Sarup 1996, 6). Cultural identity, both fluid and political, separates individuals on the basis of ingroup-outgroup differences. Further, cultural identity is not the simple addition of the components of one's cultural background. Cultural identities are cocreated and re-created in everyday interaction. Like tradition, we create our identities with those with whom we interact in a process of cocreation in the context of specific encounters. Cocreation of identity cannot occur when there is an attempt on the part of one of the communicators to consciously or unconsciously dominate the other physically or symbolically (Freire 1970; Yup 1998). Cocreation of identity becomes difficult when asymmetrical power relations exist, such as between the performer and the audience. Negotiating identities is a process involving both parties; in public folklore, among performers and between performers and the audience.

There is no question that recontextualizing tradition and foregrounding improvisation stretches and may distort the traditional worldview; in public folklore it is perhaps inevitable that worldview will be expanded. Nevertheless, this is not a one-way transaction: The audience is also changed. Like Americans, DiDinga elders could not experience the entire range of historical meanings that the songs represented for the young men because DiDinga language itself is a contextualized one; it is residential in a sense. Talking or singing in DiDinga is like a "map" because it is a topographical language. The DiDinga elders had not experienced the same journey to manhood as the Lost Boys did.

In August 2003, I called Charles, who was waiting for his DiDinga friends to arrive from other parts of the United States and Canada. On his answering machine, Charles had a new recorded greeting for them:

Iya Iya
Iya Iya
Oh Iya
Oh Iya!
Thohota nyetubot
Bring your sword!
Thohota nyetubot
Bring your sword!
Iya Iya
Iya Iya!
Oh Iya

Oh Iya!
Thohota nyetubot
Bring your sword!
Thohota nyetubot nengata hita hoto ii thoth hibaleni
Bring your sword. Over here, it's like the last time!

This bullsong "belongs" to Captain Peter Lorot, a DiDinga commander of SPLA, a liberation army fighting for independence and the rights of southern Sudanese tribes such as the DiDinga. In the American context, the lyrics convey a very different message to the DiDinga living in diaspora, thus making the song a hybrid. Assuming the role of leadership, Charles recontextualized the song: It became not a call for military intervention, but a summons to participate in an emerging tradition, an expression not of the duality of life but of a lived bifocal experience.

Appendix A

"Bull-song of Auranomi" and "The Ancient Gods: A Hymn of Initiation"

Bull-Song of Auranomi

The reedbuck calls to the roan like a young man, the reedbuck calls like a young man on the far side of the valley.
Gather ye together.
The rhinoceros stands silent at the foot of the acacia, watchful, head swaying from side to side.
Gather ye together.
The leopard crouches in the rocks, the black leopard of the forest crouches, eyes flaming, poised.
Gather ye together.
The buffalo swings his horns this way and that, scattering the mud in the river.
Gather ye together.
Ho! Akorikono of the spreading horns!
Ha! Akorikono of the spreading horns!
Ha! Akorikono, red, red as the blood which bought thee, the blood which handselled [*sic*] my manhood's spear.
As the red lightning art thou, Akorikono, as the lightning which breaks over Taala at the time of sowing.
Red, swift, terrible art thou, swifter than the leopard, stronger than the rhinoceros.
The reedbuck calls to the road like a young man, the reedbuck calls like a young man on the far side of a valley.
Gather ye together.
Ho! Akorikono of the spreading horns!
Ha! Akorikono, deep-fronted, firm-footed!
Like the flame flower art thou, Akorikono, like the flame flower of the forest, red and passionate, Akorikono.
Brother to the buffalo art thou: what other bull may stand beside thee?
The buffalo goes with his head on high,
The buffalo goes with his horns swinging this way and that.

Ha! Akorikono of the spreading horns!

The buffalo scatters mud on his brow, he churns the muddy waters.

Young men, ha!

Warriors, ho!

Young men and elders of the people, ha! eya!

Gather ye together.

He splashes mud on his ears, as he wallows in the river.

He paws the ground furiously and is not afraid.

The breath from his nostrils is a storm of wind: he breathes the lightning, and the thunder is the sound of his bellowing.

Ha! Buffalo-brother, Akorikono, the fearless, the invincible, master of the herd!

Behold him! He lashes his tail like a lion, like a lion bloody with combat. Lashes his tail menacingly.

Look well, ye cows! Your lord the bull of bulls, Akorikono, the masterful, prepares him for battle.

Beware, ye lesser bulls! The days of your presumption are ending, for Akorikono the masterful prepares him for battle.

With locked horns and heaving flanks they wrestle in combat, and one by one they withdraw torn and bleeding.

But Akorikono stands alone, he paws the earth with his hooves, he bellows loud challenges, swinging his head this way and that.

He lowers his head and charges and none may withstand him.

Froth falls from his mouth, he plunges and snorts and tears up the ground, drunken with victory, delirious with desire.

Look well, ye cows! Behold him, your master!

Ha! Akorikono, herd-master!

Kapeta knows him and Lobititang. His voice is heard at Malala and he looms red in the forested Kimodo.

Like the flame flower of the forest, red and passionate as the flame flower, red against black.

Gather ye together.

Young men and elders of the people, ha!

Maidens and warriors, ho!

Gather ye together.

The reedbuck calls to the roan like a young man, the reedbuck calls like a young man on the far side of a valley.

The reedbuck calls to the roan, for the sap is in the trees and the green corn sways with the wind and the spring has returned.

The buffalo goes with his head on high drinking the wind, in multitudes, in great herds.

The leopard crouches in his lair waiting his mate.

Look well, ye cows! for Akorikono cometh, Akorikono of the spreading horns.

Rending, tearing, frothing and champing, tossing his great horns, red-frontleted, triumphant, he comes, your master and possessor, bull of bulls the incomparable.

Ha! Akorikono!

Ho! Akorikono!

Red, swift, terrible art thou, swifter than the leopard, stronger than the rhinoceros, brave as the buffalo, bull Akorikono! (Driberg 1932b, 7)

The Ancient Gods: A Hymn of Initiation

Of the Hornless One came the red flame of desire; White brow and spreading horn.
It scorched the mountains and its rage uprooted the stars.
    Dun brow and spreading horn.
Hayeyeye! the crested crane wakes the morning:
    March we to the river, brothers!
The crested crane is the father of the morning,
    The flute sounds in the Ayago.
Oh the glistening whiteness of desire!
    White brow and spreading horn.
The white ashes of the flame-flower!
    Dun brow and spreading horn.

Of the mist of the morning were our fathers begotten:
    Oh Hornless One of Ayago.
They were borne through the stars on the pinions of vultures,
    And the flute sounded on Ayago.
The sunset wrapped them about its splendour,
And the black hood of night encompassed then:
    White brow and spreading horn.
The Great Spirit that is as the morning air
Has folded them under the wing of holiness.
    Dun brow and spreading horn.
Odonog, whose voice is in the rustling of acacia,
Summons his Mother for the ordering of the days,
That season follow season til the Spear of Perfection
Falls athwart the rainbow, and the land has rest.

Splendid with fire, as a comet trailing glory,
Herding his souls in the pastures of the blest,
Counteth his tally Orongo, great soul-Master,
Watching their return, one by one at set of sun.

Mother of souls, thy hand that plants the fallow
Shall it not know the reaping of the days?
The seed that thou sowest burgeons for resowing,
The ears are garnered and await the sowing moon.

Of the pastures of Orongo were our fathers begotten
    Lest the flute sound on Ayago!
The flame of the Hornless one has anointed them,
    March we to Ayago, brothers.

Hayeyeye! The crested crane wakes the morning:
    White brow and spreading horn.
The crested crane is the father of the morning,
    Dun brow and spreading horn. (Driberg 1932b, 29)

Appendix B

The Songs

1.

Ichayo hotongutho lota
Ichayo hotongutho lota
Ichayo gore baoko nyao
Ichayo hotongutho lota
Ichayo loholia hotonguthu lota
They fought a gun battle until they lay on the ground.
They fought a gun battle until they lay on the ground.
They fought a gun battle during the war of Nyao.
They fought a gun battle until they lay on the ground.
The children fought a gun battle until they lay on the ground.

2.

Ai Mariah hanyaki thong
Ai Mariah hanyaki thong
Ai Mariah hanyaki thong
Ai Mariah hanyaki thong
Ee tira thiga da
Arita hina gi ci ereketa
Ee Ai Mariah hanyaki thong
Mary says, I'm pregnant.
Yes, Mary says, I'm pregnant.
Mary says, I'm pregnant.
Yes, Mary says, I'm pregnant.
Yes, so let us see you give birth.
Instead she is giving birth to it [something we do not know].
Yes, Mary says, I'm pregnant.

3.

Adahit hodopuwana Lotiki likaibani
Adahit hodopuwana Lotiki likaibani
Likaiba Lotiki taminaro
Likaiba Lotika taminaro
Holo adahita
Adihit hotongutho heeni taminaro
The vultures devoured Lotiki during his past hunting expedition.
The vultures devoured Lotiki during his past hunting expedition.
Lotiki's great bushland,
Lotiki's great bushland.
Oh, they devoured.
They devoured until they slept on trees.

4.

Ee uket nohoni
Ee longo cik gang dekererik i horoma ho
Uket nohoni
Ee uki hati koruma iin meder
Why are you torturing us like this?
Yes, you guys on the hill above?
Why are you torturing us?
Yes, it will one day become a vendetta.

5.

Enek Sadiq Lugo icia
Gerengi anyaha guwa ci hauna kicaya
Kapuata ma kicaya
Kapuata tel hotia Tororita lahadi Juba ci ngati hengera huwanya iwir Sadiqi uha Khatiba
Nakeny hichayo
Muksasa ereyo icia
Khatiba Ghazali nica anyaha guwa ci Sudani
Tell Sadik to leave [the south].
Garang is coming, bringing [military] force.
We intend to bombard and liberate Kapoeta.
After we have liberated Kapoeta, we march on Torit until Juba [whereupon] we divide [munitions].

Nakeng Battalion, let us fight!
Broom Battalion, wait [for us]!
Gazelle Battalion is coming, bringing Sudan's force.

6.

Lotim holia thoti ahacaani ba ngani ngati holo akani ho
Lotim holia thoti ahacaani ba ngani ngati holo akani ho
Adak lotimi mana ci Lonyume
Lotim holia thoti ahacaani ba ngani ngati holo akani ho
Adak lotimi mana ci Kulanga
Lotim holia thoti ahacaani ba ngani ngati holo akani ho
The baboon, the black-footed. Who betrayed you from not being able to farm or cultivate?
The baboon, the black-footed. Who betrayed you from not being able to farm or cultivate?
The baboon ate Lonyume's farm produce.
The baboon, the black footed. Who betrayed you from not being able to farm or cultivate?
The baboon ate Kulanga's farm produce.
The baboon, the black-footed. Who betrayed you from not being able to farm or cultivate?

7.

Ololo Lobalu, Ololo Lobalu
Aitani cieth hutuno
Mumm Lobalu aitani cieth hutuno
Aa iin cieth carret inni
Ololo Lobalu, Ololo Lobalu.
How do you think you are building the house?
Mmm, Lobalu how are you building the house?
Why is the house [looking like] a porcupine?

8.

Lohaya hitha macuni
Ne thino tinati eto hithiha elemu borohena
Lomagal Lopuk Kutur ne thino tinati eto
I have heard of your husband my cousin.
I heard you have accepted to marry the lightning gods.
Lomagal Lobuk Kutur, what is it, daughter of man?

9.

Ee Limaluka ngani ci eheed waranga
Nganita
Ehedihi ngani
Obote
Enehi ni neegi
Kenehi ne anya ripot hithiho ne au thinit lota
Limaluka, Who wrote the letter?
It's me.
Whom did you write to?
Obete
What did you say to him?
I told him, "Give me the report and my heart will be at peace."

10.

Macineka buheyi gol ci oi huth
Hacini ya otholo thong
Hedebi ya oo thong
Kanuothi nga oo thong
Please, have you seen my girl?
I saw the moisture of urine.
I follow her footsteps just here.
I follow them while they are going.

11.

Oli cani ci marini oo ci homina
Oo! Oli cani ci marini oo ci homina
Locia eet, oli cani ci marini oo ci hamina
Ci ica aduot ci homina
Lochia eet, oli cani ci marini oo ci hamina
Illale, oli cani ci marini oo ci hamina
Lochia eet, oli cani ci marini oo ci hamina
I love my bull with its red head.
Oh, I love my bull with its red head.
Son of my uncle, I love my bull with its red head
Which no one will stone.
Son of my uncle, I love my bull with its red head.
Thank you, I love my bull with its red head.
Son of my uncle, I love my bull with its red head.

12.

Hodo hodo hodo. Ningiti mamu ho

Manga hongi modung Iyo Naita Riono
Manga hongi modung

Manga hongi modung Iyo Naita Riono
Manga hongi modung
[Ningiti mamu ho]

My! My! My! This place of water.

Stop sleeping on your stomach! Oh yes, Naita Riono
Stop sleeping on your stomach!

Stop sleeping on your stomach! Yes, Naita Riono
Stop sleeping on your stomach!
[This place of water]

13.

Ati doholeco

Duha da nibuuk cugunik
Aito gi uma ci hanyaha na
Kai kedenano thong
Na Lolima, Awo Nyakori
Lolima, Awo Nyakori
Kamuhani na iyieni nganita

Manyi doholeco

Duha da nibuuk cugunik
Aito gi uma ci hanyaha na
Kai kedenano thong
Na Lolima, Awo Nyakori
Lolima, Awo Nyakori
Kamuhani na iyieni nganita

Mother of child

You too tell your story.
There is nothing [no dowry] that I bring to you.
I am seeking a loan.
I Lolima, Awo Nyakori,
Lolima Awo Nyakori,
I was thinking of you today.

Father of child

You too tell your story.
There is nothing [no dowry] that I bring to you.
I am seeking a loan.
I Lolima, Awo Nyakori,
Lolima Awo Nyakori,
I was thinking of you today.

14.

Arukan oli cani hal

Arukan oli cani hal acina nganit manyi
Cin thida hulahaci tang ci baba

Arukan Lomagali hal ee acina nganit manyi
Cin thida hulahaci tang ci baba

My Bull roars all night.

My Bull roars all night. Because of me, the [its] owner
Observe, you poor man, the cow of my father.

Lomagal (Wide-horn) bull roars all night. Because of me, its owner
Observe, you poor man, the cow of my father.

15.

Naboyele namerirenga Limaluka
Ee Lomalachan
Nangoria
Nahomoli natihajokan
Nahomoli natihajokan
Nahomoli natihajokan

Nahomoli natihajokan
Ee Lomalachan
Eee Lomalachan
Ee Lomalachan
Naboyele, daughter of Limaluka
Beautiful eyes
Who will marry her?
The person of good heart
The person of good heart
The person of good heart
The person of good heart
Beautiful eyes
Beautiful eyes
Beautiful eyes

16.

Ee aiir loholec beninit haga
Naorekong
Mahati iiru vellek neitiha ne
Gi ci airehi beninit haga Naorekong
Oh, the young woman is fleeing,
Naorekong,
You are afraid of the music?
Even if you flee what will you do, Naorekong?

17.

Kimaria ngimoi kimaria ngimoi
Kimaria ngimoi kimaria Lowalangole
Mmmmm, kimaria ngimoi
We fought over [defeating] the enemies. We fought over the enemies.
We fought over the enemies. We fought over Lowalangole.
Mmm, We fought the enemies.

18.

Uranga loholia jaluo
Uranga loholia jaluo
Uranga loholia chiagano
Uranga loholia jaluo

The young boys who are playing jaluo
The young boys who are playing jaluo
Our young boys are playing,
Our young boys are playing jaluo.

19.

Salamakum Nadura
Salamalekum Nadura
Naduraye ee
Naduraye Nadura
Naduraye Nadura
Eneck loholech komotio gola
Eneck loholech komotio gola
Farewell to all.
Farewell to all.
At the conclusion
Conclusion
Conclusion
Tell the child [girl], "Let's meet on the road."
Tell the child, "Let's meet on the way."

20.

Iya Iya
Oh Iya
Thohota nyetubot
Thohota nyetubot
Iya Iya
Oh Iya
Thohota nyetubot
Thohota nyetubot nengata hita hoto ii thoth hibaleni
Iya Iya
Oh Iya
Bring your sword
Bring your sword.
Iya Iya
Oh Iya
Bring your sword
Bring your sword. Over there, it's like the last time!

21.

Holo holo loholia
Holo horumwa eeh eeh eeh
Homoto hatinak korumwa
Holo horumwa irkinyani
Thala oyu Canada
Holo horumwa irkinyani
Thala oyu Amerika
Holo horumwa irkinyani
Holo horumwa Kinyani
Aaya, aaya gurubi
Aaya gurbi elee ee
Hey hey boys
Hey one day, one time, hey hey
We will meet one day
Hey, one day in years [to come]
Even if you go to Canada
Hey, one day in years
Even if you go to America
Hey, one day in years
Even if you go to Kenya
Hey, yeah group.
Yeah, group, elee ee.

22.

Nalele haina jaho

Nalele haina jaho
Nalele ma anyaii bondoro na aratati eeta haino jaho

Tinati Bulani jaho
Tinati ma anyaii bondoro na aratati eeta haino jaho

Nalele, I say, keep quiet!

Nalele, I say, keep quiet!
Nalele, you have a bondoro, people molest you, I say, keep quiet.

Daughter of Bulani, keep quiet!
Daughter, you have a bondoro, people molest you, I say, keep quiet.

23.

Tuluhu naya tuluhu lochoro naya eee naya

Maku gotona naya henechi aito naya eee naya
Tuluhu naya tuluhu lochoro naya eee naya

Maku ngona naya henechi nicheni naya eee naya
Tuluhu naya tuluhu lochoro naya eee naya

Maku baba naya henechi aito naya eee naya
Tuluhu naya tuluhu lochoro naya eee naya

Maku mama naya henehi nicheni naya eee naya
Tuluhu naya tuluhu lochoro naya eee naya

Maku mara naya henehi aito naya eee naya
Tuluhu naya tuluhu lochoro naya eee naya

Maku inna naya henehi nicheni naya eee naya
Tuluhu naya tuluhu lochoro naya eee naya

Squirrel, naya squirrel who-lives-in–the-hall naya eee naya.

When my brother comes, I tell him he [fiancé] is not here.
Squirrel naya squirrel who-lives-in–the-hall naya eee naya.

When my sister comes, I tell her he is here.
Squirrel naya squirrel who-lives-in–the-hall naya eee naya.

When my daddy comes, I tell him he is not here.
Squirrel naya squirrel who-lives-in–the-hall naya eee naya.

When my mama comes, I tell her he is here.
Squirrel naya squirrel who-lives-in–the-hall naya eee naya.

When my uncle [mother's brother] comes, I tell him he is not here.
Squirrel naya squirrel who-lives-in–the-hall naya eee naya.

When my aunt [mother's sister] comes, I tell her he is here.
Squirrel naya squirrel who-lives-in–the-hall naya eee naya.

24.

Hapelingiro kumanekani ele kumaneka nathuka
Otta doholia otta loholia hoko moroto inganit doni kumaneka nathuka

Loholecieni kumanekani kumaneka nathuka
Otta doholia otta loholia hoko moroto inganit doni kumaneka nathuka

Loholecieni kumanekani kumaneka nathuka
Otta doholia otta loholia hoko moroto inganit doni kumaneka nathuka

Gotona kumanekani kumaneka nathuka
Otta doholia otta loholia hoko moroto inganit doni kumaneka nathuka

Homonec kumanekani kumaneka nathuka
Otta doholia otta loholia hoko moroto inganit doni kumaneka nathuka

Hapelingiro, prepare for me, prepare the nathuka [bedsheet tied around waist].
They are gone; the children are gone; they are gone to the bush and I am alone; prepare the nathuka.

You child, prepare for me, prepare the nathuka.
They are gone; the children are gone; they are gone to the bush and I am alone; prepare the nathuka.

You child, prepare for me, prepare the nathuka.
They are gone; the children are gone; they are gone to the bush and I am alone; prepare the nathuka.

Brother, prepare for me, prepare the nathuka.
They are gone; the children are gone; they are gone to the bush and I am alone; prepare the nathuka.

In-law, prepare for me, prepare the nathuka.
They are gone; the children are gone; they are gone to the bush and I am alone; prepare the nathuka.

25.

Otta ngitagira
Otta ngitagira
Hegereny moro hicuu odolan

Lohotha Lohichokio hatal mum hithalak

Otta doholia
Otta doholia
Hegereny moro hicuu odolan
Lohotha Lohichokio hatal mum hithalak

Otta Nyekothowa
Otta Nyekothowa
Hegereny moro hicuu odolan
Lohotha Lohichokio hatal mum hithalak

The traders [businessmen] have left.
The traders have left
Walking fearlessly through the forest [bush] in the morning
In Lohichokio [town in Kenya] where their faces brightened [shone, became smooth].

The children have left.
The children have left
Walking fearlessly through the forest in the morning
In Lohichokio where their faces brightened.

The warriors have left.
The warriors have left
Walking fearlessly through the forest in the morning
In Lohichokio where their faces brightened.

26.

Etedia toliti
Nalimaya tuhui hadim nak hasina bee shinang Nalimaya tuhui

Ero, ero, ero
Nalimaya tuhui hadim nak hasina bee shinang Nalimaya tuhui

The tolit fruit has detached itself from the tolit tree.
We would like to see Mt. Nalimaya overturn.

Ero, ero, ero
We would really like to see Mt. Nalimaya turn over.

27.

Akhaca loholec loci
Akhaca loholec loci

Loremaa
Loremaa

Haiita nan ngakhumudaa buhec ci antak nyapala nyigitee

Arita ngania umwa ci ongoli heng muuna
Arita ngania umwa ci ongoli heng butubut
Arita ngania umwa ci aburi heng heron

It is so unfortunate for this girl.
It is so unfortunate for this girl
From Lorema
From Lorema.

Since ancient time we have never seen a girl with a machete in her mouth.

Some are born with rotten hearts.
Some are born with rudeness in their blood.
Some are born with unsocial hearts.

28.

Atik Lodura caramac
Atik Lodura caramac
Atik Lodura caramac ci abuni ne inik goni eri ci abuna
Wi Lodura
Lodura kere iyee
Wi Lodura
Lodura had sex with an unmarried woman.
Lodura had sex with an unmarried woman.
Lodura had sex with a witch woman; he told his friend to take one who is not.
Oh Lodura
Lodura kere iyee
Oh Lodura.

Notes

Introduction

1. In order to preserve the privacy of the DiDinga young men, this book will not include details of encounters and social lives in Syracuse. For in-depth accounts of the daily lives of the Lost Boys in other American cities, see Bixler 2005 and B. Deng et al. 2005.

Chapter 1. Men Meet (But Mountains Do Not)

1. In the most recent textbook for cultural anthropology, Nanda and Warms define *tribe* thus: "A tribe is a culturally distinct population whose members think of themselves as descended from the same ancestor or as part of the same people" (1998, 252). Further, the DiDinga meet the following criteria: "A tribe in cultural anthropology is a theoretical type of human social organization based on small groups defined by traditions of common descent and having temporary or permanent political integration above the family level and a shared language, culture, and ideology. In the ideal model of a tribe, members typically share a tribal name and a contiguous territory; they work together in such joint endeavors as trade, agriculture, house construction, warfare and ceremonial activities. Tribes are usually composed of a number of small local communities, e.g. bands, villages or neighborhoods, and may be aggregated into high-order clusters, called nations." See "Flawed Ethnic Classifications Excerbate [*sic*] Conflict in Africa," http://www.africanfront.com/research/research1.php? (2003). There are only four miles of paved roads throughout its total area. I gathered statistical information from library sources as I was getting to know the young men who were telling me that their homeland is "fertile" and "mountainous" and "cool at night." Until I had the opportunity to locate published information, I had to assume that the information the DiDinga gave me was accurate.

Chapter 2. Encountering Ethnography

1. This was an oversight that was to prove important for the direction of my research. Had I been introduced to the combined choir of Dinka and DiDinga, I may not have realized until much later that DiDinga is the understudied group. It was only when I began to do library research that I noted that although it was easy to find published information on the Dinka language, there was almost nothing written about the DiDinga.

2. The spelling used by the young man in his written communication for Nagichot demonstrates once again the inconsistency in spelling to represent even place names in English.

3. Many Americans are unaware that as recent as the nineteenth century in the United States, most Americans did not think of time in terms of a clock: "Even though the mechanical clock had been invented nearly six hundred years before, in the eighteenth and early nineteenth centuries most Americans still mainly marked their days by the rising and setting sun, phases of the moon, cycles of hunger and sleep and the routines of rural life. They ordered their lives by the changing seasons, calendars of religious observations, and successive births and deaths" (Stephens 2002, 20). See Stephens for more on time in the United States.

4. After I rewrote Arensen's transcription so that they could read and pronounce the words aloud, the young men confirmed that Arensen's version is "good DiDinga." However, they never used double vowels or consonants to represent sounds in DiDinga, nor could they understand Arensen's standardized symbols.

5. My informants claimed that with the exception of very old people, all DiDinga have been Christianized, and rainmaking is no longer practiced. However, they were aware of the traditional method of using pebbles to divine rain. For a discussion on rainmaking, see chapter 3.

6. For a recent assessment of the war in Darfur, see Ali B. Ali-Dinar (2003).

Chapter 3. Surveying the Landscape

1. "These houses in the new larger villages are now square, but manifest the same construction techniques as the round houses. These square houses probably show the influence of the rectangular brick houses which the British built at Nagichot" (Arensen 1983, 67).

2. In a similar description of this fertile area, Stefano Santandrea provides us with a more statistical account: "The DiDinga tribe, which may number 50,000 people, live in the South-Eastern corner of Sudan, between 4 and 5 N.L. and 33–34 E.L. It is a mountainous area characterized by the DiDinga Hills, dominated by Mt. Lotukei, which is 9, 170 ft. high. In the North it borders on the Longarim or Boya, to the south with the DoDos, who live in Karamoja, Uganda, and with the Turkana of Kenya; to the east it boarders on the Toposa, and to the west the Kidepo River separates the DiDinga from the Logir and the Lorwama, also called Mining or Ketebo" (quoted in Rosato 1980, 1).

3. Arensen (1992) uses symbols to represent the sounds we do not have in English, which are similar to "ee" and "oo." Likewise, Odden (1983) includes another symbol to represent the English "ng" sound, but none adequately represent the sounds. The DiDinga in the United States do not use these linguistic symbols because it limits them when, for example, they communicate by e-mail. I therefore learned to rely on my informants' phonemic representation for DiDinga words, but frequently they disagreed among themselves. For example, an older DiDinga informant sent me a translation with the word for the dance spelled *jirikot*, but the young DiDingas repeatedly corrected it to *gyrikot*. However, when I showed one young man Odden's published quasi-phonemic system, the next time he wrote something for me, he adopted Odden's symbol to represent the letters *ng*. However, he never used it after that time.

4. Even among linguists, there are discrepancies about the phonology and phonetics of DiDinga. For example, Odden writes, "There are two tones in the language, H and L, and contrary to suggestions by Driberg or Tucker and Bryan, there is nothing which could be called stress" (1983, 151). Regarding DiDinga language itself, linguists admit, "No area of

the grammar can be said to be more than cursorily worked out" (Odden 1983, 148) because published linguistic materials on the DiDinga are scarce and inconclusive. Thus, although Bender (1977) concluded that DiDinga is a member of the larger Surma language group, which includes DiDinga-Longarim-Tenet-Murle, Odden could not confirm that DiDinga and Murle are mutually intelligible. Still, there are strong similarities in their folklore and much of their vocabularies, so much so that the DiDinga men in Syracuse told me that the Murle speak the same language as the DiDinga, with "only a few words that are their own."

5. The *nyalado* is a black leather whip, approximately five feet long with brass handles used for cattle herding (Arensen 1983, 67). DiDinga men typically carry these distinctive leather whips rather than spears, and the *nyalado* features prominently in their ceremonies and celebrations, in spite of the fact that in addition to cattle herding, hunting and slash-and-burn farming is done. It is the rhinoceros that is hunted for the skin from which the DiDinga make their cattle-herding whips, and to own one is a prestigious symbol for a young man.

6. Arensen (in Dimmendaal 1998, 201) writes that among the DiDinga-Murle the word *torombil* (car) is derived from the English word *automobile*. Therefore, the word may have come into the DiDinga lexicon indirectly from Arabic via English.

7. I found no published references on women's rainsongs with the exception of Kronenberg's brief mention of women's dance in the field (*arugu ngay mana*). See Kronenberg 1972b, 130. Driberg however, described the rain ceremony in detail:

> The local rain ceremonies are held independently in the different chieftainships if the rains are late, but the people are not convened to these by their chiefs, but by the old men. Each area has its traditional place of celebration: Patalado, for instance, at the Logutha falls in the Kaidoto river under a large fig tree; Latome under a fig tree at the head of the Kathawa river. The ceremonies do not vary essentially in the different localities. All men attend with spears and withies, but without shields, and a black bull is killed under the fig tree. It is cooked and eaten there and the undigested matter is smeared over the bodies of the men, over the withies and trunk and branches of the fig tree. The water obtained from Alukileng is then thrown up into the air from a new calabash, and the rainsongs start led by the old men, the young men joining in the refrains. They sing and dance around the tree till sunset. The person selected to kill the sacrificial bull has to repay the owner one heifer, but receives no tribute or contribution from the rest of the participants" (1922, 214).

8. Interestingly, the young men and Father Darius did not know if the DiDinga have a word for the rainstones used in this divination ritual. Further, Driberg and others who mention the DiDinga Rainmaker and the rainstones also did not record the DiDinga word. All of the DiDinga men knew the name Alukileng, whom they identified as "one of the greatest Rainmakers in DiDingland," although he had died long before they were born. I discovered this quite by accident when I was trying to learn DiDinga vocabulary. I had pointed to a sentence in Driberg's dictionary, "*Thothik alukileng anyik kanyik tamu kuchuluth*" (Tell Alukileng to make it stop raining) and most of the men told me that Alukileng was a Rainmaker from long ago. Later, when I asked other DiDinga to whom the name referred they too knew of the "greatest Rainmaker."

9. Driberg wrote, "The paramount Chief is Alukileng son of Lotum Lopungamoi son of Giramoi, Chief of the Southern Boya [who also call themselves DiDinga], clan Loborokok. Alukileng is a hereditary rainchief and is in fact the only rainmaker among the Boya and DiDinga. Every year he receives offerings of goats from DiDinga to ensure rain and in return gives them some sacred water to be used in the local rain ceremonies. Cases which are not satisfactorily decided by the local chiefs are taken by the DiDinga to Alukileng for arbitration" (1922, 214).

10. Among the DiDinga-Murle, Arensen recorded the following story (I have substituted for Arensen's original orthography one which can be read by the DiDinga in Syracuse): "Ma ayoowo eeti ki goon oma, awak *mining* karabong een yaatin karabong een baatin baal adaayitoo, ka kiiya kuruyit eet ci ona ayoowoo ki noonoo okadaak. bodo ma da goon ayoowoo eeti ki baatin, ma adaak baatine, akoo bodo abada kizi miningit, ma aku adaak ngeerin kadaak. [Translation: If a man quarrels with another, he calls the *mining*, perhaps his mother, perhaps his father who died, to come to beat the man who quarreled with him to death. Also, if a man habitually quarrels with his father, and kills his father he goes again and returns as a *miningit* and comes and kills his son to death]" (1992, 250).

11. Joseph described himself as one of the "lucky boys": at age six, the army came to his village when he was playing. He ran into the forest but an older DiDinga teenager picked him up him and carried him on his shoulders across a crocodile infested river where many boys were eaten alive. He spent 10 years in a refugee camp but got an education in the camp school. He was then "selected" to come to the United States. Although Joseph is now a teenager living with a generous foster family who took in two other DiDinga of high school age, he says, "I must hold on to my culture and language tight." Like all of the Lost Boys, Joseph planned one day to return to his homeland to help his country.

Chapter 4. Entextualization and Kinesthetic Communication

1. The young man's remark, "so the ladies will get freer with you," refers to culturally acceptable seduction of unmarried girls; see Cerullli: "Among the DiDinga, if a girl of marriageable age is seduced, it is not necessary to pay a fine unless she becomes pregnant, in which case 10 goats and five head of cattle, plus one bull which is sacrificed in the enclosure of the girl's mother, are paid. The seducer has no rights over the child, but if the girl should die in childbirth, he must pay a fine as if for murder. As a rule, however, seductions which result in pregnancy are followed by marriage, but a fine must be paid just the same to the father-in-law, who received the usual bride wealth for his daughter. Premarital relationships are extremely common" (1956, 76).

2. *Tegel* (plural *tegellwa*) means "song," but although the DiDinga knew this word, I never heard them use it. *Oli* is used for bullsong, but *oli* is also the DiDinga word for "bull." The songs sung during the dance *gyrikot* were called *gyrikot*. This is another example of the way that the genre of song cannot be easily differentiated from dance.

3. Fetterman (1992) reports that the DiDinga use the word *lorong* (string) to indicate this hierarchy but I could not confirm this usage with my informants. Although there is no DiDinga word for "age-set system," Driberg uses *nameto* (1922, 213), a word which my

DiDinga informants claim is not DiDinga. Fetterman claims that the word *nameto* has been "replaced" by the word *thapaninit*, which also refers to the ritual of spearing the bull (1992, 87). However, she also uses the word *tuturininit* interchangeably with *thapaninit* throughout her dissertation. These may be typos, another example of the problems with representing the DiDinga language in English. Kronenberg, who published his research in German, uses *zapaninit* for *thapaninit*. The Syracuse young men were not familiar with *nameto* but did recognize the word *thapaninit*, which they described in detail. Kronenberg believes that the word *naminita* is similar to Driberg's *nameto*, and he quotes a DiDinga informant: "Fruher, als wir in einer Reihe in *Naminita* (alter Platz des *nyakereget* von Lorema) sassen" (1972b, 109). [In earlier days, we sat in a row in *Naminit* in Lorema, the former site of the *nyakereget*.] When I asked the DiDinga men in Syracuse about this, they insisted that neither *nameto* nor *naminita* were DiDinga words.

4. These "thrashings" are symbolic but not painless. The boys are required to jump over a bonfire while the elders encourage them by waving whips in a threatening matter.

5. "The threat of a curse is very effective in DiDinga. Very few people are actually cursed because very few people are considered so stubborn that they would rather be cursed (*cinenit*) than punished. The two curses normally given out at *nypio* (public punishment) are, 'You will marry but your wife will not have any children,' and 'No girl will marry you.' Given the value all DiDinga place on getting married and the fact a man cannot get rich unless he is married and has children, accepting a curse at *nypio* is self-destructive. . . . Even fleeing the area of DiDinga to avoid punishment will only work if a person is willing to banish himself from DiDinga forever: no matter how many years a person is away, his punishment will be waiting for him as soon as he returns. If a person flees after being cursed, the curse goes with him so eventually, he is going to have to come back and accept his punishment so the elders can remove their curse. *Nypio* is a system devoid of loopholes" (Fetterman 1992, 97).

6. In Nilo-Hamitic cultures such as the DiDinga, both age grade and age-set systems are important. I found it confusing in Fetterman's dissertation that she makes no distinction between age grade and age-set; the latter is also called "classes." Age grade only refers to a grouping according to stage of life because among DiDinga birth dates are not calculated and birthdays are not celebrated. In the United States the DiDinga referred to the age assigned to them by immigration officials, but that figure is only an estimate of their chronological age since the DiDinga do not determine age by birth date. Instead, certain duties and rights are associated with age grade as a young boy matures. Every three to five years, any boys around the age of eight are placed together to form an age grade. These boys play and work together until they are married. However, within the age grade groupings is a further subgroup gradation based on initiations which is the age-set system, also called "bull classes": "The classes are of two kinds, the age classes proper and the 'bull classes' which in due course absorb them" (Nalder [1937] 1970, 70). Among all of the tribes in southern Sudan, when males are formally divided into grades according to their ages and resultant capabilities and duties, the members in these groups are like brothers who assist and support one another in every way. A typical series ranging from the least to the most prestigious place in the hierarchy would be:

Children, who tend the goats
Youths (uninitiated), who "fag" for their elders and betters

Warriors (initiated, in age grade Nyikothowach), who fight and hunt
Elders, who talk and advise
Dotards, who just sit. (Nalder [1937] 1970, 18–19)

Nalder and others assert that the warrior tradition was originally a fighting organization, an explanation confirmed by my informants. However, this fighting organization is not to be equated with a military organization. The former is now a symbolic one attached to the young man's desirability in the eyes of young women. Although there are some all-female dances, mostly lewd humorous dances performed publicly at the coeducational *nyakorot*, the main function of girls and women is to assemble in order to provide admiration for the male dancers by clapping and singing. There are women's dances from which men are entirely forbidden. Not only can they not participate, but it is taboo to observe the women while they are dancing, and it is a serious offense for a boy or man to be caught doing so. Although the men knew about women's dances, they had never observed them because it is taboo.

7. The spelling of the word for these dance-songs, *gyrikot*, was consistent among the young men in Syracuse. However, in an e-mail message, Paul Atanya insisted that the word be more adequately represented in English as *jirikot*. Fetterman alternates *girkot* with *gyrkot*.

8. This tradition was documented by Scott Randall, who published a Tennet insult song lyrics online that included audio of the text in Tennet. See http://members.telocity.com/scottrandal/tennet/tennet.html. In the Tennet song, the singer mocks his rival by singing about how the girl will feel if she selects the other man. "Chaluwai" refers to her age group, to which the DiDinga told me girls and women also belong:

Anya Baba mach
Hey, girls, my father gave me a man.
Hey, women of Chaluwai, my father gave me a man
He showed me this man
Look, Dad, I tried to kill him
Look, Mom, my heart is vomiting.

9. My informants said that they could not dance *lokembe* in the United States because "there are no ladies here." When *lokembe* was first introduced from Uganda to Sudan and Kenya, Fetterman writes, it met with disapproval by parents, who thought such a dance encouraged premarital sex (1992, 186). The young men in Syracuse disagreed by telling me that their parents often held dances at their homes where the parents also danced *lokembe*.

10. Paul Atanya supported the young men's statements about *lilia* in an e-mail message: "It is a song usually sung after nine or ten hours of *nyakorot* has elapsed; a dawn hymn that warns the warriors to stop indulging in the act of love-making, It is taboo to be caught with a lover making love in broad daylight." The words to the *lilia* recorded by Kojo, which the young men sang are:

Oo Kiwala nyahopo halohide
Kiwala nyahopo kalohide
Oo Kiwala robo.

However, none of the young men in Syracuse could translate these words, other than to tell me that these are typical DiDinga sounds used in song.

Chapter 5. Memory, Childhood, and Restored Behavior

1. Ankle bells, not drums, are traditional DiDinga percussion instruments, but DiDinga-Murle still use drums. Fetterman mentions that, in DiDingaland during her field-work in 1980 and 1981, drums had been introduced to the DiDinga. This may be a result of the DiDinga exile in Uganda. In an interview on August 16, 2003, Paul Atanya, who met Fetterman in Sudan, told me, "I'm the first to introduce drums into DiDinga music." His claim is substantiated by my interviews with the young men and by Mack and Robertshaw, who suggested in 1982 that the significance of drums extends beyond entertainment in related groups such as the Lotuxo, who populate the plains between the Lafit Mountains in the north and the Imtong and Dongotona ranges in south and southeast Sudan. Lotuxo is classified in the Eastern Nilotic branch of the Nilo-Saharan language family, usually classed with Maa languages spoken in Kenya and Tanzania and groups west of the Lotuxo, the Lokoya and Bari. However, Mack and Robertshaw find that the Toposa and other Itung'a people do not have drums at all, and there are even taboos against using them. Most Surmic speakers such as the Murle do have drums, which are at the base of their sociopolitical system, called a "drumship." The DiDinga, by contrast, did not use drums even for social occasions until recently:

There is a tradition that they once had six drums which were used in curative rites and which they kept in a drum house. They are also identified as an introduced tradition with a clear implication that the source was Lotuxo. However, in a period of famine the efficacy of these drums was called into question and, in what amounts to a classic illustration of witchcraft accusation, they were identified as the source of the evil and were buried in a riverbank. Nowadays the only drums in use among the DiDinga are rudimentary ones of skin stretched over a pot. The place of burial is known as Katarinon, meaning a place where something was forgotten, a reminder of the time when in denial of tradition, objects and institutions of exotic origin were flirted with (Driberg, quoted in Mack and Robertshaw 1982, 113–14).

Mack and Robertshaw assess Driberg's account thus: "Again, there is not perhaps enough to dwell on the historical accuracy of such accounts (though Driberg dates the events to the latter part of the nineteenth century and thus implies their actual occurrence). What is significant is that a material association with the Lotuxo should thus be evaluated, particularly so when it relates to drums whose absence is so general a feature of Itung'a rather than Surma material culture" (Mack and Robertshaw 1982, 114). However, Fetterman noted in 1980 that during "*gyrkot*," men as well as women still played calabashes with sticks or drums, yet my informants told me that they recalled that sometimes someone would play a drum in the middle of the circle.

Notes

Chapter 6. Cultural Intervention and Mediation

1. Prior to the civil war, unlike the Toposa, the Dinka were not considered enemies by the DiDinga because the two groups did not come into contact. However, the Dinka and Murle, who live in northeastern Sudan, are traditional enemies, and, at the same time, they intermarry.

Chapter 7. Gendered Performance

1. Bride price is not the same as dowry. The bride's family pays dowry to her husband.

DiDinga-English Glossary

adak nyeloki: last night of the month

ahat: porridge of ground maize

aikorra lokora: high noon

arra: ceremonial place

aruk cawa: divination with sandals

athapan: cleansed

bokyo: woman's belt

bolohinit: leaf; flower

bondoro: weapon

butubut: a plant with an unpleasant smell

buyagit: evil person; witch

ceremi: women's traditional dress

chobechit: hair decoration no longer worn

chodoyi-otoni: one-horned

churgurena: jingle bells

cinenit: cursed

dae eth, dae khon: give sheep, give goat (children's game)

di toromech; di toroomi: warriors

eet chi egenyithi: man who is gifted

eet chi maka: older respected man

eet chi obia: man who holds a respected position

egenyith eeti nicie gerret: man who is very clever

egero: poison

ekothowait: warrior (see also *di toromech*)

et ci aga hena: traditional healer

galac: white man, foreigner, respected man

golu: road

gyrikot (jirikot): percussion dance

haputh: kale

hedemeta: percussion instrument of dried gourds

hohomala: blackberries

holiorichul: black cow with white tail

horometa (korometa): steep hills

ichayo: fighting

ikari: not castrated

irkit: year

iryeemani: crossed horns
kahurii (*kaúri*): ostrich feathers
kari: dappled red and white cow
kavurenit: flower (Longarim)
kebek kor: full moon
kehngeromegeer: dried meat (Murle)
Kikiya kora lukora: 8:00 a.m.–9:00 a.m.
kodhorui: cow with dark shoulders and back
labaci: black cow with white belly
liilu: river
lilan: elation, shrill
lilia: slow dance signaling end of *nyakorot*
lill: valley
lobolobyagit: glutton
lo hato: world of the *mining*
lohirto: hyena
loholia: children
lokembe: modern African dance; thumb piano
lolo: season of beginning rains
lomotin: harvest time
lorong: string
lotiki: one with big ears
lotim: baboon
mango: mango
mani: cream- or yellow-colored cow
mariki (*marihi*): cow with red heard
marikiorichul: red cow with white tail
marikioto: red horns
merti: beer
min: love
miningit, pl. *mining*: ghost
mirohit (*murohit*): others; enemy (non-DiDinga)
modenit: others; enemies
mugur: dark moon
muguri-o: born without horns
muuna: waste product of local fermented beer
muur, pl. *muuruk*: mountain
nataka: woman's metal belt
nathuka: women's attire; folded cloth skirt
ngane lotima: baboon; uninitiate
ngare: diviner; shaman
nglec: one horn curved forward, one backward
ngohit: first level in age-set system
ngothi: jumping

nyadhogol: both horns upright

nyahuta: wedding

nyakereket: initiation

nyakododh: horns curved forward and downward

nyakorot: formal community celebratory dance

nyalado: cowtail fly whip

nyelok: new moon; month

nyeluk: spreading or drooping horns

Nyerkinit ci nyelogo: "breaking open" of the month

nyikothowach, pl. *nyikothowa*: member of the age grade "warrior" (see also *ekothowait*)

nypio (*napyio*): ritual thrashing

obi: big

oli (ole'): bull; bullsong

olo: long-haired cow

ora: white cow

oribi: gazelle

orioto: white-horned

oroo: bull with white head

ortin: white moon; new moon

ortini omoto: tenth night of the white moon

otak: mouth

padan: dance step in which females bump against males

paipai: papaya

pelo: short whistle made of stem of dried gourd

pereanui: traditional game with seeds or stones

rama ci nyelogo: second night of the month

rehinit: courtship meal

rita: traditional woman's apron

ruko tooto: to take omens

tagis: rainy season

tarabal: gentle or tame cow

tegel: song

temedik: traditional hairstyle no longer worn

thapaninit: ritual spearing of a bull

thuan: courtship

tina: cows

toboe e: children's game like London bridge

tolit: sausage tree (*kigelia pinnata*)

tongoleekou: baldheaded cow

tooeri: wooden trumpet

tooto: divination

tukula: curved or bent horns

tukul tang ngon: waning moon

tulki: striped cow
tuluhu: squirrel
toromile: car
umya (*umoya*): archaic dance of old men and old women
weka: okra

Bibliography

Abeles, Marc, and Marie-Christine Peltier-Charrier. 1979. Migration forcée et transformation d'une société du Soudan meridional: Les DiDinga. *Journale des africanistes* 49 (1): 127–62.

Abrahams, Roger D. 1972. The Complex Relations of Simple Forms. In *Folklore Genres*, ed. Dan Ben-Amos, pp. 193–214. Austin: University of Texas Press.

———. 2005. *Everyday Life: A Poetics of Vernacular Practices*. Philadelphia: University of Pennsylvania Press.

African Institute of South Africa. 1998. Operation World: Africa at a Glance. http://www.liaafrica.org/sudan_articles/sudandata.htm.

Ahial, Abraham, and DiAnn Mills. 2004. *Lost Boy No More: A True Story of Survival and Salvation*. Nashville, TN: Broadman and Holman, Pub.

Akabwai, Darlington. 2001. *The Turkana-Topsoa-Nyang'atom-DiDinga Alokita: The Women's Peace Crusade*. Produced by OAU/IBAR [CAPE Unit of the Pan African Programme for the Control of Epizotics], August.

Ali-Dinar, Ali B. 2003. Aspirations and Discontent: Examining the Government Role in the Current Armed Conflict in Darfur. Paper presented at the Fourth International Sudan Studies Conference, Georgetown University, Washington, DC (July 31–August 2).

Almagor, U. 1977. Raiders and Elders: A Confrontation of Generations among the Dasseanetch. In *Warfare among East African Herders: Papers Presented at the First International Symposium*, ed. Katsuyoshi Fukui and David Turkon, pp. 119–45. Osaka: National Museum of Ethnology.

Amankulor, James, N. 1980. Dance as an Element of Artistic Synthesis in Traditional Igbo Festival Theater. *Okike: An African Journal of New Writing* 17 (Feb.): 42+.

Amselle, Jeanu-Luc, and Elikia M'Bokolo. 1985. *Au coeur de l'ethnie, tribalisme et état en Afrique* Paris: Editions la Découverte.

Andretta, E. H. 1989. Symbolic Continuity, Material Discontinuity and Ethnic-Identity among Murle Communities in the Southern Sudan. *Ethnology* 28 (1): 28–31.

Appadurai, Arjun. 1991. Global Ethnoscapes: Notes and Queries for a Transnational Anthropology. In *Recapturing Anthropology: Working in the Present*, ed. Richard G. Fox, pp. 191–210. Sante Fe, NM: School of American Research Press.

Arensen, Jonathan E. 1983. *Sticks and Straw: Comparative House Forms in Southern Sudan and Northern Kenya*. Dallas, TX: International Museum of Cultures.

———. 1987. The God of the Sky: The Supreme God Concept among the Eastern Sudanic Peoples of Southern Sudan. *Notes on Anthropology* 9 (March): 4–21.

———. 1988. Names in the Life Cycle of the Murle. *Journal of the Anthropological Society of Oxford* 192: 125–30.

———. 1992. *Mice Are Men: Language and Society among the Murle of Sudan*. Dallas: International Museum of Cultures.

———. 1998. Murle Categorization. In *Surmic Languages and Cultures*, ed. Dimmendaal, Gerrit, and Last, pp. 181–218. Cologne: Ruediger Koeppe.

Asante, Kariamu Welsh. 2001. Commonalities in African Dance: An Aesthetic Foundation. In *Moving History/Dancing Cultures*, ed. Ann Dils and Ann Cooper Albright, pp. 144–51. Middletown, CT: Wesleyan University Press.

Baron, Robert. 1999. Theorizing Public Folklore Practice—Documentation, Genres of Representation, and Everyday Competencies. *Journal of Folklore Research* 36 (2/3): 185–201.

———. 2003. Amalgams and Mosaics, Syncretisms and Reinterpretations: Reading Herskovits and Contemporary Creolists for Metaphor of Creolization. *Journal of American Folklore* 116:88–115.

Baron, Robert, and Nicholas R. Spitzer. 1992. *Public Folklore*. Washington, DC: Smithsonian Institution Press.

Barz, Gregory. 2004. *Music in East Africa: Experiencing Music, Expressing Culture*. New York: Oxford University Press.

Basch, L. et al. 1994. *Nations Unbound: Transnational Projects, Postcolonial Predicaments and Deterritorialized Nation-States*. Basel: Gordon and Breach.

Bateson, Gregory. 1955. The Message, "This Is Play." In *Group Processes*, ed. B. Schaffner, pp. 145–242. New York: Josiah Macy.

Bauman, Richard. 1978. *Verbal Art as Performance*. Rowley, MA: Newbury House.

———. 1986. *Story, Performance and Event: Contextual Studies of Oral Narrative*. Cambridge: Cambridge University Press.

———. 1989. American Folklore Studies and Social Transformation: A Performance-Centered Perspective. *Text and Performance Quarterly* 9.3 (July): 175–84.

———. 2004. *A World of Others' Words: Cross-Cultural Perspectives on Intertextuality*. Oxford: Blackwell Publishing.

Bauman, Richard, and Charles L. Briggs. 1990. Poetics and Performance as Critical Perspectives on Language and Social Life. *Annual Review of Anthropology* 19:59–88.

Bauman, Richard, Patricia Sawin, and Inta Gail Carpenter. 1992. *Reflections on the Folklife Festival: An Ethnography of Participant Experience*. Bloomington, IN: Special Publications of the Folklore Institute No. 2.

Bausinger, Hermann. 1992. Tradition und Modernisierung. In *Tradition and Modernization: Plenary Papers Read at the Fourth International Congress of the Société International d'Ethnologie et de Folklore*, ed. Reimund Kvideland, pp. 9–22. Turku, Finland: Nordic Institute of Folklore Publications.

Baxter, P. T. W., and Uri Almagor, eds. 1978. *Age, Generation and Time: Some Features of East African Age Organizations*. New York: St. Martin's Press.

Belcher, Stephen P. 1999. *Epic Traditions of Africa*. Bloomington: Indiana University Press.

Ben-Amos, Dan. 1972. Towards a Definition of Folklore in Context. In *Toward New Perspectives in Folklore*, ed. Americo Paredes and Richard Bauman, pp. 3–15. American Folklore Society Bibliographical and Special Series, 23. Austin: University of Texas Press, for the American Folklore Society.

———. 1975. *Sweet Words: Storytelling Events in Benin*. Philadelphia: Institute for the Study of Human Issues.

Bender, Lionel. 1977. The Surma Language Group: A Preliminary Report. *Studies in African Linguistics*. Supplement 7.

Berger, Harris M., and Giovanna P. Del Negro. 2002. Bauman's Verbal Art and the Social Organization of Attention: The Role of Reflexivity in the Aesthetics of Performance. *Journal of American Folklore* 455 (115): 62–91.

Berkeley, Bill. 2001. *The Graves Are Not Yet Full: Race, Tribe and Power in the Heart of Africa*. New York: Basic Books.

Berlin, Brent. 1978. Ethnobiological classification. In *Cognition and Categorization*, ed. Eleanor Rosch and Barbara B. Lloyd, pp. 9–26. Hillsdale, NJ: Lawrence Erlbaum.

Bixler, Mark. 2005. *The Lost Boys of Sudan: An American Story of the Refugee Experience*. Atlanta: University of Georgia Press.

Boyer, Pascel. 2001. *Religion Explained*. New York: Basic Books.

Briggs, Charles L. 1986. *Learning How to Ask: A Sociolinguist Appraisal of the Role of the Interview in Social Science Research*. Cambridge: Cambridge University Press.

———. 1988. *Competence in Performance: The Creativity of Tradition in Mexicano Verbal Art*. Philadelphia: University of Pennsylvania Press.

Campbell, Carol A., and Carol M. Eastman. 1984. Ngoma: Swahili Adult Song Peformance in Context. *Ethnomusicology* 28 (3):467–93.

Cantwell, Robert. 1993. *Ethnomimesis*. Chapel Hill: University of North Carolina Press.

Cashman, Ray. 2000. "Young Ned of the Hill" and the Reemergence of the Irish Rapparee: A Textual and Intertextual Analysis. *Cultural Analysis* 1:51–68.

Castles, Stephen, and Alistair Davidson. 2000. *Citizenship and Migration: Globalization and the Politics of Belonging*. London: Macmillan.

Cerulli, Ernesta. 1956. Peoples of South-West Ethiopia and Its Borderland. *Ethnographic Survey of Africa: North-Eastern Africa*, part 3: 11–228.

Chernoff, John Miller. 1979. *African Rhythm and African Sensibility: Aesthetics and Social Action in African Musical Idioms*. Chicago: University of Chicago Press.

Clifford, James. 1997. *Routes: Travel and Translation in the Late Twentieth Century*. Cambridge, MA: Harvard University Press.

Cohen, Ronald, and John Middleton, eds. 1970. *From Tribe to Nation in Africa: Studies in Incorporation Processes*. Scranton, PA: Chandler.

Condé, Maryse. 1998. "Creolite" without Creole Language? In *Caribbean Creolization, Reflections on the Cultured Dynamics of Language, Literature and Identity*, ed. Kathleen M. Balutansky and Marie-Agnes Sourieau, pp. 101–9. Gainsville: University of Florida Press.

Connerton, Paul. 1989. *How Societies Remember*. Cambridge: Cambridge University Press.

Conquergood, Dwight. 1994. Performance Theory, Hmong Shamans and Cultural Politics. In *Playing Boal*, ed. Janelle G. Reinelt and Joseph R. Roach, pp.41–64. New York: Routledge.

Csikszentmihalyi, Mihalyi. 1974. *Flow: Studies of Enjoyment*. PHS Grant Report. University of Chicago.

Dau, John Bul, and Michael Sweeney. 2007. *God Grew Tired of Us: A Memoir*. Washington, DC: National Geographic.

de Jong, Nicky. 2004. Didinga Orthography. *Occasional Papers in the Study of Sudanese Languages* 9: 145–64.

Deng, Benison, et al., 2005. *They Poured Fire on US from the Sky: The True Story of Three Lost Boys from Sudan.* New York: PublicAffairs.

Deng, Francis Mading. 1973. *The Dinka and Their Songs.* Oxford: Clarendon Press.

———. 1995. *War of Visions: Conflicts of Identities in the Sudan.* Washington, DC: Brookings Institution.

Deng, Gabriel Bol. 2006. The Narrow Escape: The Facts of My Life. *Voices: The Journal of New York Folklore* 32 (Fall-Winter): 20–25.

Dils, Ann, and Ann Cooper Albright. 2001. *Moving History/Dancing Cultures.* Middletown, CT: Wesleyan University Press.

Dimmendaal, Gerrit J. 1982. Contacts between Eastern Nilotic and Surma Groups: Linguistic Evidence. In *Culture History in the Southern Sudan: Archaeology, Linguistics and Ethnohistory*, memoire no. 8, ed. John Mack and Peter Robertshaw, pp. 101–10. Nairobi: British Institute in Eastern Africa.

Dimmendaal, Gerrit J., and Marco Last. 1998. *Surmic Languages and Cultures.* Cologne: Ruediger Koeppe.

Ditota, Donna. 2003. "Run to Freedom: Former Sudanese Refugees Find Peace and Joy in Tully." *Syracuse Post-Standard* December 25: D-1+.

Dorst, John D. 1995. "Sidebar Excursions to Nowhere": The Vernacular Storytelling of Errol Morris and Spalding Gray. In *Folklore, Literature, and Cultural Theory: Collected Essays*, ed. Cathy Lynn Preston, pp. 119–34. New York: Garland.

———. 1999. Which Came First, the Chicken Device or the Textual Egg? Documentary Film and the Limits of the Hybrid Metaphor. *Journal of American Folklore* 112 (445): 268–81.

Drewal, Margaret T. 1992. *Yoruba Ritual: Performers, Play, Agency.* Bloomington: Indiana University Press.

Driberg, J. H. 1919. Rain-making among the Lango. *Journal of the Royal Anthropological Institute of Great Britain and Ireland* 49: 52–73.

———. 1922. A Preliminary Account of the DiDinga. *Sudan Notes and Records* 5: 208–22.

———. 1923. *The Lango: A Nilotic Tribe of Uganda.* London: T. Fisher Unwin, Ltd.

———. 1925. DiDinga Customary Law. *Sudan Notes and Records* 8: 153–75.

———. 1927a. The DiDinga Mountains. *Geographical Journal* 69 (May): 385–401.

———. 1927b. Notes on Dreams among the Lango and the DiDinga of the South-Eastern Sudan. *Man* 27 (August): 94+.

———. 1928. Primitive Law in East Africa. *Africa* 1: 63–72.

———. 1929. Inheritance Fees. *Man* 64 (May): 87–90.

———. 1930. *People of the Small Arrow.* London: George Routledge and Sons.

———. 1931. The DiDinga Language. *Afrikanische Studien*, part 3: 139–82.

———. 1932a. *At Home with the Savage.* London: George Routledge and Sons, Ltd.

———. 1932b. *Initiation: Translations from Poems of the DiDinga and Lango* Tribes. Great Britain: Golden Cockerel Press.

———. 1932c. The Status of Women among the Nilotics and Nilo-Hamitics. *Africa* 5 (4): 404–21.

————. 1933. Divination by Pebbles. *Man* 33 (January): 7–9.

————. 1934. *Engato, the Lion Club*. New York: Dutton.

————. 1935. The "Best Friend" among the DiDinga. *Man* 35 (July): 101–02.

————. 1939. A Note on the Classification of Half-Hamites in East Africa. *Man* 39 (February): 20–21.

Drumtra, Jeff. 1999. *Follow the Women and the Cows: Personal Stories of Sudan's Uprooted People.* Washington, DC: U.S. Committee for Refugees.

Echerou, Michael J. C. 1994. Redefining the Ludic: Mimesis, Expression, and the Festival Mode. In *The Play of the Self*, ed. Ronald Bogue and Mihal I. Spariosu., pp. 137–56. Albany: State University of New York Press.

Eggers, Dave. 2004. *Lost Boy: Valentino and the Lost Boys of the Sudan.* London: Penguin.

Ellis, C., and A. Bochner. 1996. *Composing Ethnography: Alternative Forms of Qualitative Writing.* Walnut Creek, CA: AltaMira Press.

European-Sudanese Public Affairs Council. 2001. SPLA Responsible for Sudan's Lost Boys. http://www.twf.org/News/Y2001/0121-SudanBoys.html.

Evans, David. 1982. *Big Brother Blues.* Berkeley: University of California Press.

Evans-Pritchard, E. E. 1928. The Dance. *Africa* 1 (October): 446–62.

————. 1929. Some Collective Expressions of Obscenity in Africa. *Journal of the Royal Anthropological Institute of Great Britain and Ireland* 59: 311–32.

————. 1940. *The Nuer.* Oxford: Oxford University Press.

Feld, Steven. 1982. *Sound and Sentiment: Birds, Weeping, Sound and Sentiment in Kaluli Expressions.* Philadelphia: University of Pennsylvania Press.

Fetterman, Marilyn Harer. 1992. Drought, Cattle Disease, Colonialism and Lokembe: One Hundred Years of Change among the Pastorialist DiDinga, Eastern Equatoria Province, Sudan. PhD diss., Brown University.

Fitzgerald, Mary Anne. 2002. *Throwing the Stick Forward: The Impact of War on Southern Sudanese Women.* Nairobi, Kenya: UNIFEM and UNICEF.

Foley, John Miles, ed. 1980. *Oral Traditional Literature: A Festschrift for Albert Bates Lord.* Columbus, Ohio: Slavica Publishers.

————. 1995. *The Singer of Tales in Performance.* Bloomington: Indiana University Press.

————. 2002. *How to Read an Oral Poem.* Urbana: University of Illinois Press.

Fried, Morton H. 1975. *The Notion of Tribe.* Menlo Park, CA: Cummings.

Freire, P. 1970. *Pedagogy of the Oppressed.* New York: Continuum.

Galaty, J.G. om, and P. Bonte. 1991. *Herders, Warriors and Traders: Pastoralism in Africa.* Boulder, CO: Westview Press.

Glassie, Henry. 1995. Tradition. *Journal of American Folklore* 108 (430): 395–412.

Goodall, H. L. 2003. What Is Interpretive Ethnography? An Eclectic's Tale. In *Expressions of Ethnography: Novel Approaches to Qualitative Methods*, ed. Robin Patric Clair, pp. 55–64. Albany, NY: State University of New York Press.

Gosso, Yumi, Emma Otta, Maria de Lima Salum e Morais, Fernando José Leite Ribeiro, and Vera Silvia Raad Bussab. 2005. Play in Hunter-Gatherer Society. In *The Nature of Play*, ed. Anthony D. Pellegrini and Peter K. Smith, pp. 213–53. New York: Guilford Press.

Gourlay, K. A. 1972. The Ox and Identification. *Man* 7: 244–54.

Gow, Greg. 2002. *The Oromo in Exile: From the Horn of Africa to the Suburbs of Australia.* Melbourne, Austral.: Melbourne University Press.

Graves, James Bau. 1998. Rules of Engagement: Facilitating Community Cultural Programs. *Journal of Applied Folklore* 4: 79–90.

———. 2005. *Cultural Democracy: The Arts, Community and the Public Purpose.* Urbana: University of Illinois Press.

Gunmar, Liz. 1995. *Politics and Performance: Theory, Poetry and Song in Southern Africa.* Bloomington: University of Indiana Press.

Hall, Edward T. 1976. *Beyond Culture.* Garden City, NY: Doubleday-Anchor Books.

Hampton, Barbara L. 2004. "Kulu Mele: Legacy and Transnational Practice." *Works in Progress*, volume 17, number 3, p 15. Philadelphia: Philadelphia Folklore Project.

Hanna, Judith L. 1977. African Dance and the Warrior Tradition. In *The Warrior Tradition*, ed. Ali A. Mazrui, pp. 113–33. Leiden: Brill.

———. 1989. African Dance Frame By Frame. *Journal of Black Studies* 19 (4): 422–41.

Hannerz, Ulf. 1989. Notes on the Global Ecumene. *Public Culture* 1 (2): 528–49.

Hayley, T. T. S. 1947. *The Anatomy of Lango Religion and Groups.* New York: Negro Universities Press.

Herskovits, M. J. 1926. The Cattle Complex in East Africa. *American Anthropologist* 28: 230–72; 361–88; 494–528; 633–64.

Hill, Richard Leslie. 1951. *A Biographical Dictionary of the Anglo-Egyptian Sudan.* Oxford: Clarendon Press.

Holtzman, Jon. 1999. *Nuer Journeys, Nuer Lives: Sudanese Refugees in Minnesota.* Boston: Allyn and Bacon.

Hrvatin, Emil, and Peter Senk. 2004. Refugee Camp for First World Citizens. *Janus* 16: 77–79.

Huffman, R. 1931. *Nuer Customs and Folklore.* London: Oxford University Press.

Humesco, Seyoum Y. 1997. *Ethnicity in Africa: Towards a Positive Approach.* London: TSC.

Huntingford, G. W. B. 1953. *The Northern Nilo-Hamites.* London: International African Institute.

Hymes, Dell. 1972. The Use of Anthropology: Critical, Political, Personal. In *Reinventing Anthropology*, ed. Hymes, pp. 3–79. New York: Penguin.

———. [1975] 1981. Breakthrough into Performance. In *Folklore: Performance and Communication*, ed. Dan Ben-Amos and Kenneth S. Goldstein, pp. 1–74. The Hague: Mouton.

Inda, Jonathen Xavier, and Renato Rosaldo. 2002. Introduction: A World in Motion. In *The Anthropology of Globalization*, ed. Inda and Rosaldo, pp. 1–34. Malden, MA: Blackwell.

Iwasaka, Michiko, and Barre Toelken. 1994. *Ghosts and the Japanese: Cultural Experience in Japanese Death Legends.* Logan: Utah State University Press.

Jok, Madut. 2001. *War and Slavery in the Sudan: The Ethnography of Political Violence.* Philadelphia: University of Pennsylvania Press.

Kapchan, Deborah. 1995. Performance. *Journal of American Folklore* 108 (430): 479–508.

Kearney, Michael. 1995. The Local and the Global. *Annual Review of Anthropology* 24: 547–65.

Kemper, Yvonne. 2005. Youth in War-To-Peace Transitions: Approaches of International Organizations. *Berghof Report Nr. 10*, January. Berlin: Berghof Research Center for Constructive Conflict Management.

Bibliography

Kirshenblatt-Gimblett, Barbara. 1983. Studying Immigrant and Ethnic Folklore. In *Handbook of American Folklore*, ed. Richard M. Dorson, pp.39–47. Bloomington: Indiana University Press.

Kratz, Corinne A. 1990. Persuasive Suggestions and Reassuring Promises: Emergent Parallelism and Dialogic Encouragement in Song. *Journal of American Folklore* 103 (January–March): 42–67.

Kronenberg, Andreas. 1961. Longarim Favorite Beast: Kush. *Journal of the Sudan Antiquities Service* 9: 258–77.

———. 1972a. The Bovine Idiom and Formal Logic. In *Essays in Sudan Ethnography Presented to Sir Edward Evans-Pritchard*, ed. J. Cunnison and W. James, pp. 71–86. London: C. Hurst.

———. 1972b. *Logik und Leben: Kulturelle Relevanz der DiDinga und Longarim, Sudan.* Wiesbaden, Ger.: Franz Steiner Verlag.

Labov, William. 1966. *The Social Stratification of English in New York City.* Washington, D.C.: Center for Applied Linguistics.

Lamb, David. 1983. *The Africans.* New York: Vintage Books.

Langton, D. 1984. Vulnerable Breadwinners: Larim Women in East Africa. *IDRC Reports* 13 (2): 8–9.

Lewis, B. A. 1947. Murle Folk Tales. *Sudan Notes and Records* 28: 135–47.

———. 1972. *Murle: Red Chiefs and Black Commoners.* Oxford: Clarendon Press.

Leinhardt, Godfrey. 1961. *Divinity and Experience: The Religion of the Dinka.* Oxford: Oxford University Press.

Logan, M. H. 1918. The Beirs. *Sudan Notes and Records* 1 (4): 238–48.

Lokonobei, Lino Locek, and Nicholas de Jong. 1989. On the Position of Boya in Relation to Murle and Didinga. *Occasional Papers in the Study of Sudanese Languages* 6: 77–93.

Mack, John, and Peter Robertshaw. 1982. *Culture History in the Southern Sudan: Archaeology, Linguistics and Ethnohistory, memorie no. 8.* Nairobi: British Institute in Eastern Africa.

Matheson, Ishbel. 2002. The "Lost Girls" of Sudan. http://news.bbc.co.uk/2/low/africa/2031286.stm.

Mayer, Philip. 1971. *Townsmen or Tribesmen: Conservatism and the Process of Urbanization in a South African City.* London: Oxford University Press.

Mazrui, Ali A. 1977a. The Warrior Tradition and the Masculinity of War. In *The Warrior Tradition in Modern Africa*, ed. Ali A. Mazrui, pp. 69–81. Leiden: E.J. Brill.

———. 1977b. *The Warrior Tradition in Modern Africa.* Leiden: Brill.

McMahon, Felicia. 2002. Emerging Tradition: Dance Performances of the Sudanese DiDinga in Syracuse. *Voices: The Journal of New York Folklore* 28 (Fall-Winter): 32–37.

———. 2005. Repeat Performance: Dancing DiDinga with the Lost Boys of South Sudan. *Journal of American Folklore* 465 (Summer): 356–79.

Meeker, Michael E. 1989. *The Pastoral Son and the Spirit of Patriarchy: Religion, Society, and Person among East African StockKeepers.* Madison: University of Wisconsin Press.

Merriam, Alan J. 1953. The Game of Kubuguze among the Abatusi of North-East Ruanda. *Man* 53 (November): 169–72.

Merriam, A. P. 1982. *African Music in Perspective.* New York: Garland Publishing.

Molinaro, Luigi. 1935. I DiDinga, tribu dell'africa orientale. *Anthropo* 30: 421–31.

Montville, Joseph. 2002. Fear and Loathing: The Burdens of History on the Israeli-Palestinian Conflict. Paper presented at "Evaluating Track II Dilomacy," Program on the Analysis and Resolution of Conflicts, Syracuse University, Syracuse, NY (April 5).

Nalder, L. F., ed. [1937] 1970. *A Tribal Survey of Mongalla Province*. New York: Negro Universities Press.

Nanda, Serena, and Richard L. Warms. 1998. *Cultural Anthropology*. Belmont, CA: Wadsworth Publishing.

N'Diaye, Diana Baird. 1997. African Immigrant Culture in Metropolitan Washington, DC: Building and Bridging Communities. http://www.folklife.si.edu/resources/festival1997/afrindi.htm.

Nesdale, D., R. Rooney, and L. Smith. 1997. Migrant Ethnic Identity and Psychological Distress. *Journal of Cross-Cultural Psychology* 28: 569–88.

Noyes, Dorothy. 1995. Group. *Journal of American Folklore* 108 (430): 449–78.

Odden, David. 1983. Aspects of DiDinga Phonology and Morphology. *Nilo-Saharan Language Studies* 13: 148–76.

Owens, Maida. 1999. Festivals, Cultural Tourism and the Louisiana Folklife Program. http://www.louisianafolklife.org/LT/Articles_Essays/creole_art_fests_tourism.html.

Palmer, Gary B., and William R. Jankowiak. 1996. Performance and Imagination: Toward an Anthropology of the Spectacular and the Mundane. *Cultural Anthropology* 11 (2): 225–58.

Pelligrini, Anthony D., and Peter K. Smith. 2005. *The Nature of Play: Great Apes and Humans*. New York: Guilford Press.

Pipher, Mary. 2002. *The Middle of Everywhere: The World's Refugees Come to our Town*. New York: Harcourt.

Ranger, T. O. 1975. *Dance and Society in Eastern Africa 1890–1970*. Berkeley: University of California Press.

Roach, Joseph. 1996a. *Cities of the Dead: Circum-Atlantic Performance*. New York: Columbia University Press.

———. 1996b. Kinship, Intelligence, and Memory as Improvisation: Culture and Performance in New Orleans. In *Performance and Cultural Politics*, ed. Elin Diamond, pp. 219–38. London: Routledge.

Rone, Jmera. 1995. *Children in Sudan: Slaves, Street Children and Child Soldiers*. New York: Human Rights Watch.

Rosato, Michele. 1980. *Didinga=Didina Grammar and Dictionary*. Rome.

Rosenberg, Neil V. 2002. Repetition, Innovation and Representation in Don Messer's Repertoire. *Journal of American Folklore* 115 (456): 191–208.

Rynearson, Ann M. 1996. Living within the Looking Glass: Refugee Artists and the Creation of Group Identity. In *Selected Papers on Refugee Issues IV*, ed. Rynearson and James Phillips, pp. 20–44. Arlington, VA: American Anthropological Association.

Safran, William. 1991. Diasporas in Modern Societies: Myths of Homeland and Return. *Diaspora* 1 (1): 83–99.

Said, Beshir Mohammed. 1965. *The Sudan: Crossroads of Africa*. London: Bodley Head.

Salamone, Frank A. 1993. Creolization, Music, and Opposition to National Policy: A Nigerian Case. *Journal of Play Theory and Research* 1 (40): 281–97.

Salih, M. A. Mohamed. 2001. Tribal Militias, SPLA/SPLM and the Sudanese State: "New Wine in Old Bottles": Management of the Crisis in the Sudan. Background Papers Presented to the Bergen Conference. http://www.fou.uib.no/fd/1996/f/7/2001/backevid.htm.

Sarup, M. 1996. *Identity, Culture and the Postmodern World.* Athens: University of Georgia Press.

Schechner, Richard. 1985. *Between Theater and Anthropology.* Philadelphia, PA: University of Pennsylvania Press.

———. 1988. Playing. *Play and Culture* 1 (1): 3–27.

———. 2002. *Performance Studies: An Introduction.* London: Routledge.

Scroggins, Deborah. 2002. *Emma's War.* New York: Pantheon Books.

Seligman, C. G., and B. Z. Seligman. 1950. *Pagan Tribes of the Nilotic Sudan.* New York: Humanities Press.

Sheehy, Daniel. 2002. Crossover Dreams: The Folklorist and the Folk Arrival. In *Public Folklore*, ed. Robert Baron and Nicholas R. Spitzer, pp. 217–29. Washington, D.C.: Smithsonian Institution Press.

Sherzer, Joel. 1983. *Kuna Ways of Speaking: An Ethnographic Perspective.* Austin: University of Texas Press.

Shostak, M. 1976. A !Kung Woman's Memories of Childhood. In *Kalahari Hunter-Gatherers: Studies of the !Kung San and Their Neighbors*, ed. R. B. Lee and I. DeVore, pp. 246–77. Cambridge: Harvard University Press.

Small, Christopher. 1998. *Musiking: The Meanings of Performance and Listening.* Middletown, CN: Wesleyan University Press.

Stephens, Carlene E. 2002. *On Time: How America Has Learned to Live by the Clock.* Boston: Little, Brown & Co.

Strother, Z. S. 2001. Invention and Reinvention in the Traditional Arts. In *Moving History/ Dancing Cultures*, ed. Ann Dils and Ann Cooper Albright, pp. 152–64. Middletown, CN: Wesleyan University Press.

Svoboda, Teresa. 1985. *Cleaned the Crocodile's Teeth: Nuer Song.* New York: Greenfield Review Press.

Szwed, John F. 2003. Metaphors of Incommensurability. *Journal of American Folklore* 116 (459): 9–18.

Tedlock, Dennis. 1983. *The Spoken Word and the Work of Interpretation.* Philadelphia: University of Pennsylvania Press.

Theroux, Paul. 2003. *Dark Star Safari: Overland from Cairo to Cape Town.* Boston: Houghton Mifflin.

Thompson, Robert Farris. 1974. *Art in Motion.* Los Angeles: University of California Press.

Titon, Jeff Todd. 1995. Text. *Journal of American Folklore* 108 (430): 432–48.

Tucker, Archibald N. 1933a. Children's Games and Songs in the Southern Sudan. *Journal of the Royal Anthropological Institute of Great Britain and Ireland* 63: 165–87.

———. 1933b. *Tribal Music and Dancing in the Southern Sudan [Africa] at Social and Ceremonial Gatherings.* London: New Temple Press.

Tucker, Archibald N., and David A. Turton. 1981. Le groupe DiDinga-Murle ou Surma: Group isole. In *Les langues dans le monde ancien et moderne*, ed. Jean Perrot, pp. 333–34. Paris: Centre national de la recherche scientifique.

Turner, Victor. [1974] 1982. Liminal to Liminoid in Play, Flow, and Ritual. In *From Ritual to Theater*, ed. Richard Schechner, pp. 20–60. New York: Performing Arts Journal Publications.

——. 1986. *The Anthropology of Performance*. New York: PAJ Publications.

Unseth, Peter. 1987. "A Typological Anomaly in Some Surma Languages." *Studies in African Linguistics* 18 (3): 357–61.

van Garsse, Yvan. 1972. *Ethnological and Anthropological Literature on the Three Southern Sudan Provinces: Upper Nile, Bahr el Ghazal, Equatoria*. Vienna: Acta Ethnologica et Linguistica.

Walgren, Judy. 1998. *The Lost Boys of Natinga: A School for Sudan's Young Refugees*. Boston: Houghton Mifflin.

Wahlbeck, Osten. 1998. Transnationalism and Diasporas: The Kurdish Example. Paper presented at the International Sociological Association Fourteenth World Congress of Sociology, Montreal, Canada (July 26–August 1).

Whisnant, David. 1983. *All That Is Native and Fine: The Politics of Culture in an American Region*. Chapel Hill: University of North Carolina Press.

Williams, Mary. 2005. *Brothers in Hope: The Story of the Lost Boys of Sudan*. New York: Lee and Low Books.

Wynn, Walter C. 1943. An Examination of the Sociological Aspects of African Spiritism. Thesis, Kennedy School of Missions, Hartford Seminary Foundation.

Yup, Gust A. 1998. My Three Cultures: Navigating the Multicultural Landscape. In *Readings in Cultural Contexts*, ed. Judith N. Martin, Thomas K. Nakayama, and Lisa A. Flores, pp. 79–84. Mountain View, CA: Mayfield Publishing.

Zhou, M., and C. L. Bankston, III. 1994. Social Capital and the Adaptation of the Second Generation: The Case of Vietnamese Youth in New Orleans. *International Migration Review* 28: 821–45.

Zutt, Johannes. 1994. *Children of War: Wandering Alone in Southern Sudan*. New York: UNICEF.

Index

a cappella, 125
Abrahams, Roger, 179
abuse songs (mocking), 14, 25, 26, 50, 92
active tradition bearer, 54
aesthetics, 9, 12, 115; horn taming, of bulls, 92–93; and performance, 16, 18
African Americans: and Africans, 7, 8, 49–50, 117–18; "aftermath" and performance, 118, 134–41
age-set (age grades), 17, 72, 90, 106, 108, 145, 149ff., 205–6; and names, 109
apiti (women's dance), 164ff., 172
Arabic (language), relationship to DiDinga, 55, 73–74, 154–55
Arensen, Jonathan, 37–41, 55, 58, 64, 66, 74, 78, 203–4
armies, Sudanese, children and conscription, 146–47
audience(s), and performance, 6, 7, 16, 18, 85, 115, 117, 119, 135, 180, 181, 182
authenticity, cultural, 6, 7, 22, 180, 182

Baron, Robert, 6, 7, 180
Basch, L., 5
Bateson, Gregory, 175
Bauman, Richard, 6, 14, 16, 117, 154, 180
Bausinger, Hermann, 181
Berger, Harris, 16
Beshir, Omar, 46
body language, 115
bride price, 157, 205, 209
Briggs, Charles, 6, 14, 30
bull names, and warriors, 89
bullsongs, 14, 26, 48, 86ff., 205; as artistic resource, 93; Dinka, 92; male identity,

90; marriage, 69–70; as pastoral tradition, 87–88; types, 124

call and response, 23, 89, 90, 137
Campbell, Carol, and Carol Eastman, 169
Cashman, Ray, 14, 16, 177
Catholic Charities, 3
cattle raiding, 19, 42, 118; song traditions, 73; and women, 27, 148, 149, 160ff.
"cattle raiding complex," 145
childhood: and adulthood, 119, 141; performance, 23, 175; play, 26; play groups, 17; song games, 27
children: forced conscription, 146; games, 22, 118–19, 181; nicknaming, 44–45; riddling, 54; songs, 146
Clifford, James, 49
code-switching, 49
collaboration, 28, 117, 120, 180
collective authority, 21
commodification, resistance to, 181
competence: communicative, 117; in performance, 6
composition, spontaneous, 86
Connerton, Paul, 141
Conquergood, Dwight, 120
context, 6, 7, 9, 15, 19, 117, 118, 121, 140, 155, 170, 182, 183
creolization, 74
cross-cultural exchange, 73
cultural adaptive ability, 89
cultural conservation, 6, 8
cultural intervention, 5, 27, 142ff., 180
cultural self-esteem, 5–6

225

Index

culture: children's, 15, 119, 175; and
collectivity, 21, 177–78; and globalization,
5; hunter-gatherer, 118–19; localization,
5; and orality, 7; and refugees, 7, 9, 82,
177–79; and song, 10, 23
curse, 206

dance: deep description, 129–32; DiDinga,
70–73, 117ff.; Dinka, 84–85; group
solidarity, 23; social structure, 23;
warrior, 147–48; and work, 114; Yoruba,
124; Zande, 21
Darfur, 174, 203
de Jong, N., 37
decontextualization, of tradition, 181
Del Negro, Giovanna, 6, 16
Deng, Francis Mading, 30, 103
diaspora: definition, 8; identity and, 182
DiDinga: differientiated from Dinka,
16–17; language, 34–37, 64–67, 74–75;
women, 67
DiDingaland, 22; economy, 55; geography,
55–56, 60–61, 203
Dimmendaal, Gerrit, 37, 73, 204
Dinka, 16–17, 55, 62, 66, 143–44, 149ff.;
women, 67
Dinkaland, 55
disco dance, African, 112
divination, 79–82
dowry, and cattle, 75
Dreiberg, J. H., 61, 102, 109, 114, 204–5;
cultural groups by, 66–67
Drewal, Margaret T., 124, 132
drums, introduced to DiDinga, 208

emergence, 21, 95, 154, 156, 167, 181–84; as
dynamic process, 6, 14, 149; of identity,
126, 154, 175, 183; in parallel structure,
102–3
entextualization, 8, 14, 86ff., 116, 142, 177
Ethiopia, 4
ethnoaesthetics, 92
ethnography, 29ff.
Evans-Pritchard, E. E., 20–21, 66, 136

Feld, Steven, 169
Fetterman, Marilyn H., 10, 41, 56, 64, 66,
72, 76, 78, 106, 107, 108, 205, 206, 207,
208
flexibility, and survival, 89–90
Foley, John Miles, 17–18, 25
folklore: definition, 6; public-sector, 7
folklorists: and cultural intervention, 5;
public-sector, 5, 7
folktales, DiDinga, 38–41, 45–46
frame(s), framing, 82, 155, 180; performance,
6, 7, 15, 28, 117, 154, 180, 181

games, differentiated from divination, 81
Garang, John, 46–47
gender, and performance, 169ff.
Glassie, Henry, 6
globalization, 5, 11, 177, 179
Gosso, Yumi, 15, 17, 120
Gow, Greg, 177, 179
Graves, James Bau, 5, 143, 155

Hall, Edward, 180
Hanna, Judith, 147, 148
hazing, ritual, 106
Herskovits, Melville, 145
high context, vs. low context, 117
Huffman, R., 66, 71, 90
humor, in song, 25
hybrid: identity, 27, 85, 133, 134–35, 141,
146, 155, 179; music event, 181; tradition,
23, 26
Hymes, Dell, 6, 14, 16, 23, 170, 181

identity, 5, 27, 75, 182; age group, 109;
ancient, 51; audience, 183; authenticity,
7; co-creation of, 182, 183; diasporic, 138;
emerging, 182–83; group, 51; hybrid,
7, 51, 126, 178, 179; non-Western, 178;
power, 183; racial, 7, 8, 27, 49–50, 117–18;
song, 146; transnational, 5; women's, 174
improvisation, in song, 89, 101, 121, 122,
124, 137, 138
initiation songs, 107, 109

9/22

CPSIA information can be obtained
at www.ICGtesting.com
Printed in the USA
BVHW042338240722
642748BV00001B/4

9 781604 734157